DevOps on the
Microsoft Stack

■■■

Wouter de Kort

Apress®

DevOps on the Microsoft Stack

Wouter de Kort
Ordina Microsoft Solutions
GRONINGEN, The Netherlands

ISBN-13 (pbk): 978-1-4842-1447-3   ISBN-13 (electronic): 978-1-4842-1446-6
DOI 10.1007/978-1-4842-1446-6

Library of Congress Control Number: 2016939388

Managing Director: Welmoed Spahr
Lead Editor: James DeWolf
Development Editor: Douglas Pundick
Technical Reviewer: Josh Garverick and Willy-Peter Schaub
Editorial Board: Steve Anglin, Pramila Balen, Louise Corrigan, James DeWolf, Jonathan Gennick,
    Robert Hutchinson, Celestin Suresh John, Michelle Lowman, James Markham, Susan McDermott,
    Matthew Moodie, Jeffrey Pepper, Douglas Pundick, Ben Renow-Clarke, Gwenan Spearing
Coordinating Editor: Melissa Maldonado
Copy Editor: Kezia Endsley
Compositor: SPi Global
Indexer: SPi Global
Artist: SPi Global

Distributed to the book trade worldwide by Springer Science+Business Media New York, 233 Spring Street, 6th Floor, New York, NY 10013. Phone 1-800-SPRINGER, fax (201) 348-4505, e-mail orders-ny@springer-sbm.com, or visit www.springer.com. Apress Media, LLC is a California LLC and the sole member (owner) is Springer Science + Business Media Finance Inc (SSBM Finance Inc). SSBM Finance Inc is a Delaware corporation.

For information on translations, please e-mail rights@apress.com, or visit www.apress.com.

Apress and friends of ED books may be purchased in bulk for academic, corporate, or promotional use. eBook versions and licenses are also available for most titles. For more information, reference our Special Bulk Sales–eBook Licensing web page at www.apress.com/bulk-sales.

Any source code or other supplementary material referenced by the author in this text is available to readers at www.apress.com. For detailed information about how to locate your book's source code, go to www.apress.com/source-code/.

Printed on acid-free paper

Contents at a Glance

Foreword xi

About the Author xiii

About the Technical Reviewers xv

Acknowledgments xvii

Preface xix

■Part I: Getting Started 1

■Chapter 1: What Is DevOps? 3

■Chapter 2: Introducing Azure and Visual Studio Team Services 9

■Part II: Plan 17

■Chapter 3: Agile Project Management: The Importance of Communication 19

■Chapter 4: Managing User Feedback: Knowing What to Build 43

■Chapter 5: Advanced Agile Project Management 55

■Chapter 6: Dashboards and Reporting 77

■Part III: Code and Build 97

■Chapter 7: Setting Up Version Control 99

■Chapter 8: Managing Technical Debt 137

■Chapter 9: Implementing Continuous Integration 161

■Chapter 10: Creating and Sharing Packages 189

■**Part IV: Test, Deploy, and Monitor**.. **203**

■**Chapter 11: Integrating Testers into DevOps**................................... **205**

■**Chapter 12: Implementing Continuous Delivery with Release Management** **231**

■**Chapter 13: Using Application Insights** **261**

■**Chapter 14: The Path Forward**.. **277**

Index.. **283**

Contents

Foreword xi

About the Author xiii

About the Technical Reviewers xv

Acknowledgments..xvii

Preface xix

■Part I: Getting Started.. 1

■Chapter 1: What Is DevOps? 3

Why Are We Doing DevOps? 3

Assessing Your DevOps Capability 6

Summary... 8

■Chapter 2: Introducing Azure and Visual Studio Team Services 9

Understanding the Microsoft Cloud: Azure 9

laaS, PaaS, and SaaS...10

Security 11

Using Visual Studio Team Services.. 14

Security 15

The Need for Training 16

Summary... 16

■Part II: Plan 17

■Chapter 3: Agile Project Management: The Importance of Communication 19

Agile Project Management 19

Agile Tooling 22

    Sprints 22

    Product Backlog Items 24

    Tasks 27

    Impediments 28

    Bugs 30

    Capacity 32

Team Rooms 36

Achieving Traceability with Developers 39

Summary 41

■Chapter 4: Managing User Feedback: Knowing What to Build 43

Why We Need Better Communication 43

Creating Storyboards with PowerPoint 44

Involving Stakeholders in Feedback Management 47

Summary 53

■Chapter 5: Advanced Agile Project Management 55

Kanban and Lean 55

Portfolio Management 67

Summary 75

■Chapter 6: Dashboards and Reporting 77

Queries 77

    Using the Search Box 77

    Work Item Queries 79

    Charts 83

Code Search 89

Dashboards 92

Alerts and Notifications 93

Summary 96

■**Part III: Code and Build** **97**

■**Chapter 7: Setting Up Version Control** **99**

Introducing Version Control 99

Using Team Foundation Version Control (TFVC) 103

Workspace 103

Checking in a Changeset 106

Get Latest and Merge Conflicts 110

History, Annotations, and CodeLens 111

Shelvesets and Suspending Your Work 114

Branches 119

Check-In Policies 122

Using the Git Version Control System 124

Clone 124

Commit and Push 125

Fetch and Pull 127

Branch 128

Pull Request 130

Choosing a Branching Strategy 134

Branch Scenarios 134

Feature Toggles 135

Summary 136

■**Chapter 8: Managing Technical Debt** **137**

Running Code Analysis 138

Code Metrics 141

Lines of Code 142

Cyclomatic Complexity 144

Coupling.. 144

Depth of Inheritance 146

Calculating Code Metrics.. 146

Finding Duplications.. 147

Validating the Architecture 149

Create and Run Unit Tests 152

Creating Custom Code Analyzers with Roslyn.. 156

Summary.. 160

■Chapter 9: Implementing Continuous Integration 161

Configuring a Continuous Integration Build.. 162

Installing and Configuring Build Agents 173

Creating Custom Tasks.. 175

Using SonarQube.. 181

Summary.. 187

■Chapter 10: Creating and Sharing Packages 189

What Are Packages? 189

Package Management for Visual Studio Team Services 195

Summary.. 201

■Part IV: Test, Deploy, and Monitor.. 203

■Chapter 11: Integrating Testers into DevOps................................... 205

Manual Testing Through Web Access 205

Microsoft Test Manager.. 216

Automated Testing.. 220

Summary.. 229

■Chapter 12: Implementing Continuous Delivery with Release Management 231

Understanding the Deployment Pipeline 231

Setting Up Automatic Releases with Release Management.............................. 232

Deploying Web Sites 246

Understanding Containers 256

Summary 259

■Chapter 13: Using Application Insights 261

What Is Application Insights? 261

Configuring Monitoring for Your Application 263

Availability Monitoring 269

Usage Monitoring 272

Diagnose Failures and Exceptions 274

Summary 275

■Chapter 14: The Path Forward 277

The Basics 277

Stepping It Up 280

Finishing Touches 281

Summary 282

Index 283

Foreword

Team Foundation Server (TFS) and Visual Studio Team Services (VSTS) from Microsoft are two incredible products for enabling DevOps. They both offer everything you need, from planning to continuous delivery.

Their features and capabilities are available regardless of the language you program in or the platform you target. From on-premises to the Cloud, PC to Mac, and Android to iOS, nothing is out of reach.

With built-in web access, you can track your project from any web-enabled device.

TFS and VSTS can seem intimidating at first because they contain the largest breadth of features in the industry. However, Wouter gives you a guided tour of the features and capabilities so you can start using them on your DevOps journey.

I have had the pleasure to work with Wouter on several ALM Ranger projects and I am very impressed by his knowledge and experience. I was very pleased to hear that Wouter was writing a book on DevOps because I trust his abilities in this area implicitly.

DevOps is the union of people, process, and products to enable the continuous delivery of value to our end users. DevOps on the Microsoft Stack teaches you the products that will shape your process and enable your people to build amazing applications.

—Donovan Brown
Senior DevOps Program Manager
Microsoft

About the Author

Wouter de Kort started with software development when he was seven years old and his dad brought home the family's first computer. It was a 286 monochrome laptop. After discovering Windows, Solitaire, and Paint, he came across Quick Basic. And then things became interesting. He can still remember one of the first programs he wrote that helped students practice their multiplication tables. He didn't know much about programming at that time and his code looked something like this:

```
if ( current_table = 1 )
        if ( current_question = 1) checkifanswer(1 * 1)
        if ( current_question = 2) checkifanswer(1 * 2)
```

All the way to the table of ten. Of course this was littered with goto statements and labels to keep his procedural program working. Proud as he was, he asked a friend of his parents—a software developer—to have a look at his code. He looked at his code, smiled, and then opened up a program where he wrote a couple of lines and was able to calculate all possible multiplications you could imagine.

And that's how it started. Now de Kort works as the Principal Consultant Microsoft at Ordina in the Netherlands. He helps organizations stay on the cutting edge of software development on the Microsoft stack and focuses on Application Lifecycle Management and software architecture. He still loves to write code and solve complex problems, but especially loves helping other developers grow. He has authored a couple of other books, is a Microsoft Certified Trainer, and an ALM Ranger. You can find him on Twitter at @wouterdekort and on his blog at http://wouterdekort.com.

About the Technical Reviewers

Josh Garverick is a Microsoft MVP in Application Lifecycle Management, a Visual Studio ALM Ranger, a solutions architect, and self-proclaimed cross-platform nerd. When he's not fulfilling his duties on the job or with his family, he finds enjoyment in his Frankenbuild lab, making new creations from old hardware. Follow the Frankenbuild adventure at http://frankenbuild.net, Josh's blog at http://joshgarverick.blogspot.com, and his antics on Twitter at @Jgarverick.

Willy-Peter Schaub started his IT career in the early 1980s during his electrical engineering studies, focusing on the BTOS/CTOS operating systems, until he moved over primarily to Microsoft technologies in the early 90s. Since then, his passion has been to investigate, research, and evangelize technology, striving for simplicity and maintainability in software engineering. Apart from writing books such as *.NET Enterprise Solutions: Best Practices*, *.NET Enterprise Solutions: Interoperability for the Connoisseur*, *Software Engineers on their way to Pluto*, and *Managing Agile OSS Projects with Microsoft Visual Studio Online*, his varied and extreme interests include scuba diving, cycling, science fiction, astronomy, and most importantly, his family. You can follow him on Twitter at twitter.com/wpschaub.

Acknowledgments

I would like to thank the following persons for their support and help:

- My wife Elise. Thanks for letting me work on this book!

- The team at Apress who helped me create this book, especially James DeWolf, Melissa Maldonado, and Douglas Pundick.

- Willy-Peter Schaub. Thank you for making me a part of the ALM Rangers and for all your advice on this book.

- Josh Garverick. Thanks for your support and all the reviewing work you did.

- Donovan Brown. Your enthusiasm for DevOps is incredible and really contagious. Thanks for your feedback and encouragement.

- All the members of the Microsoft Product Group who reviewed chapters and helped me with all the small details only they know. Especially Jean-Marc Prieur, Rohit Bansal, Jeff Levinson, Ravi Shanker, Gopinath Chigakkagari, Shruti Poddar, Biju Venugopal, and Vijay Machiraju.

- My colleagues at Ordina who listened to my plans and reviewed the material: Eelco Koster, Daniel van der Starre, Jeroen Ploeg, Jasper Jak, and Peter de Nijs.

Preface

While learning about Agile and DevOps, I read some great books. I studied the different parts that make up the Application Lifecycle Management (ALM) toolkit from Microsoft, like Visual Studio Team Services and Azure, and learned how they worked. I also read books on the issues you face when helping an organization implement DevOps and Agile.

However, what I always missed was a book that answered questions like these:

- When should I introduce which part of the Microsoft tooling?

- How do the various parts work together?

- How can I help my people understand the benefits of ALM, Agile, and DevOps?

And that's why I wrote this book. This book is here to show you not only how the tooling is used but also how you can make everything work together and make sure that your team wants to use it. This book focuses not only on individual tools but also on the collaboration between tools and how to help your whole team with them.

So mainly, I wrote this book because this is what I would love to have known when I started with DevOps.

Who Should Read this Book

This book focuses on Agile, DevOps, and Application Lifecycle Management techniques on the Microsoft development stack. It shows you how to use VS Team Services, Visual Studio, and Azure. The book is mainly targeted at experienced developers who develop applications with .NET using Visual Studio. Prerequisite knowledge of Team Foundation Server, Azure, and VS Team Services is not required. Knowing the basics of Scrum is a plus.

However, developers are not the only audience for this book. The book not only explains the tools, but it also shows you what DevOps can do for an organization and what is currently possible with state-of-the-art technology. This means that this book is an interesting read for everyone who's fascinated by DevOps, be it on the Microsoft stack or on another development platform. You can choose to read any part of this book that interests you in any order you want. That's all up to you.

Prerequisites

To follow along with the examples in this book, you will need access to a VS Team Services account or an on-premises installation of Team Foundation Server 2015 with the latest updates (or newer). You can use a free account of VS Team Services and enable all the features during the trial. If the trial ends, you can use a Basic license for most of the examples. Only some advanced examples require an MSDN subscription. You also need an installation of Visual Studio 2015 with the latest updates (or newer). To learn about Application Insights and some of the deployment options, you also need an Azure subscription. This can be a trial, MSDN, or pay-as-you-go subscription.

Knowledge of C# and the .NET Framework is preferred for the chapters on continuous integration and technical debt management.

■ ■ ■

Getting Started

In this first part, you'll learn what DevOps is and why it should interest you. You will be introduced to Microsoft's tooling in the form of Visual Studio Team Services and Microsoft Azure.

CHAPTER 1

■ ■ ■

What Is DevOps?

You might lately have heard a lot about the term DevOps. Gartner even stated that 2016 is the year of DevOps (http://www.gartner.com/newsroom/id/2999017). Is DevOps more than a marketing term? Or is it just some hype that someone created?

Why Are We Doing DevOps?

Software development is still a young industry. As an industry, it's rapidly evolving and trying to become better. And growth is really necessary. The software development industry doesn't have a very good reputation when it comes to producing software on time and on budget. In what's now called a *waterfall* process, software was developed in a couple of discrete steps. In Figure 1-1 you see the steps a typical project used to have to develop software. All these phases follow each other and the total timespan could be several months or even years.

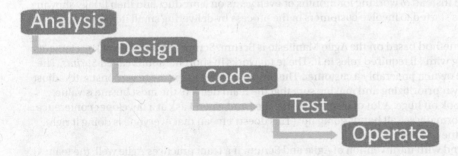

Figure 1-1. Stages in a waterfall project

Other industries use the same kind of distinct steps. For example, consider a city block where all houses are being built to look alike. It makes sense to have a clear specification of all the steps that go into building a house and then repeat those steps for all houses until the block is finished. Software is different. Customers don't ask developers to build them multiple copies of the same product. Instead, each project is unique. Development teams are always building something new. The problem with wanting something new is that you don't know exactly what you want since you first have to come up with an idea. Software development organizations thought the solution was to create better specifications. The documents that were created became bigger and bigger. And of course, creating a detailed upfront specification takes a lot of time. So customers were asked to sign those documents and then treat them as the absolute truth.

Electronic supplementary material The online version of this chapter (doi:10.1007/978-1-4842-1446-6_1) contains supplementary material, which is available to authorized users.

After the first analysis phase ends with a detailed specification, design, code, and test phases follow. After the first pass through the steps, a working version is demoed to the customer. The first time a customer sees a working version of his idea, he gets a better idea of what he actually needs. Maybe the customer wants some small changes or maybe he decides he wants something completely different. This has plagued the software industry for a long time and led to the reputation that the software industry builds the wrong thing, while missing deadlines and costing more than was promised. This is when a big step in the software industry was made: the beginning of Agile.

In 2001, the Agile Manifesto was released. The Agile Manifesto can be seen as a response to the state that software development was in. The Agile Manifesto stated a couple of simple values:

> *We are uncovering better ways of developing*
> *software by doing it and helping others do it.*
> *Through this work we have come to value:*
> *Individuals and interactions over processes and tools*
> *Working software over comprehensive documentation*
> *Customer collaboration over contract negotiation*
> *Responding to change over following a plan*
> *That is, while there is value in the items on*
> *the right, we value the items on the left more.*

—The Agile Manifesto

The Agile Manifesto caused a lot of change in the software industry. Instead of writing thick documents, development teams started actually working with the customer. The fact that a customer changes his mind was no longer viewed as something that a team needed to avoid. Instead, teams accepted that customers change their minds and that it's their right to do so. Software development teams started working together with their customers. So instead of working for months or even years on a product and then finally showing it to the customer, teams started to involve customers in the process by delivering small iterations and responding to changes.

The most popular method based on the Agile Manifesto is Scrum. Scrum has a couple of key elements. A team is self-organizing with all required roles in it. The team works in short iterations called *Sprints*. The team is led by a product owner, preferably a customer. The product owner helps the team constantly adjust to changes by constantly reprioritizing and making sure that the team delivers the most business value.

Scrum took off. It took off huge. A lot of teams liked the idea and when I ask at a developer conference who is doing Scrum, I normally see all hands going up! (This doesn't mean that everyone is doing it right. Some teams only think they are doing Scrum.)

The story doesn't end with the invention of Agile and Scrum. If a team practices Agile well, the team will pick up speed. The developers, helped by the product owner, will create a steady release of new features. Agile is part of the solution but we needed more. Successful Agile teams still have barriers.

Testers often struggle in an Agile organization. They are always trying to keep up with the developers. The discipline of testers is changing and I see the distinction between testers and developers blurring. Testers and developers often pair up or blend into a multi-skilled developer role. While testers struggle to keep up, the situation is even worse for the operations team. These teams are often in another department. They are responsible for running the datacenter and are tasked with deploying applications that the development team creates while making sure that everything keeps running. This leads to silos, which are different teams in different departments reporting to different managers with different responsibilities. The operations team is responsible for making sure the software is stable. The development team is responsible for getting out new features as fast as possible. The testers are caught in between and the business only sees that the things they need take too long to become available.

In the years since the introduction of Agile, the software world has changed even more. Mobile systems and the cloud were big game changers. Customers have changed the way they interact with companies and startups take advantage of this. A company like Uber suddenly competes with the regular taxi world. PayPal, which is a software company, competes with banks. Netflix has revolutionized the way people watch TV. How have these companies succeeded?

This is where DevOps come in. DevOps helps Agile to fully realize its potential. The opinions on what DevOps is differ, but I like the following definition:

> *DevOps is the union of people, process, and products to enable continuous delivery of value to our end users.*

—Donovan Brown, DevOps Senior Program Manager at Microsoft

The key phrase is continuous delivery of value. Where Agile helped the software industry respond to customer needs and keep up with changes, DevOps is the key to actually delivering the value to the hands of the end users. DevOps is more than tooling. DevOps is about the whole organization working together to deliver value to its customers. This makes DevOps as much about people and processes as it is about choosing the right tools. DevOps helps you in optimizing what's called the *software delivery pipeline*, which involves taking software from an idea to the hands of the end user. By putting DevOps patterns into practice, organizations like Netflix, Facebook, Amazon, Twitter, Google and Microsoft are achieving levels of performance that were unthinkable while using Agile. These organizations don't deploy once a year or even once a week. Instead they deploy multiple times a day while delivering a stable and reliable user experience.

The word DevOps is a clipped compound of developers and operations. In Agile, you don't hear anyone about the operations team. But they are really needed for delivering a successful application. DevOps breaks down the silos between the development team and operations. Organizations that practice DevOps take the principles of Agile and extend it to involve all parties—business, development, testers, and operations—into creating, deploying, and running successful applications.

Although DevOps is not only about tooling, tooling is important. This tooling must support the Agile process and optimize the delivery pipeline. Tooling can help with automating the error-prone, time-consuming tasks like deploying applications and running regression tests. This book helps you with discovering the tooling that Microsoft offers. You will learn how Microsoft supports both your Agile and your DevOps processes and makes sure that they blend together into a delivery pipeline that optimizes the value for your end users. Figure 1-2 shows a visual overview of how Microsoft sees DevOps.

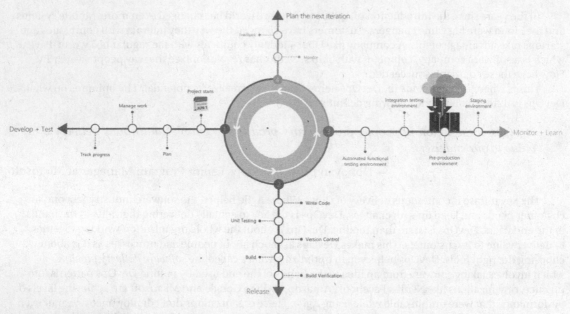

Figure 1-2. *The different parts that make up a DevOps process*

A team that implements both Agile methodologies and DevOps processes is a team that can do incredible things. They can respond to changes so quickly that the build software becomes a business advantage. Teams and organizations that do this successfully are high-performing organizations.

And that's why Agile, DevOps, and the whole process of Application Lifecycle Management is not hype nor just empty marketing terms. They are real techniques with real value. However, implementing them is not as easy as it may seem.

Assessing Your DevOps Capability

To understand what you need to do to implement DevOps, you first need to know where you are now. A good way to get started is by looking at the practices a DevOps team typically has (see Figure 1-3).

A team starts with an Agile schedule and with being a true Agile team. This means they have self-control and have all the people and roles they need. They follow an Agile schedule, meaning they work in short iterations and constantly try to adapt to changing customer demands, changing markets, and other circumstances. They also try to constantly improve everything they do. The second thing you should look at is the quality of your work. If you create lots of bugs and your code is impossible to maintain, but you improve your speed, this could mean that you are creating even worse code and releasing more bugs.

A DevOps team tries to create a continuous flow of value. Flow of value means that you can move swiftly from an idea all the way to production. To realize this, silos disappear and multidisciplinary teams are created. By automating deployments, testing, and infrastructure operations, new features can reach production in minutes.

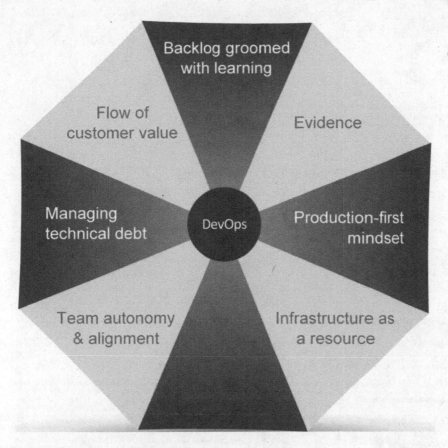

Figure 1-3. Practices of a DevOps team

Agile helps teams create a *backlog*, which is a prioritized list of features that have real customer value. The product owner has the difficult task of prioritizing features. Having insight into what customers do helps the product owner prioritize the right features. By creating a hypothesis (if I change feature X, Y more users will Z) and then measuring in production if this is actually true, you create a hypothesis-based backlog. Instead of guessing what the customer wants, you start creating small experiments and run these with real customers. This can drive the direction your product is going.

Being able to quickly deploy changes, monitor results, and scale according to real world use is a business advantage. To achieve this agility, a flexible infrastructure is an enormous advantage. This is why the Cloud is mentioned as one of the practices of a DevOps team. Microsoft offers you an excellent Cloud solution that you can use privately, publically, or in a hybrid way, called Microsoft Azure. Microsoft Azure contains a wide variety of infrastructure services that allow you to utilize quick deployments, monitor results, and then scale on demand. A flexible infrastructure that delivers these services really helps your company become a DevOps organization.

As you can see, DevOps is a huge subject. Knowing which practices you already have and where you can improve can be difficult. To help you with this, Microsoft has released a self-assessment tool that you can use to score yourself in the seven key areas of DevOps. You can find this assessment at http://devopsassessment. azurewebsites.net (see Figure 1-4). I encourage you to take this assessment to get a sense of what DevOps can do for your organization. This will also place the coming chapters into context.

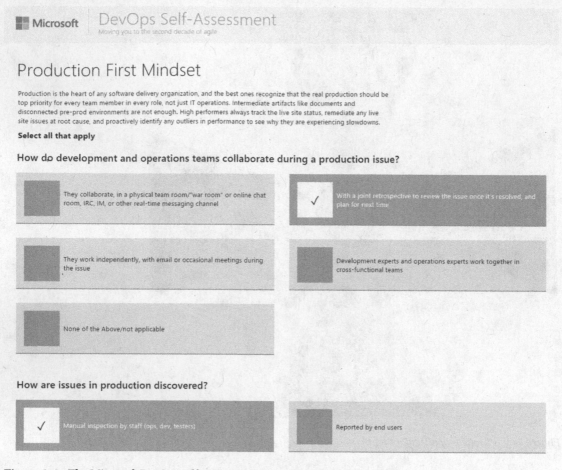

Figure 1-4. *The Microsoft DevOps self-assessment is a great way to get started*

Summary

In this chapter, you've read a short history of the movement of the software industry, from waterfall to Agile to DevOps. You've learned that organizations that practice DevOps have a huge advantage and deliver end user value at a much higher rate. You've seen that DevOps is not only about tooling but also about breaking down silos and optimizing the flow of value from the idea to the hands of the end users. You've also taken the DevOps assessment to help you get started.

Before you dive into DevOps, the next chapter introduces you to two essential tools that you'll use throughout the rest of the book: Azure and Visual Studio Team Services.

CHAPTER 2

■ ■ ■

Introducing Azure and Visual Studio Team Services

DevOps is the union of people, process, and products that enables continuous delivery of value to our end users. As a company, you bring the people and Microsoft helps you define your process and a great set of products. The foundation of Microsoft's DevOps tooling is Team Foundation Server (TFS) and Visual Studio Team Services. These are a complete suite of products that help you with DevOps.

Team Foundation Server is installed on-premises on your own servers or on virtual machines running in a Cloud environment. You configure the environment and do the maintenance and you have full control over the environment. Microsoft has also released a new way using of Team Foundation Server called VS Team Services. VS Team Services runs on top of the Microsoft Cloud platform, called Microsoft Azure. In this book, the examples use VS Team Services, but you can also use Team Foundation Server if you have an on-premises installation.

In this chapter, you'll learn what the Cloud, and specifically Microsoft Azure, is. You'll get started with using Azure and be able to explain the benefits of using the Cloud. After that, you'll get started with VS Team Services. You'll be able to reason about security when it comes to both Azure and VS Team Services and you'll be able to make an informed decision based on your situation.

Understanding the Microsoft Cloud: Azure

How is your company hosting its applications? Your company might be running its own infrastructure, hosted in a datacenter or in a space of its own. Maybe you're renting servers from a specialized company and they configure and maintain your environments.

When a new application needs to be deployed, you work out the number of servers you need and the specifications you require. You then submit a request to your internal or external hosting party. After some time, varying from days to weeks or even months, the servers are delivered. You then pay a fixed price for the servers you buy or lease.

Most companies I've worked with use these types of hosting. While looking at the steps you need to take, you immediately see some disadvantages. What if you want to scale your capacity based on load? What if you just want a few servers to run an experiment on? What if you want to pay only for what you actually use? And why would you want to run a complete server to only host a web application?

Flexibility, both in pricing and in capacity, has proven to be a huge advantage for companies trying to implement DevOps. And that's what the Cloud offers.

© Wouter de Kort 2016
W. de Kort, *DevOps on the Microsoft Stack*, DOI 10.1007/978-1-4842-1446-6_2

IaaS, PaaS, and SaaS

Microsoft Azure offers you an almost unlimited amount of resources. You can use those resources, like servers or storage, and pay only for what you use. This means that you can start treating infrastructure as a service. Requesting a virtual machine takes a couple of minutes. When using storage, you only pay for what you use. The moment you don't need a resource, you just stop using it and stop paying for it.

So what kind of resources does Azure offer you? You can group all the Azure resources in two categories: Infrastructure as a Service (IaaS) and Platform as a Service (PaaS).

Figure 2-1 shows the differences between IaaS and PaaS. On top of the IaaS and PaaS resources, you have Software as a Service (SaaS). Complete applications that are maintained by the company that built them.

Figure 2-1. *IaaS, PaaS, and SaaS components of Azure*

IaaS is on the level of servers, network, and identity. You don't have to worry about the underlying infrastructure. You don't need to buy servers, route cables, and deal with hardware failures. IaaS looks like a typical datacenter, with the difference that Azure IaaS offers you complete self-service and lets you pay per minute.

PaaS has an even higher level of abstraction. With IaaS you're still required to run an operating system (OS), install updates, and deal with actual virtual machines. PaaS doesn't bother you with those things. Take for example SQL Azure. Instead of installing one or more servers running SQL Server, configuring accounts, security, backups, and all the other things, you just use SQL Azure. Azure will automatically create database servers for you, arrange backups, and make sure that you have certain performance characteristics. This is way easier than running your own SQL Server instance.

Another example of PaaS is Azure Web apps, a web site hosting platform. Azure completely manages the underlying machines, updates, and availability for you. The only thing you have to do is create a new Web App, publish your web site to it, and you're done. Things like managing Internet Information Services (IIS), the OS, patches, and updates are all done for you. If a machine crashes, your web site automatically starts on a new machine. So instead of worrying about infrastructure, Azure allows you to focus on building your application.

Security

An important discussion topic when it comes to the Cloud is security. Where does my data reside? Who is responsible for it? Who has access to it? Can I move away from the Cloud? These are important questions that you need to answer for your specific situation. Depending on the type of applications you build and the data you store, you will have different requirements.

Microsoft understands that security is a key concern for organizations to move to the Cloud. Because of this, Microsoft takes a lot of steps to guarantee safety of your data. For example, Microsoft uses the Security Development Lifecycle. This is a company-wide, mandatory process that embeds security requirements into the entire software lifecycle. Azure offers strict identity and access control mechanisms. Two factor authentication, encryption of data both in motion and at rest, network security, and threat management are all part of Microsofts approach. Another thing that can help with adopting Azure is the global reach of the datacenters that Azure uses. Microsoft is constantly investing in new datacenters and even offers specialized versions for government use.

If you want to know more about security and Azure, you can find more information at http://azure. microsoft.com/en-us/support/trust-center/. If you work in a strictly controlled organization, don't dismiss Azure from the beginning. Investigate if you can use certain security features or other options to allow the use of the public Cloud.

If it turns out this is absolutely not possible, you can also turn to a private Cloud solution. Microsoft offers Azure Stack for on-premises datacenters that want to install Azure features on-premises. This means that you get a number of IaaS and PaaS services that you can run in your own datacenter. Microsoft is making sure that management, configuration, and deployment of applications can be done in a similar way in both the public and private Cloud.

This book uses a lot of Azure. An Azure subscription is necessary if you want to take full advantage of all the examples in this book. You can quickly sign up for your own Azure account. If you own an MSDN subscription, you get free monthly credits for Azure. Otherwise, you can sign up for a trial or a pay-as-you-go subscription with a credit card.

Follow these steps if you own an MSDN subscription:

1. Go to https://account.windowsazure.com/signup?offer=Azure_MSDN.

2. Accept the terms.

3. Click on Buy.

4. Wait for the signup process to finish.

Take this step if you want to create a free trial that lasts one month or pay $200:

1. Go to http://azure.microsoft.com/en-us/pricing/free-trial/.

2. Sign up for the free trial.

Take this step to create a new pay-as-you-go Azure subscription:

1. Go to http://azure.microsoft.com/en-us/pricing/purchase-options/.

2. Select Buy Now for the Pay-As-You-Go option.

3. Complete the signup process.

In addition to these three options, you can also purchase an Azure subscription through your Enterprise Agreement (EA). If you are an Enterprise organization that has an EA with Microsoft, you should use it to buy Azure credits at a discounted price.

When working with Azure, you will use the Azure Portal that you can find at http://portal.azure.com. Figure 2-2 shows the Azure Portal. You see the wealth of the different datacenters spread around the world. You also see a tile that shows how much credit I've left on my MSDN subscription credits, a link to the marketplace, and to Help and support. You can create new resources by clicking on the green plus icon in the top left. This opens a *blade* (that's what the different sections in Azure are called) that lets you pick a category of resources. For example, a virtual machine is part of the Compute category. Figure 2-3 shows the settings you need to configure to create a new virtual machine. After entering your settings, all you have to do is click on Create. The actual process to create your new virtual machine takes a couple of minutes. When it's finished you can navigate to the blade of your virtual machine to manage settings and start and stop the machine. You can also set up a Remote Desktop connection so you can use the user interface of your new machine from your own PC.

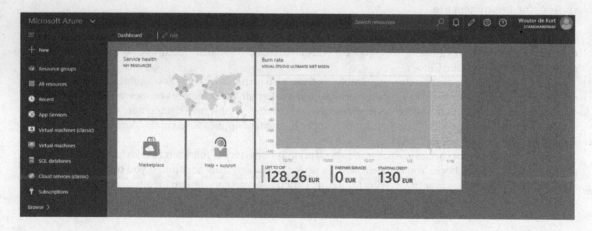

Figure 2-2. *The Azure Portal*

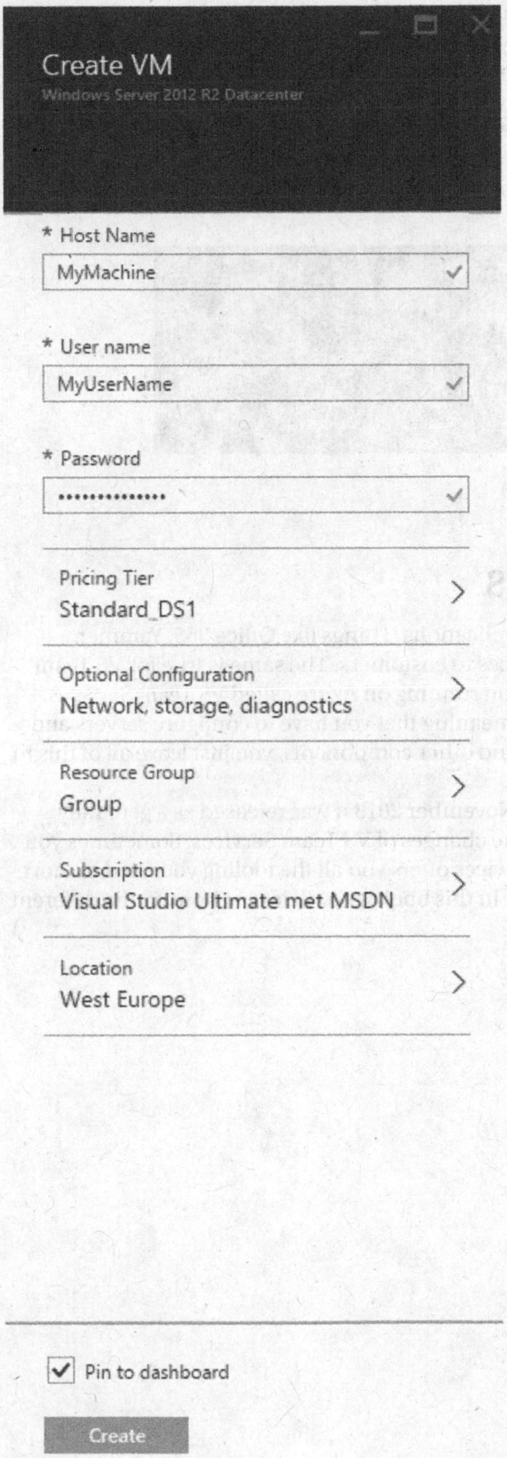

Create VM
Windows Server 2012 R2 Datacenter

* Host Name

MyMachine ✓

* User name

MyUserName ✓

* Password

••••••••••••• ✓

Pricing Tier
Standard_DS1 >

Optional Configuration
Network, storage, diagnostics >

Resource Group
Group >

Subscription
Visual Studio Ultimate met MSDN >

Location
West Europe >

☑ Pin to dashboard

Create

Figure 2-3. *You need to configure a couple of settings when creating a new virtual machine*

What's important to understand is that you pay per minute for the virtual machine you just created. This means that if you let the machine run, you continue paying for it. By selecting the Shut Down option (Figure 2-4), you close the machine and you stop paying for the compute resources. You will only pay a small amount of money for the storage of your virtual machine's hard disk. This is only a fraction of what you can do with Azure. Microsoft has also created an automation service that you can use to schedule automatic resource shutdown. You can create services ranging from storage to machine learning in the portal. You can deploy complex applications or use Azure as a Dev/Test environment.

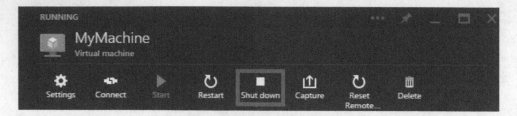

Figure 2-4. *You can shut down your machine to save costs*

Using Visual Studio Team Services

On top of Microsoft Azure, Microsoft has built all kinds of applications. Things like Office 365, Yammer, Bing, and Skype run on top of Azure and are offered as services to customers. The same is true for VS Team Services. Team Foundation Server is offered as a SaaS solution running on Azure called VS Team Services. Instead of installing Team Foundation Server on-premises, meaning that you have to configure servers and then install SQL Server, application services, build servers, and other components, you just leave all of this to Microsoft and use VS Team Services.

VS Team Services started as a preview in June 2013. In November 2013 it was released as a generally available service. Figure 2-5 shows the timeline and the name changes of VS Team Services. Sometimes you will see the older names in the documentation. VS Team Services offers you all the tooling you need to move your organization to a full-fledged DevOps implementation. In this book you will learn about all the different elements of VS Team Services and how they work.

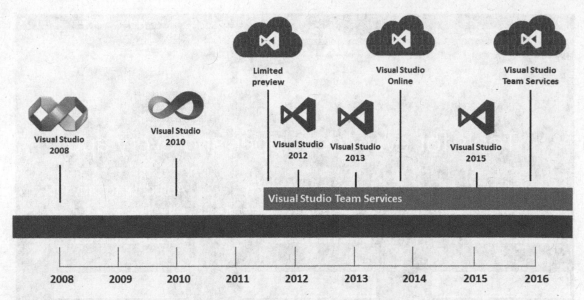

Figure 2-5. *Visual Studio Team Services' timeline*

Security

Just as with Azure, you need to be aware of the security options you have when using VS Team Services. Microsoft is working hard on making sure that VS Team Services has the certifications and policies in place that allow all kinds of organizations to safely use it.

A big advantage of building on top of Azure is that all the built-in security mechanisms from Azure automatically apply to VS Team Services. Things like identity management, DDoS protection, and data replication are all part of the Azure infrastructure and are used by VS Team Services. Microsoft is also applying to get VS Team Services certified. Early 2015 Microsoft earned the ISO 27001 (information security management) certification. Microsoft continues to invest in additional certifications.

Microsoft uses VS Team Services for its own development. The developer division that builds Visual Studio and VS Team Services has migrated from an on-premises TFS to VS Team Services. Microsoft is actively tracking and fixing any issues that occur on VS Team Services. You can follow the VS Team Services Twitter account (@vsonline) and the Service Blog (http://blogs.msdn.com/b/vsoservice/) for any issues and updates. You can also install the News for Visual Studio plugin in your Visual Studio IDE (https://visualstudiogallery.msdn.microsoft.com/ace247af-962d-41a2-b6a3-7b0510690bf6). This allows you to get news directly in your IDE.

Microsoft is very open about its quality of services. Whenever a serious incident occurs, Microsoft always publishes a root cause analysis. This is done by Brian Harry, the vice-president responsible for VS Team Services. These reports contain details about the issue, such as why it happened and which steps Microsoft has taken to make sure it can't happen again. All these things are done to improve the service and to make sure that you can trust VS Team Services (see http://aka.ms/VSOSecurity for more information).

You can create a VS Team Services account by navigating to http://visualstudio.com. Figure 2-6 shows the landing page. Notice in the middle of the page is the option to get started for free. All you need to do is sign in with a Microsoft account and come up with a name for your account. Your account gets a URL with the form https://<youraccountname>.visualstudio.com. You need to choose a source control type (Git or Team Foundation Version Control). For now, just select the default. In Chapter 7, which covers version control, you'll learn the differences and which options to choose. You can also choose a location for your VS Team Services account. This is the Azure datacenter where your account data will be stored. This setting defaults to the location that is closest to you.

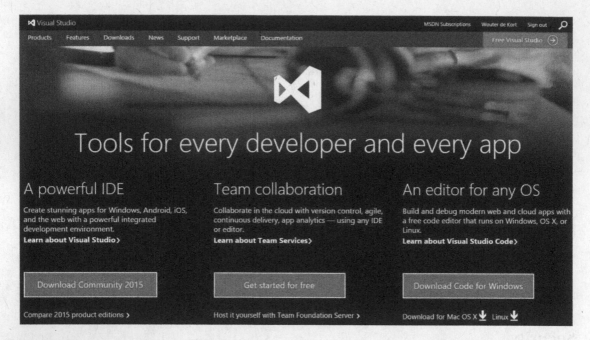

Figure 2-6. The Visual Studio web site offers access to your VS Team Services account, documentation, and other resources

The Need for Training

Because of the sheer impact of Agile, DevOps, and ALM implementation, I see a lot of implementations fail. Companies often don't see the bigger picture when it comes to DevOps. They only focus on installing some tools and then forcing their teams to use those tools. Azure and VS Team Services are great tools for helping your organization implement DevOps. But without the proper training in using those tools and working on the cultural changes, your DevOps implementation is doomed to fail.

Don't expect that having an Azure subscription and a VS Team Services account is enough. Make sure that every member of your team is trained in using these tools. If you incorporate multidisciplinary assignments in your training, you will break down silos and work together with your whole team. This will give you the complete benefit that Azure and VS Team Services can offer you.

Summary

This chapter introduced Microsoft Azure and VS Team Services. You now know the differences among IaaS, PaaS, and SaaS. You've seen how easy it is to create a resource such as a virtual machine. You've also seen that VS Team Services is a SaaS offering of Team Foundation Server that Microsoft runs on top of Azure. Finally, you've seen how to create an account.

This concludes the introduction. In the following chapters, you will dive much deeper into VS Team Services and Azure and learn how to implement a DevOps process using these tools.

PART II

Plan

Every project starts with an idea. Getting from that idea to a working application is the challenge you face when developing software. Visual Studio Team Services helps you a lot in tracking requirements, adapting to change, and improving the communication among your team members. This part details different processes, techniques, and tools you can use for improving the planning activities of your project.

CHAPTER 3

■ ■ ■

Agile Project Management: The Importance of Communication

When managing a software project, communication is one of the most, if not the most, important aspect of software development. In this chapter you'll learn the excellent features that Visual Studio Team Services offers you for managing your project. Stimulating communication, keeping track of the work that needs to be done, and making sure that all team members work together are important aspects.

You will learn the project management tooling that VS Team Services offers you directly in the Web Access. You will see how you can use these tools to track work, plan resources, and optimize your team. You will also look into *team rooms*, which is a chat environment that you can use to stimulate discussions and keep track of all the work that's being done. Finally, you'll take a first step in Visual Studio by seeing how developers integrate into these processes.

Agile Project Management

When building software there are a lot of parties involved. First, you have the customer with all their different stakeholders. In a typical project you also have business analysts, user experience designers, architects, developers, testers, operations, managers, and maybe you can come up with some more roles for your project.

In what's now called a *waterfall* project, the project is divided into distinct phases (see Figure 3-1). First, the analyst works with the customer in creating a detailed specification of what the customer actually wants. This is often called a *functional design*. Sometimes user stories or other types of documentation are created. This document is discussed with the customer and worked on until the customer agrees that this is what he wants.

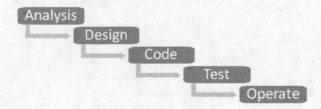

Figure 3-1. *Stages in a waterfall project*

© Wouter de Kort 2016

W. de Kort, *DevOps on the Microsoft Stack*, DOI 10.1007/978-1-4842-1446-6_3

The next phase is *coding*. The functional specification is then translated into a technical specification. The architect is involved in creating the architecture diagrams and doing all kinds of planning for topics like security, scalability, and modularity. These plans are then passed on to the developers. They try to actually code all the features while interpreting the functional and technical specifications.

Hopefully this is also when the testers get involved. Although in some scenarios, you see that the testers are only involved after the developers are finished. The testers try to map the specifications to the actual implementation and find any bugs and incorrect implementations. After this phase, you should have a correct working application that needs to be deployed to a production environment. The operation team is called in to configure the correct servers, deploy the application, and make sure that everything works.

Waterfall has the big disadvantage that feedback comes really late in the cycle. What if the developers came up with something that is insecure when deployed in production? What if the business analyst interpreted a customer request incorrectly and the customer sees the mistake months later? What if the testers find a bug in a part of the code and in the meantime the developers have moved to a totally different part of the code base?

Shortening the feedback loop is key to improving communication. This is where both processes and tooling can help. Agile is all about shortening cycles, improving communication, and thereby improving value for the customers. VS Team Services has built-in support for running general Agile projects or a project based on the Scrum methodology.

If you look at Scrum as one of the popular methodologies (if you're unfamiliar with the Scrum terminology, read the official Scrum guide at http://www.scrumguides.org and see Figure 3-2 for the most important terms), you often see teams start without any tooling support. Teams use a whiteboard with post-its or some other physical medium to run their projects. Daily Scrums are done with all team members gathered at a single location and other metrics like the burn down are calculated by hand.

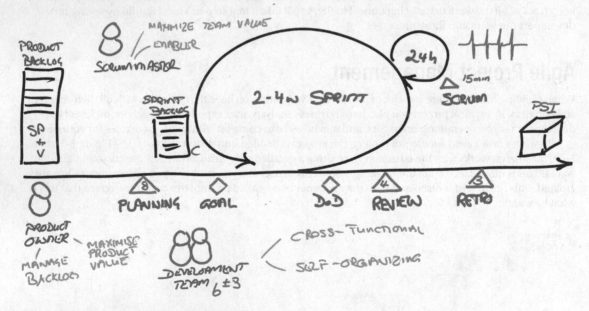

Figure 3-2. *Scrum is a popular Agile methodology that uses a couple of key principles*

This works. For small, starting teams this can even be a good thing because it allows them to focus on the process and collaboration instead of getting lost in tooling and all the possibilities they discover. I would even encourage you, if you're just getting started with Scrum, to run a couple of sprints manually just to make sure you focus on the process. After this, you will understand the areas where tooling can help you. Using VS Team Services for the planning phase will make even more sense.

Implementing Scrum does not only affect the team. It should affect the whole organization and be something that's supported all the way to the top. However, that's easier said than done. Management commitment is the area where Scrum implementations often fail. Especially when nearing deadlines, the pressure from above can become so intense that teams lose the idea behind Scrum and end up in a mix between Scrum and waterfall: Scrummerfal. This is essentially running a waterfall project with a notion of short iterations.

You need to be aware that in no project, especially a Scrum project, can you have fixed time, features, and resources. But all too often this is what organizations want. The biggest problem with Scrum adoptions is that organizations adopt Scrum and take all their old baggage with them. Organizations are sometimes afraid of change. But for Scrum, and in the same line DevOps, management needs to give teams freedom. The freedom to experiment, try new processes, and iterate on their own process to become better and better. Try to avoid the ScrumBut: we do Scrum but we're not doing all of it because <substitute your particular reason>. Of course Scrum is not the Holy Grail and you shouldn't adopt it without thinking things through. Scrum is, however, a complete framework with parts that complement each other.

■ **Note** Willy-Peter Schaub, one of the technical reviewers and the Program Manager for the Microsoft ALM Rangers, pointed out that he doesn't like the term *ScrumBut*. "Scrum is a framework, 'but' nowhere does it state that a user has to implement every aspect of the framework as outlined. As long as we have the key artifacts as in the previous image; for example, backlog, sprint, events, and a potentially shippable increment, we are practicing Scrum. Using ScrumBut always gives me the impression that unless I implement everything as outlined, I am one of the BUT users." I understand what Willy is saying. The reason I don't agree is that I've often seen teams before they even tried one sprint already declare that some part of Scrum is not going to work for them because they are different. And then after a couple of sprints, they abandon Scrum because it doesn't work.

Using tooling becomes especially important when a team starts to grow. Having a distributed team with physical whiteboards with post-its is complex to keep synchronized. Having a digital equivalent of the whiteboards that can be accessed by all team members all over the world is much easier. And of course a whiteboard doesn't track changes. If the post-its fall from the wall (or are nicely stacked by a helpful cleaner!), you have to recover everything from memory. If you are in a business with auditing requirements, you probably need a more sophisticated solution than a plain whiteboard.

These and other reasons are a sign that tooling can be helpful for you. Of course, VS Team Services won't make you a perfect Scrum team. But using the tooling the way that it's meant to be used definitely helps you in improving your process. VS Team Services and Visual Studio have some great tooling support when it comes to Agile and Scrum. The whole idea behind VS Team Services as a solution for your application lifecycle management implementation is that you can achieve full traceability and visibility throughout your process.

This is done by storing all your work items in a central location. Everyone can see them; everyone can work with them (with the necessary permissions, if you require that). All members of your team can use their favorite tools. Product owners and other stakeholders have easy access through a web interface. Developers directly manage their tasks from within Visual Studio. Testers have their own tools (see Chapter 11 on testing for more information). All their work integrates in the backend, thus allowing for a full overview of the process.

Let's first have a look at the Agile Tooling Web Access interface.

Agile Tooling

When creating a new project, you select a process to base your project on. By default, this can be Scrum, CMMI, and Agile. The differences in these processes come down to different types of work items you can create, out of the box queries and reports, and the states that your work goes through. In essence, all processes are just templates that are built on a shared foundation.

When running an Agile project, it's often easiest to start with the Scrum template. The Scrum template is the most lightweight template and has some small differences from the Agile template. For example, the Agile template uses terminology like User Story where Scrum uses the more generic Product Backlog Item. The Agile template has states like Resolved (Code Complete and Unit Tests passes) that encourage the separation between developers and testers, while the Scrum template just has an In Progress state. I encourage teams to start with the Scrum template to avoid a team adapting its terminology and process to the Agile template.

The Scrum templates gives you the following important items:

- Sprints

- Product backlog items

- Tasks

- Impediments

- Bugs

- Capacity planning (you can use this regardless of the template you use)

Team Web Access is the portal that you can use to access all those items on VS Team Services. This is the Work tab in your menu (see Figure 3-3).

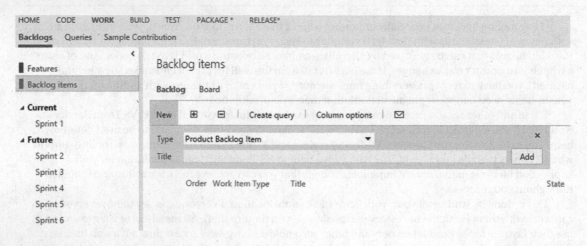

Figure 3-3. *Team Web Access showing the Work page*

Sprints

Sprints are the foundation of your Scrum project. You need to decide on the length of your sprint and the day you start a new sprint. A sprint is nothing more than a start and end day. Within this period, you schedule work, track progress, and manage the capacity of your team.

The Scrum guide states that a Sprint should be no longer than four weeks. Typical teams that I encounter run sprints of two or three weeks. This is something that you should decide on as a team and as an organization. Having one sprint schedule across the entire organization improves communication and makes it easier to schedule releases across multiple teams. When configuring your sprints in VS Team Services, you can group them in releases if you want. You can also assign start and end dates to each sprint. This will be used to automatically create the burn down and do capacity planning (see the "Capacity" section later in this chapter).

When you open your Team Project, you start at the Overview page. In the Other Links section, you see a link titled Configure schedules and iterations (Figure 3-4). If you don't see the Other Links section, add it to your dashboard as a widget.

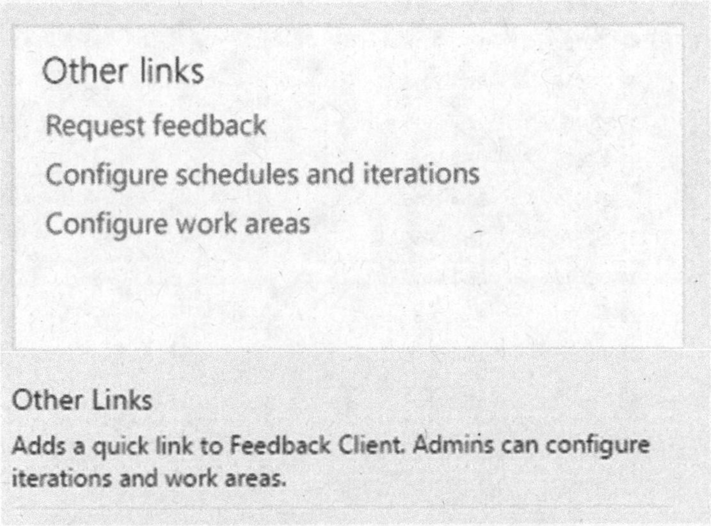

Other links

Request feedback

Configure schedules and iterations

Configure work areas

Other Links

Adds a quick link to Feedback Client. Admins can configure iterations and work areas.

Figure 3-4. *The Configure schedules and iterations link in the Other Links section*

By default, there are six sprints visible. By using the New and New Child buttons, you can create a hierarchy of releases and sprints. By default, the iterations are named *sprints*. This is because you're using the Scrum template. If you are using the Agile template, they're named *iterations*. For each sprint, you can set the start and end date. After setting the first sprint, VS Team Services helps you by suggesting equal sprint lengths for the other sprints. Figure 3-5 shows a configured iteration schedule with two releases and nine sprints. The selected sprints are the ones that are visible for the team. When time passes, you probably want to select new sprints and hide older sprints to maintain a clear overview.

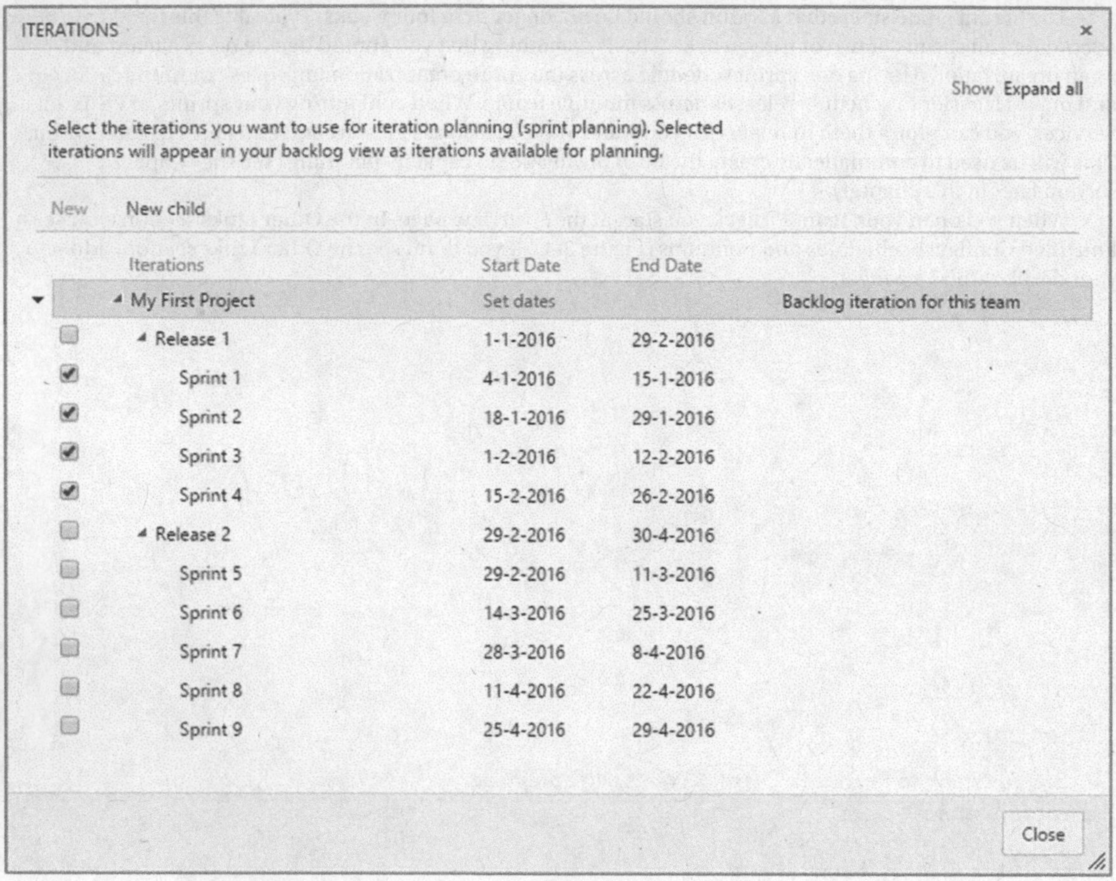

Figure 3-5. *A configured sprint schedule*

Product Backlog Items

A Scrum team works off a backlog, which is a prioritized list of work that needs to be done. VS Team Services helps you to track your product backlog by letting you create product backlog items (PBIs). As you can see in Figure 3-6, a product backlog is a nicely formatted list of items. (In Chapter 5 on Advanced Agile Tooling you'll look at the Kanban board) You can configure the columns you want to see, such as title, effort, business value, and other fields.

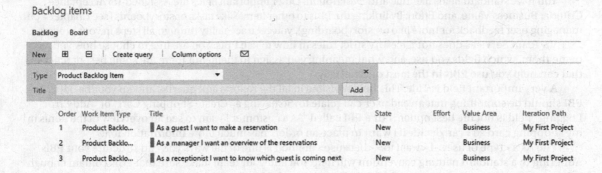

Figure 3-6. *An overview of the product backlog*

Product backlog items can contain a lot of details. Figure 3-7 shows the detail view for a PBI.

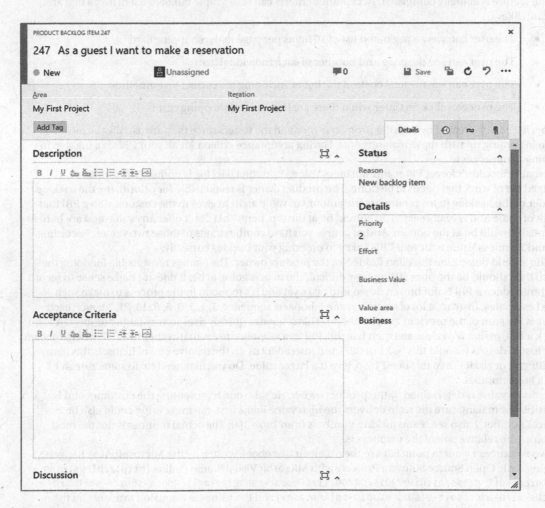

Figure 3-7. *Details for a product backlog item*

You have standard fields like Title and Description. Other important fields are Assigned To, Acceptance Criteria, Business Value, and Effort. By linking the PBIs to other items, like tasks or storyboards (see Chapter 4 on managing user feedback for more info on storyboarding), you get traceability through all steps in your process.

VS Team Services does not force any strict rules in how to use PBIs. You are free to choose how you name them, which fields you use, and what meaning you assign to them. But there are some best practices that can help you use PBIs in the most optimal way.

A very important field is Title. This field is visible in all the reports and queries and on your backlog. A PBI should be something that an end user can relate to. So having a "Create Shopping Cart" or "Add Error Logging" field is not the best option. But a PBI called "As a customer I want to see an overview of the items in my shopping card so I can decide if I want to place an order" has much more information in it.

The As a <type of user> I <want to> <because> method is one of the ways you can structure your PBIs. Adhering to a standard naming convention will help you and your team make sure that PBIs contain enough information and are easy to understand. The Description field is also one you shouldn't forget. This is a rich text field that you can use to add information that the team needs to implement the feature.

One field that I often see teams forgetting is the Acceptance Criteria. The information in this field should help a developer know when he's finished coding the feature. A tester can use this information to test if the feature is actually completed. Acceptance criteria can be a simple bulleted list of items that are important, like:

- The user can view a paginated list of 10 items per page in the shopping card

- The user can see the price and number of each individual item

- The user can see the total costs of the items, including the correct VAT amounts

- The user can click on Order when there are items in the shopping cart

This list can be created by both the product owner and the testers since they are usually the most capable in coming up with these requirements. Having acceptance criteria for all your PBIs is a big step in improving your process.

You also shouldn't forget Effort and Business Value. A product backlog is nothing more than a prioritized list of work that needs to be done. The product owner is responsible for prioritizing the backlog. The order of the backlog items represents the amount of value an item gives to the customer. So a PBI that has a lot of value and is really easy to do should be at the top. Items that don't offer any value and are hard to accomplish should be at the bottom. And of course you have combinations of those two values. Recording Effort and Business Value with your PBIs is key to ordering your backlog correctly.

Who should determine the Effort field? Not the product owner. The team is responsible for doing the work, so they should be the ones stating how difficult the item is going to be. It doesn't make sense to record this in hours since a PBI is not broken down into tasks yet and it's too soon in the process to make such detailed estimates. Instead, a lot of teams use the Fibonacci sequence: 1, 1, 2, 3, 5, 8, 13, 21, 34, etc. (each number is the sum of the previous two numbers). This sequence quickly rises to very large numbers. A team can pick a PBI, assign it a value, and then use this PBI as a reference to estimate other PBIs. This helps a team not get lost in details (should this be 21 or 22?) and instead focus on the relative size of items. Is this item more difficult or riskier than this item? If so, give it a larger value. Do you first need to do some research? Give it a large number.

Business value is determined by the product owner. He's the one representing the customer and is responsible for making sure the team delivers the high value items first. Business value could also be a Fibonacci number. I also see teams picking numbers from 1 to a 100. The actual number is not the most important. The relative size of the numbers is.

Two resources I want to point out are the excellent free ebook written by the Microsoft ALM Rangers: Managing Agile Open Source Software Projects with Microsoft Visual Studio Online (http://blogs.msdn.com/b/microsoft_press/archive/2015/04/09/free-ebook-managing-agile-open-source-software-projects-with-microsoft-visual-studio-online.aspx) and the Estimate extension available on the

VS Team Services Marketplace (https://marketplace.visualstudio.com/items/ms-devlabs.estimate). One of the topics the ebook discusses is how the Rangers estimate and how they use normalized estimations. The Estimate extension enables you to play Planning Poker with your team and estimate items this way.

Some other useful features that I often see teams not using are the Discussion field and Tags fields. Team members can use the Discussion field to comment on a PBI and store those comments directly with it. Other team members can view them and respond to them. Tags can be used to add a collection of labels to a PBI. Think of the area a PBI falls in (mobile, frontend, Windows 10, etc.) or some other category that you want to assign. You can add as many tags as you want and you can easily filter PBIs on the tags you assign to them (see Figure 3-8).

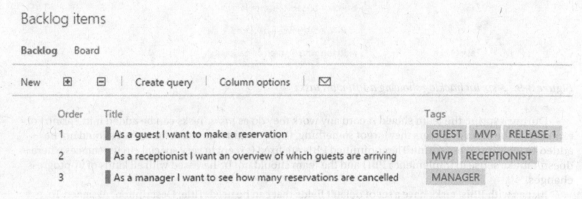

Figure 3-8. *Product backlog items with tags*

While viewing the backlog, you can easily add new PBIs by title. At the top of the backlog, you see the New work item pane. If you change the Type drop-down, you can also create a bug. All you need to do is enter the title and click Add. This adds the PBI to the top of your backlog. You can then double-click on the PBI to open the details view. The order of your backlog is very important. You can easily adjust this by using drag and drop on the PBIs.

Tasks

Product backlog items are features that directly provide value to a customer. To implement a PBI, work needs to be done. This could be things like working out the user experience, writing code, and adding logging and tracing or other work specific to each PBI. These tasks are picked up by your team and executed during the sprint.

The Scrum planning meeting at the beginning of each sprint is used by the product owner to explain the PBI to the team. The team has already taken some time in the previous sprint to check if the PBI is complete or if they need more info. This is the time to discuss this with the product owner. The team breaks up the PBI in tasks and agrees to commit to doing the work. By assigning a PBI to a sprint, the team can manage their tasks in the sprint backlog and on the sprint board. Figure 3-9 shows an example of a sprint backlog. You see the parent PBI (with a blue rectangle) and the tasks (with a yellow rectangle) as children beneath it.

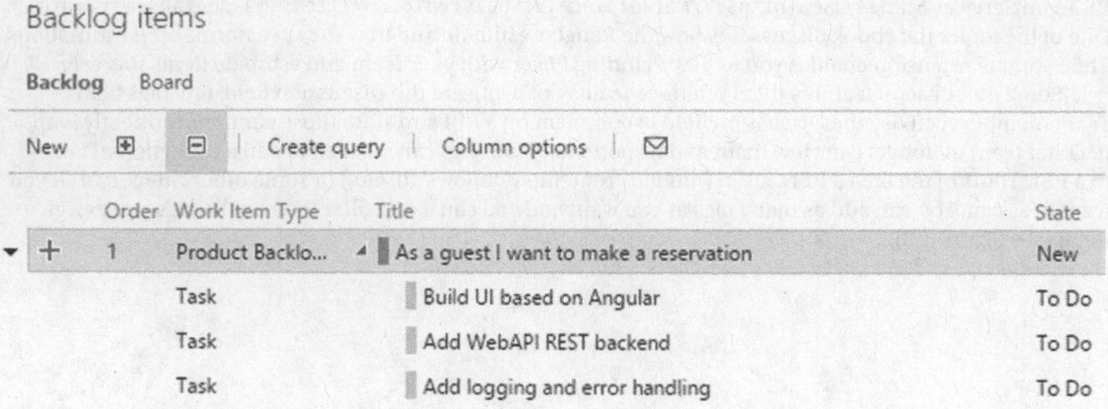

Backlog items

		Backlog	Board				

New	⊞	⊟	Create query	Column options	✉

	Order	Work Item Type	Title		State
▼ +	1	Product Backlo... ◢ ▌	As a guest I want to make a reservation		New
		Task	▌ Build UI based on Angular		To Do
		Task	▌ Add WebAPI REST backend		To Do
		Task	▌ Add logging and error handling		To Do

Figure 3-9. *A sprint backlog showing a PBI with tasks*

During a sprint, the team should record any work they do as *tasks*. Tasks can be added mid-sprint. For example, if the team discovers they forgot something, they can add a new task for it. PBIs should not be added to an in-progress sprint. The committed PBIs are fixed (except in very special circumstances where it doesn't make sense to implement a PBI) and the team should not be harassed with all kinds of in-progress changes.

Just as with PBIs, tasks have a set of default fields that can be used. Title, Description, Assigned To, and State are the most important ones. A field that can be used to track progress is Remaining Work. This is a number that the team member who's working on the tasks updates regularly to show how the task is progressing. When the task is moved to the done state, the remaining work is set to zero.

When the team agrees to schedule a PBI, you set the state of the PBI to Committed. After that, you can use drag and drop or set the iteration field to the sprint you want. By using the green + icon in front of the PBI, you can add tasks that need to be executed.

Impediments

The role of the Scrum Master is to facilitate the team in all the work they need to do. Sometimes a team member runs into issues that he can't solve himself. The Scrum Master is there to help. These problems are called *impediments* in Scrum and VS Team Services helps you to track them. Impediments can be all kinds of things, ranging from a broken laptop to not having enough access to the product owner to ask questions.

Impediments have a description and resolution in addition to default fields like the State, Title, and Tags. Figure 3-10 shows the details for a new impediment.

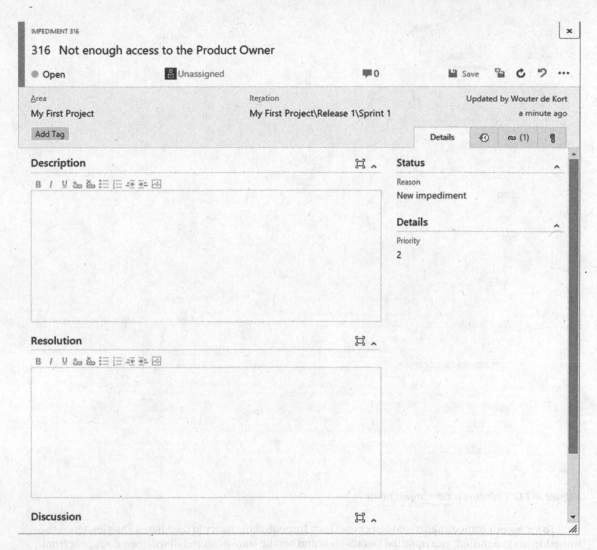

Figure 3-10. Details for a new impediment

An impediment does not show on the product backlog or the task list. This is because impediments are something that need to be worked on by the Scrum Master and shouldn't take up space or time on the team's backlog. There are two options to create an impediment. The first one lets you create a new impediment from the Queries tab next to your backlog, as shown in Figure 3-11. The second option is to use the New Work Item widget that you can place on your dashboard.

Figure 3-11. *Creating a new impediment*

To view your impediments, you select the Open Impediments query in the Shared Queries. Once the impediment is handled, you open the Details view and set the state to Closed. It will then disappear from the Open Impediments query results. Another way to keep track of your open impediments is to use a dashboard tile that shows the number of open impediments (see Chapter 6 for more information).

Bugs

Every project has bugs. Bugs represent work that needs to be tracked. This means that you can choose to show bugs on your backlog and prioritize them just as you do with other work. Some bugs need to be fixed immediately; others are scheduled for a later time. This decision should be made by the product owner.

Bugs can be introduced in various ways. You can add them manually to the backlog through Team Web Access or let testers add them through Microsoft Test Manager. Bugs can also be added automatically for failing automatic builds (see Chapter 9 on builds for more information). When using the Scrum template, bugs show by default on your backlog and your requirements board. If you want, you can easily configure this to not show the bugs or show them on the task board. (Chapter 5 goes into the details of customizing your backlog and Kanban board.)

■ **Note** There is an Open Source extension available at GitHub (https://github.com/microsoft/mail2bug) that lets you create bugs from e-mail threads.

Bugs have their own unique fields (see Figure 3-12), such as:

- Steps to reproduce
- Priority
- Severity

Figure 3-12. *Detail view of a new bug*

If the bug is created through Microsoft Test Manager, additional information about the system where the bug occurred on, IntelliTrace data, or other data sources is added (see Chapter 11 on testing for more information). Traceability is achieved by linking bugs to PBIs. This way, you get data on which PBIs are stable and which have a lot of bugs in them. Bugs go through a workflow where the bug is first approved (meaning that it's a real bug that needs to be worked on). A team then commits to fixing the bug (just as with other work), and finally the bug is done, meaning it has been fixed and tested.

You can create bugs directly from your backlog by using the New panel and changing the drop-down to Bug. This creates a new bug that's not linked to a PBI. To link a bug to a PBI, you open the details of the bug, select the Link tab, and create a link to an existing item. You then set the parent relationship and select the PBI as parent (see Figure 3-13).

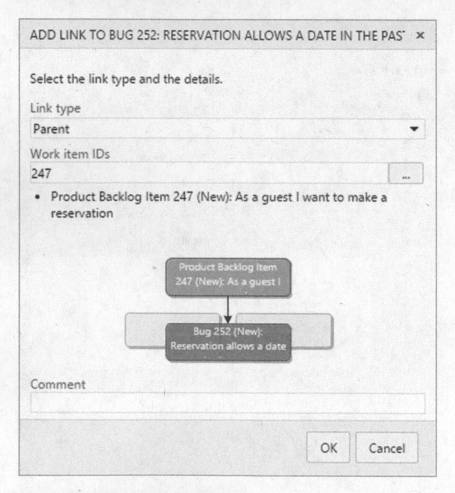

Figure 3-13. *Linking a bug to an existing PBI*

Capacity

Now that you have sprints, PBIs, and tasks, you want to get a sense of how much work your team can commit to. In Scrum, velocity is the standard way of tracking the amount of work a team can do during each sprint. The velocity is based on experience of the previous sprints and shows how much PBIs a team typically delivers in a sprint.

As a product owner, you can do a forecast of the time it's going to take your team to implement features. When you've assigned effort values to PBIs, you can then use the Velocity feature to calculate which items can be finished in which sprint. Since velocity is an ever-changing number, it's wise to do an optimistic and pessimistic forecast so you get a sense of what's possible. Figure 3-14 shows a forecast for a backlog with four PBIs. The forecasting-based value is a value the product owner can enter. With a velocity of 8, the first item will take a whole sprint. The second and third item will be done in sprint 2 and the last item in sprint 3. For sprint 4, there isn't any work scheduled at the moment.

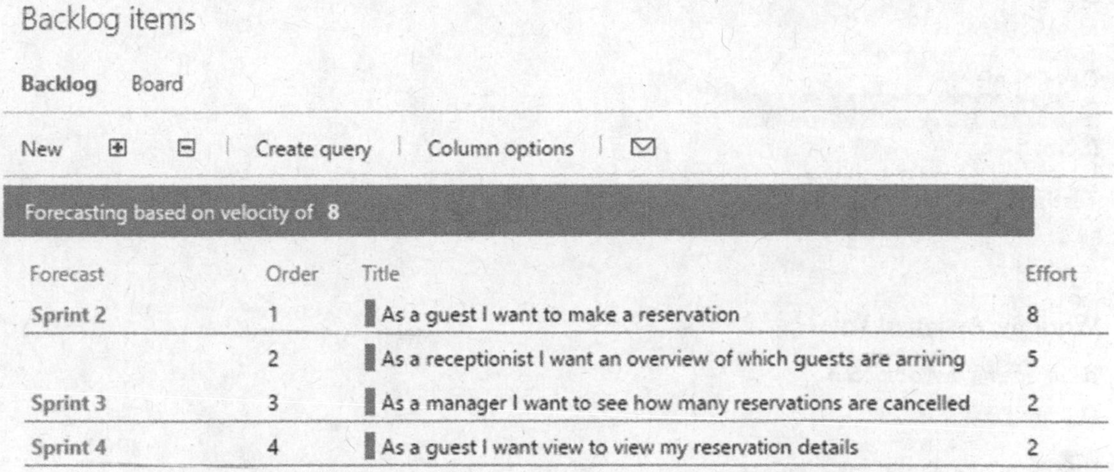

Backlog items

Backlog   Board

New   ⊞   ⊟ | Create query | Column options | ✉

Forecasting based on velocity of 8

Forecast	Order	Title	Effort
Sprint 2	1	▌ As a guest I want to make a reservation	8
	2	▌ As a receptionist I want an overview of which guests are arriving	5
Sprint 3	3	▌ As a manager I want to see how many reservations are cancelled	2
Sprint 4	4	▌ As a guest I want view to view my reservation details	2

Figure 3-14. *Forecasting sprints*

Velocity is not the only measure to help you plan a sprint. Some team members work part-time, during the year you have holidays, and maybe you need to set aside time for other events. Capacity planning helps you get a quick overview of the hours your team is working and what types of work they can do. For example, if your team has only one Java developer who happens to be on holiday, you shouldn't try to schedule any Java work for the next sprint, no matter what your velocity was the last couple of sprints. Figure 3-15 shows an example of a capacity planning for a team with two developers and one tester. The development bar is red because there is more development work than there is capacity available.

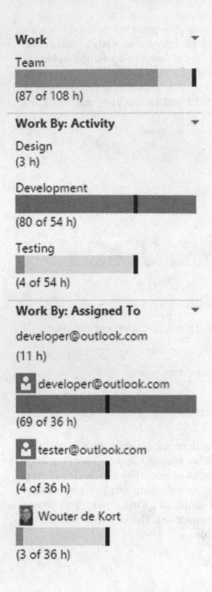

Work

Team

(87 of 108 h)

Work By: Activity

Design
(3 h)

Development

(80 of 54 h)

Testing

(4 of 54 h)

Work By: Assigned To

developer@outlook.com
(11 h)

developer@outlook.com

(69 of 36 h)

tester@outlook.com

(4 of 36 h)

Wouter de Kort

(3 of 36 h)

Figure 3-15. *Capacity overview of current sprint*

VS Team Services helps you plan your working days (by default, Monday to Friday) and by assigning hours and days off to each team member for each sprint. You can also assign a work category, such as development or testing, to different team members to further help you with planning. This data is then used to show how much work your team can take on and differentiate this from the different types of activities you have in your team. Capacity is something that's uniquely entered for each sprint.

To see some interesting capacity information, you need multiple team members in your team. If you open a project, click on the Team Members widget to open the Manage Members dialog box. Add a couple of users by e-mail address. In Figure 3-16, you see two fictitious users being added to the team.

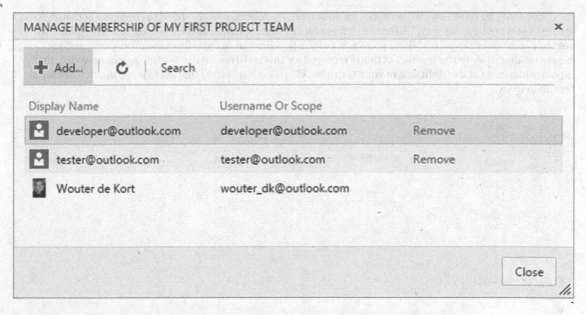

Figure 3-16. *Managing the members of your team*

Now that you have a couple of team members in your team, you can start scheduling their capacity for the coming sprint. Select Work ➤ Backlogs ➤ Sprint 1. You now the see the sprint backlog and the a Capacity option (see Figure 3-17). You can now configure activities for your team members, set their working hours, and schedule days off (see Figure 3-18). As you can see, a team member is not restricted to only one activity. You can add multiple activities per team member and specify the time they have available for each activity. You can also configure days off for individual team members and for the whole team.

My TFVC Project Team Sprint 1

Backlog   Board   **Capacity**

Figure 3-17. *Capacity planning per sprint*

User	Days Off	Activity	Capacity Per Day
developer	0 days	Development ▼	6
tester	0 days	Testing ▼	6
Wouter de Kort	0 days	Requirements ▼	4
		Development ▼	2
Team Days Off	0 days	These days off apply to the whole team.	

Figure 3-18. *A sample capacity plan*

Now that you have selected activities for your team members, you also need to configure activities for the tasks you create. This way, VS Team Services can calculate the hours for each activity and display this next to the available team members you have. For a task, select an Activity from the drop-down and set the remaining work to the number of hours required for this task (see Figure 3-19). You can now view the capacity planning at the right side of your sprint backlog. Red bars signal that there is too much work for a certain activity.

Details ^

Priority
2

Remaining Work
8

Activity
Development

Blocked

***Figure 3-19.** Assign hours and an activity to a task*

Capacity is configured per sprint. When you're starting a new sprint, you can enter new numbers for your team's capacity or you can choose to copy the data from the previous sprint and then adapt it.

Team Rooms

Communication is key. To help you with this, VS Team Services offers *team rooms,* which are online chat rooms where your team members can leave messages. Team rooms are more than simple chat rooms. However, team rooms are definitely not the only solution. Some teams I encounter use Slack, a popular messaging application, or other solutions. Especially when working cross-platform, it's important to choose an application that's easy for your team to use.

You can configure team rooms to show messages for different events that happen during your project, such as work item state changes, developers checking in code, testers filing bugs, and other events. This means that a team room gives you a complete transcription of what's happening in a project. This makes it easy to track what your team members are doing, especially if you missed a couple of days. Some teams even track the notes of their daily standup in a team room. You can create different team rooms with different events they track. You can also configure which team members you want to see the events for.

■ **Note** Team rooms are troublesome if you are working in multiple teams. You can install the following extension to get a summary in one place of all the team rooms you're part of: `https://marketplace.visualstudio.com/items/tfc.TeamRoomSummary`.

When you open the Overview page of your project, you can add the Team Room widget to display a list of available team rooms in your project. When you create a new project, a single team room is created for you automatically. You can click on the name of the room to navigate to it (see Figure 3-20).

Figure 3-20. *The Team Room widget on the dashboard*

Figure 3-21 shows what the team room looks like. The easiest thing to do is send a simple chat message. You can use the textbox at the bottom to enter the message and click Send to share it with your team.

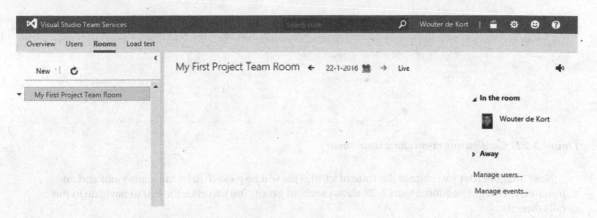

Figure 3-21. *A team room in VS Team Services*

Besides chat, team rooms can also display events. If you click on Manage Events, you can select event types that you want to be displayed in your team room. You can also add users to the team room so they can view the events. Be aware, however, that this could mean that team members see events of things they normally wouldn't have access to. Figure 3-22 shows how to configure your team room to display an event for every work item update in the project (both by members of the team room and by other team members).

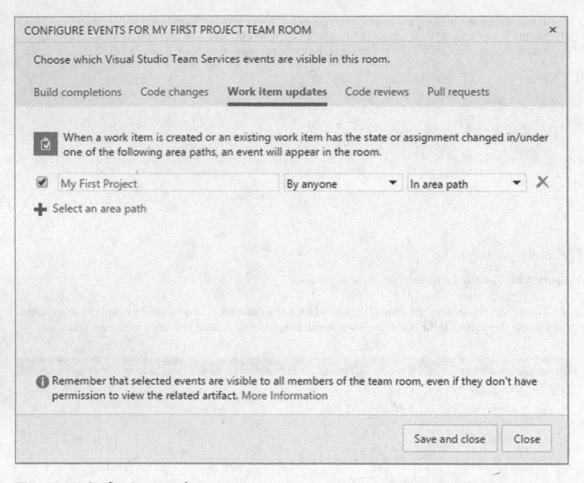

Figure 3-22. *Configuring events for a team room*

Now imagine that you change the state of a PBI. This will be picked up by the team room and an automated message is added. Figure 3-23 shows such an event. You can click the PBI to navigate to the details directly.

Figure 3-23. *An automated message showing that a PBI has been updated*

Achieving Traceability with Developers

One of the best features of VS Team Services is the way it lets all team members interact and use the tooling that's best for them. This is definitely true for developers. Although a developer should be able to use the Web Access features to participate in team rooms, planning sessions, and other events, Visual Studio is the tool of choice for Microsoft developers. And for not Microsoft developers, VS Team Services offers integration with tools like Eclipse and IntelliJ or cross-platform command-line tools that can be used everywhere.

When a developer works with Visual Studio, she uses the Team Explorer (see Figure 3-24) to connect to VS Team Services. One of the things you can do with the Team Explorer is show work items that are assigned to you and work with them.

Figure 3-24. *The Team Explorer in Visual Studio*

The best thing about this is that when a developer makes a code change and sends these changes to the server, she can directly correlate her changes with the work item she's working on. This creates full traceability between code and work done. Later on, the traceability information will be extended to reviews, tests, builds, and releases.

A developer can see which work items are available for her and select a work item to work on. Even better, when a developer gets interrupted, she can save the whole state of her development environment (being code changes, work items, window layout, breakpoints, and other settings), switch to another task, and then return to the saved state to continue working on the task at hand. In the Code part, you will also see how to ask for code reviews directly from Visual Studio. This will create a work item in VS Team Services and track this until the code review is performed.

Opening a project in Visual Studio is easily done from within Web Access. If you check the Overview page of your Team Project, you see the Visual Studio Widget (see Figure 3-25) with an option to directly open the project in Visual Studio. Your browser will show some security questions when you do this. Since you trust both VS Team Services and Visual Studio, you can accept the security warning to launch Visual Studio.

Figure 3-25. *The Visual Studio widget on the Overview dashboard*

After Visual Studio is launched, you see the Team Explorer panel (if not, go to View ➤ Team Explorer). Select the My Work tile to view any tasks that are assigned to you directly in Visual Studio. If you don't see anything, this means that no tasks are assigned to you. You can use the Web Access to assign a task to you. If there is a task you want to start working on, you can use drag and drop to move it from Available Work Items to In Progress Work (see Figure 3-26). This updates the work item state and makes the new state immediately visible in Web Access. This way, a developer doesn't have to leave Visual Studio while still keeping others updated on her work.

Figure 3-26. *The My Work panel in Visual Studio*

During this book you will learn about other tools, like Microsoft Test Manager, that integrate testers into the traceability chain.

Summary

VS Team Services has a lot to offer when it comes to Agile Tooling. The Web Access interface makes it easy for your whole team to cooperate and work on one single backlog. You can track sprints, product backlog items, tasks, impediments, and bugs. If you want, you can also let VS Team Services help you with capacity planning.

Team rooms are there to facilitate your team in communicating and keeping track of what's happening in your project. Especially for distributed teams or for members who want a quick update, team rooms are the way to go. You also had a first look at how developers integrate into the Agile process. You worked with the My Work panel in Visual Studio and got a glimpse of how your whole team can cooperate.

But this is only the tip of the iceberg. In the following chapter, you'll see how you can cooperate with all stakeholders by easily getting their feedback and making sure they can follow along with your process.

CHAPTER 4

■ ■ ■

Managing User Feedback: Knowing What to Build

This chapter introduces you to *storyboarding* and *feedback management* with Visual Studio Team Services. Both are important ways of stimulating communication with your stakeholders and making sure that you're building the right thing.

Why We Need Better Communication

Having a good backlog with product backlog items that have detailed descriptions and acceptance criteria is a huge step in the right direction. This will help your team know what to build and build it correctly. That doesn't mean that things will always go as you hope. Figuring out what the customer really wants can be a difficult task. Sometimes you end up building the wrong thing. This costs time and money and damages the relationship with your stakeholders. Helping customers get a clear picture of what they want is difficult, but this chapter will help you by explaining how you can easily share ideas with your customers and get their feedback.

You probably know the saying, "A picture is worth a thousand words". Seeing a mockup of a user experience can help a developer or tester get a much better sense of what they need to build and test. Discussing a mockup with a stakeholder is much faster than spending time building user interfaces

Decreasing cycle time is key. Discussing a couple of mockups in a rapid timeframe, brainstorming ideas, and iterating on them is what Agile and DevOps are about. What often goes wrong is the timing of this process. Teams running a Scrum process schedule their work in sprints. At the start of each sprint, they have a planning meeting where they discuss the work for the next sprint with the product owner.

When should the mockups be created? Since the mockups directly relate to the product backlog item, shouldn't they be created in the sprint? But how can the team then fully understand what they need to build? This is something I see going wrong with teams. There is no rule that forbids a team to look at the PBIs that are coming in the next sprint. To run a successful project, this is essential. The team should spend some time every day making sure that the PBIs they're going to work on in the near future are clear enough. This time can be used by team members to create mockups, define acceptance criteria, and make sure that the team knows all they need to know to run the planning meeting. Having a user experience expert create the mockups is definitely a plus, especially since most developers are not specialized in UX.

Having good mockups and clearly defined PBIs is one part of building software that your users actually want. After delivering a PBI, you need to validate what you build. The role of a product owner is to constantly interact with stakeholders and make sure that the team is building the right thing. And the same principle applies: shorter cycle times are key. Truly immerging stakeholders in the DevOps process is a big win for your flow of value.

For both scenarios—creating mockups and getting user feedback—there are a lot of tools on the market. Fortunately, Microsoft has created tools that directly integrate with VS Team Services.

© Wouter de Kort 2016
W. de Kort, *DevOps on the Microsoft Stack*, DOI 10.1007/978-1-4842-1446-6_4

Creating Storyboards with PowerPoint

Have you ever used PowerPoint? I think that almost everyone who has been to a meeting has seen PowerPoint in action. And that's mostly because PowerPoint is very easy to use. Create a couple of slides, add some animations and other graphics, and you can easily create something that looks pretty nice.

Microsoft realizes that most users have PowerPoint and that it is very easy to use. This is why Microsoft created an extension for PowerPoint that helps you easily create mockups and link them back to work items in VS Team Services (see Figure 4-1).

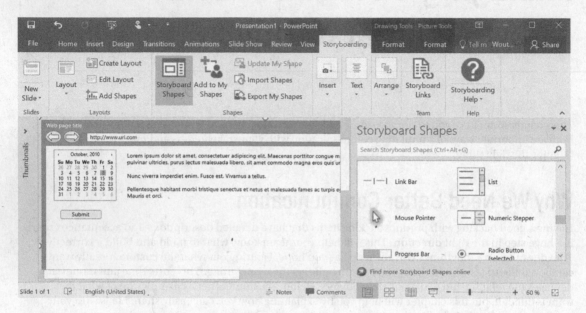

Figure 4-1. *Storyboarding plugin for PowerPoint*

The PowerPoint plugin gives you a set of often-used shapes like a web browser, standard controls, and other elements that you'll probably use when creating mockups. You can also add your own set of shapes and share those with your team, such the default layout of your web page, your company's logo, or some custom control that you often use. By adding them to your shapes library, you create a consistent look and feel throughout all your mockups.

End users can easily view your mockups in PowerPoint even if they don't have the plugin installed. And for those who don't have PowerPoint, they can install a free PowerPoint viewer that allows them to view your slides.

The best thing about these storyboards is that you can link them to your product backlog items. Team members can open the storyboard directly from the PBI information and use it while working on their tasks.

To create a storyboard, you start by opening PowerPoint. If you have installed Visual Studio on your PC, you will already have the Storyboarding plugin installed. Users who don't want to install Visual Studio can install the standalone Team Foundation Server Office Integration plugin. This is a free download that everyone can use (see https://www.microsoft.com/download/details.aspx?id=49992 for the download details).

Inside PowerPoint, you'll now have the Storyboarding tab visible on your ribbon (see Figure 4-1). If you select this tab, you can start creating storyboards. The Storyboard Shapes panel contains a couple of standard controls you probably want to use, such as a web browser, text fields, buttons, etc.

If you want to create some mockup text for your storyboard, add a text field, enter the text =Lorem(), and press Enter. This will fill your textbox with a couple of lines of Lorem Ipsum text. You can also extend the default shapes library. You can add shapes of your own and download sets of shapes from the Visual Studio Gallery site.

■ **Note** *Lorem Ipsum* is a pseudo-Latin text that's often used by printers and designers. You can easily create a large amount of text but since the text is not actually readable it doesn't distract your audience from the overall design.

Since you are working in PowerPoint you can also easily add animations. One animation that's particularly useful is the Click shape that's available in the Storyboard Shapes gallery. The Click shape uses a path animation. You configure where the pointer starts, where it should move to, and finally what it clicks on. This allows you to create animations that show how the storyboard will work once implemented. Figure 4-2 shows the Click shape on a slide.

Figure 4-2. *You can use the animated Click shape in your storyboards*

After finishing your storyboard, you want to share it with your team and with stakeholders. If you look at the ribbon, you see a button there called Storyboard Links in the Team group (Figure 4-3).

Figure 4-3. *You can link your storyboard to a work item in VS Team Services*

Clicking this button opens a window that allows you to link your storyboard to a work item in your project. If you look at Figure 4-4, you see how a predefined query is used to find the product backlog items in your project. You can then select a PBI and click OK to establish the link (Chapter 6, on Dashboards and Reporting, explains more about queries).

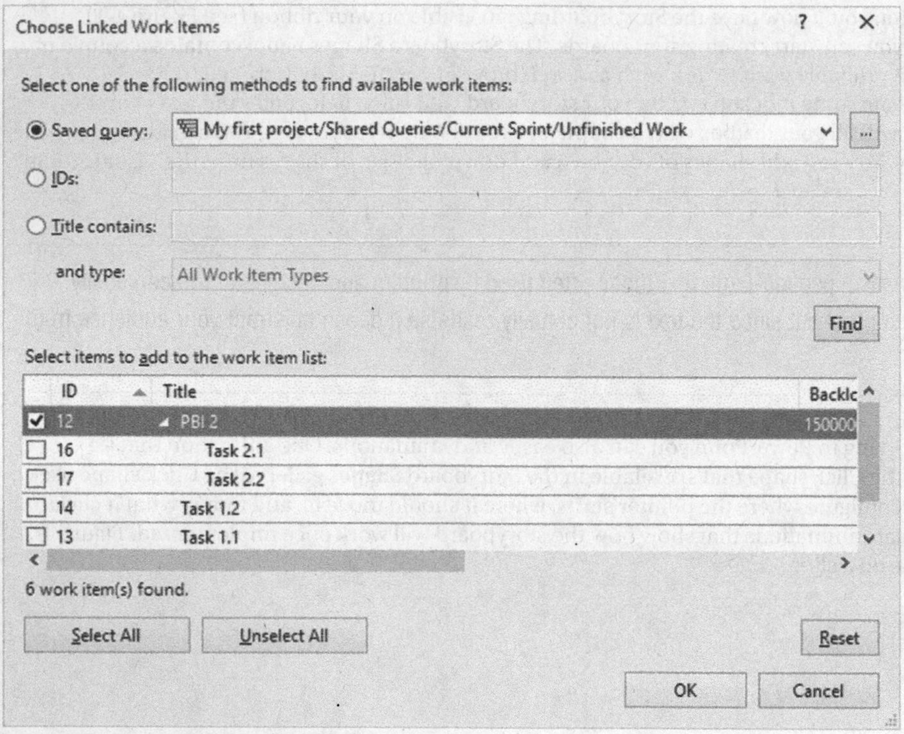

Figure 4-4. *You can choose a work item to link to your storyboard*

If you now open your VS Team Services project in the browser, you can view the link to the storyboard. If you open the details for a PBI work item, you see the Storyboards tab in the bottom left. Figure 4-5 shows such an example link. What's important to notice is that the link contains an actual URI to a network share or an Internet address. In this case, the storyboard is stored on OneDrive to make it available to the whole team. The files are therefore not stored inside VS Team Services.

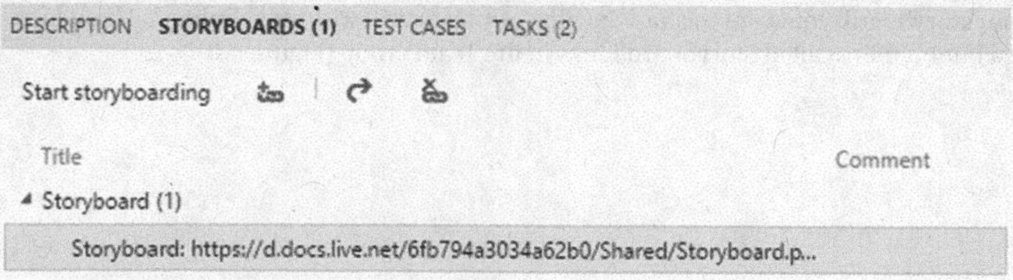

Figure 4-5. *In the details of the PBI, you can view the storyboard's link*

Involving Stakeholders in Feedback Management

Getting feedback from users is extremely important. You want a continuous cycle of build, measure, and learn. The best way would be to always have your customer available with you in the room. Every time you want some feedback, they are there to help. In reality, customers won't always be available. Maybe you give them a call or send them an e-mail asking them to look at something. You then need to document their reaction and manually add it to VS Team Services.

Because this is something that happens frequently, Microsoft added the Feedback Management tool to VS Team Services. This allows you to create a feedback request from within the Web Access. You add the required info, like what it is you want the recipient to look at, how they can access your application, and other information that's important. You then just click Send and VS Team Services does the rest. The recipient gets an e-mail detailing your request and a link that starts the feedback session. The first time they do this, a specialized tool will be installed that will help the user in giving the feedback. This tool opens on the side of the screen and guides the user through the steps you want him to take. While doing this, users can easily add feedback such as screenshots or even video or voice. Users can also add comments and give a simple 1- to 5-star rating.

All this data is collected and attached to the feedback response. After submitting the feedback, you can retrieve the data from within VS Team Services. This creates full traceability from request to response and links this data to the PBIs you want feedback on.

VS Team Services creates a Feedback Request work item for each item you want the user to look at. Figure 4-6 shows a request that contains two feedback items.

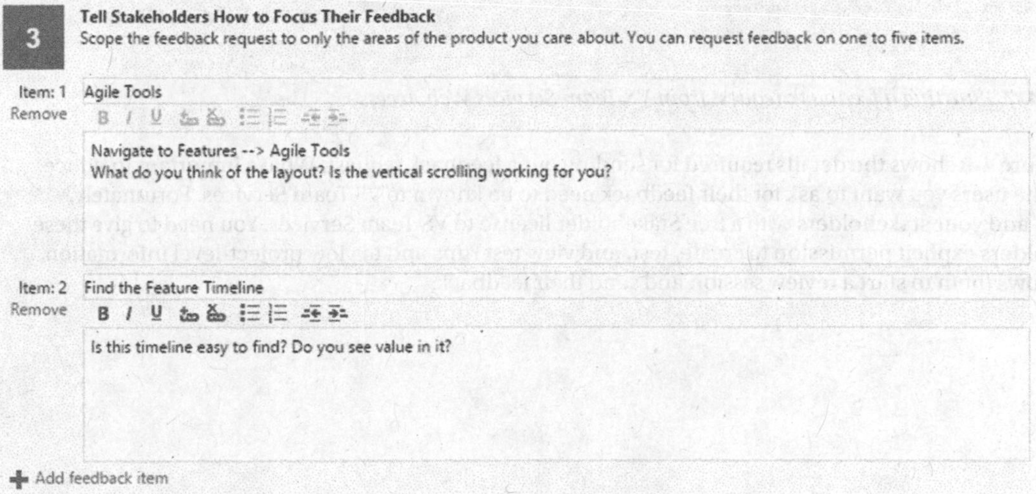

Figure 4-6. Requesting feedback on multiple items

After sending the feedback request, VS Team Services generates two work items for you that contain all the details. What's nice is that your feedback request is linked to the work items in VS Team Services. This means that when you update your feedback request in VS Team Services, users will automatically see these updates when they start their feedback response.

Of course, it can happen that a user does not respond to your feedback request. You can view the feedback requests you send in VS Team Services. As long as the State is Active, you know the user hasn't responded. The URL that gets sent with the feedback request stays active and the user can still use the Feedback Client to respond.

Sending a feedback request is easy. If you go to the Overview page of your VS Team Services Team Project, you see a small section named Other links (see Figure 4-7). If you click on Request feedback, the Request Feedback windows open. If you don't see the Other Links group, add the widget to your dashboard (see Chapter 6, on Dashboards and Reporting, for how to do this).

Figure 4-7. *Starting a feedback request from VS Team Services Web Access*

Figure 4-8 shows the details required for sending out a feedback request. What's important to notice is that the users you want to ask for their feedback need to be known to VS Team Services. Fortunately, you can add your stakeholders with a free Stakeholder license to VS Team Services. You need to give these stakeholders explicit permission to create, test, and view test runs and to view project-level information. This allows them to start a review session and send their feedback.

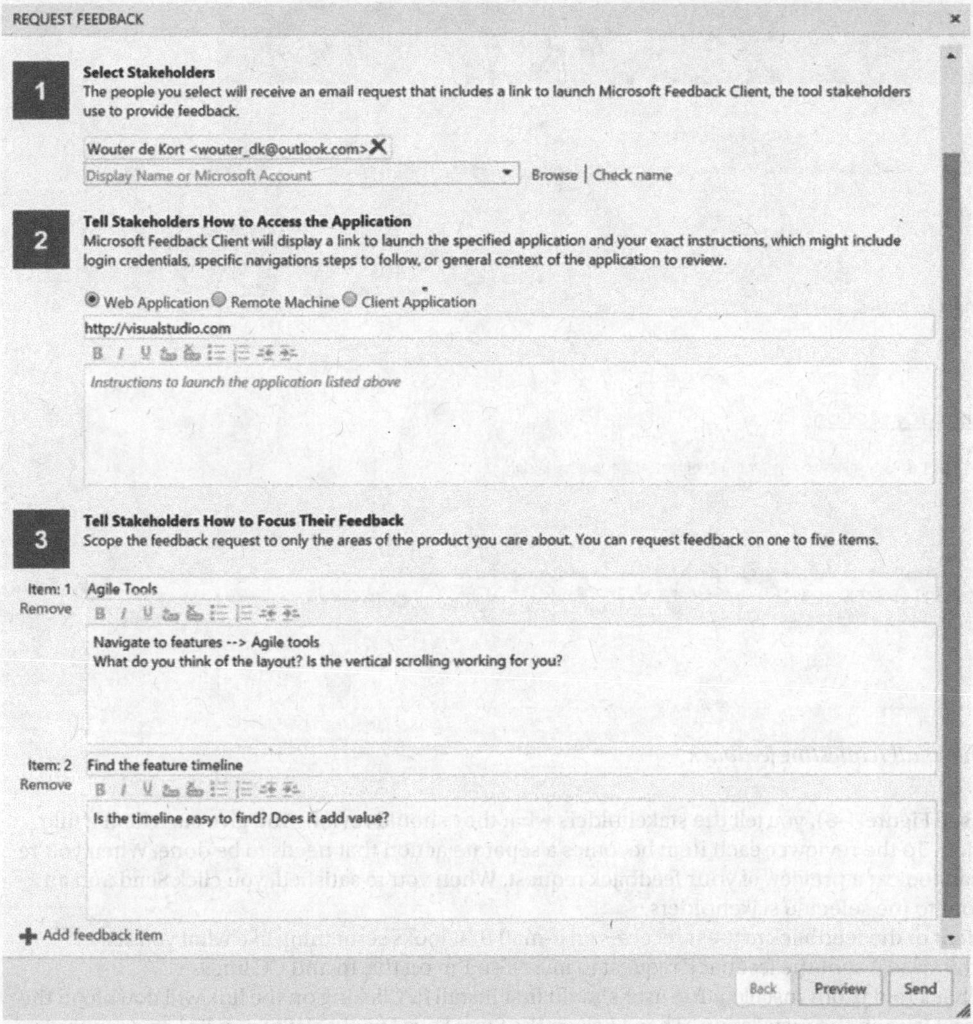

Figure 4-8. *Configuring a feedback request*

In addition to the stakeholders that you want to send the request to, you of course have to tell them what to do. In step 2 (see Figure 4-8), you specify how they can reach your application. If it's a web application, you can add the URL and you have a free text field where you can specify details such as username and password or other things they should know when accessing your application. If you have a remote machine, you can enter the name of the machine. For a client application, you should enter the full path to the application.

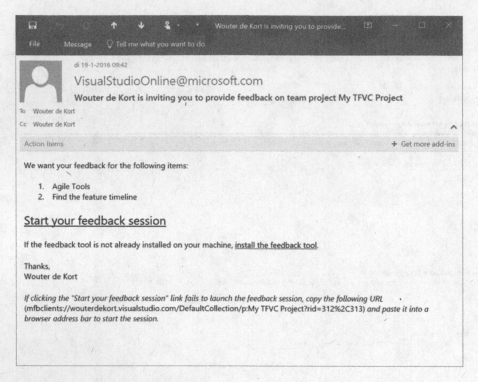

Figure 4-9. *An e-mail requesting feedback*

In step 3 (see Figure 4-8), you tell the stakeholders what they should review. You give each item a title and a description. To the reviewer, each item becomes a separate action that needs to be done. When you're finished, you can look at a preview of your feedback request. When you're satisfied, you click Send and an e-mail will go out to the selected stakeholders.

The recipient of the feedback request receives an e-mail that looks something like what you see in Figure 4-9. In this case, I sent the feedback request to myself so I'm on the To and CC lines.

If the feedback tool is not installed, the user should first install it. Clicking on the link will download the feedback tool and launch the installation. Then click on the Start Your Feedback Session link to open the feedback tool and begin the feedback response.

You now get an instance of the feedback tool running at the left side of your screen. Figure 4-10 shows what this tool looks like. The first page of the tool shows information on how to access the application. In this case, a URL is shown that points to `http://visualstudio.com`. After the user has opened the application, click Next to see the first feedback item.

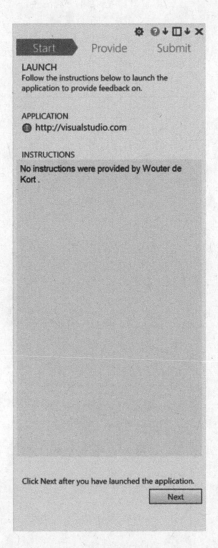

Figure 4-10. *The Feedback Response tool with information on how to access the application*

While giving their feedback, users can add screenshots, record video of their screen, add audio from a microphone, add comments, and give a star rating to each item. This information is captured for you and automatically sent to VS Team Services when the user finishes. Figure 4-11 shows the first step for this request and all the actions a user can take.

Figure 4-11. *The Feedback Response tool showing a feedback item*

After the user finishes the feedback request, the data is sent to your VS Team Services project. The Feedback Response work item now contains all the data that the user entered. This includes any video, audio, screenshots, or other data the user added.

If you open your project and go the Work tab and then to the Queries sub-tab, you see a query named Feedback in Shared Queries (see Figure 4-12). After selecting the query, you see a list of feedback responses. You can view each item, inspect the details, and create new work items based on the feedback.

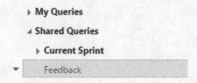

Figure 4-12. *The Feedback query in your team project*

The feedback client is a great way to involve your stakeholders in the process. In Chapter 11, you'll also see that there is a plugin for the Chrome web browser (and in the future other browsers) that you can use to do exploratory testing on an application and send the results back to VS Team Services.

Summary

Knowing what your customers want and building the right solutions for them is still one of the hardest aspects of software development. In this chapter, you learned about some easy-to-use tools that can help you with this.

You've seen how to create mockups with PowerPoint, link these to work items, and share those with your stakeholders. You've also seen how the Feedback tool that's a part of VS Team Services lets you send requests for feedback and work with the results as a part of your process.

In the next chapter, you'll dive into other parts of Agile tooling, namely Kanban and Portfolio Management. These tools will help you optimize the value your team delivers and scales out to multiple teams, all using VS Team Services.

CHAPTER 5

■ ■ ■

Advanced Agile Project Management

In the chapter on Agile project management, you were introduced to the Agile tools that Visual Studio Team Services offers you. You've seen how to plan work with your team and keep track of what's happening. These tools are very useful and will be part of your daily routine.

There is even more to the Agile tools in VS Team Services. To optimize the flow of value through your project, VS Team Services implements support for Kanban and Lean techniques. And when you're working with multiple teams, you can use the portfolio management tools to get an overview of what all your teams are doing and distribute work across them. This chapter goes into the details of the Kanban and portfolio management tools and shows you how to apply them effectively.

Kanban and Lean

Most teams I see that want to move to DevOps are already doing some form of Agile. Scrum is the most popular process that I see around. When doing Scrum, work is planned in sprints of equal length. At the beginning of the sprint, work is planned, and at the end of the sprint you review what you've built and try to improve on your process.

When effectively applied, Scrum has a lot of benefits for a team. Teams start delivering more regularly, improve together, and offer more value to stakeholders. However, the strict sprint length can also bring challenges. Teams face questions like: How much work can we do this sprint? What if all the planned work is finished before the end of the sprint? How can we further optimize our process?

Imagine the following situation where you are Scrum Master in a team. Your team runs sprints of two weeks. You have a team with five developers, two testers, a designer, and a part-time architect. The team has worked together for a couple of sprints and they are starting to get familiar with the project and are picking up speed. In the second week of the last sprint, the developers come to you and happily explain that they have finished all their development work for this sprint. What do you do?

You can of course have the developers pick up some more tasks that are scheduled for the next sprint. Or maybe you have some technical debt in the system and you want them to work on that. Now ask yourself the question: would having the developers do more work increase the value offered to the customer?

Well, what is value for the customer? The customer gets value from your work only when they can actually use it. This means that code needs to be written, tested, and deployed. So yes, you can let the developers do more work. But when is this work going to end up in the hands of the customer? If you see your project as a flow of value through the different phases, the customer value is determined by how fast a single item goes from the beginning of your pipeline to the end. This immediately implies that the speed of

© Wouter de Kort 2016
W. de Kort, *DevOps on the Microsoft Stack*, DOI 10.1007/978-1-4842-1446-6_5

the pipeline is determined by the slowest factor: the bottleneck. Figure 5-1 demonstrates this concept. No matter how much you do at the start of your pipeline, the speed after your bottleneck stays equal until you remove the bottleneck.

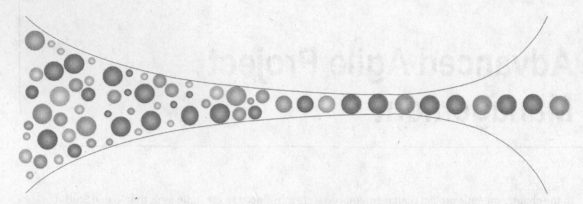

Figure 5-1. *The speed of the pipeline is determined by the bottleneck*

So, should you give your developers more work? If the developers are the bottleneck, giving them more work will improve flow of value. But what if the testers are the bottleneck? Giving the developers more work will only increase the amount of work that's waiting for the testers before it can go the customer. That does not increase value for the customer. Instead it increases waste. You waste resources on having a queue of items that only gets bigger. Instead, focus on the bottleneck: the testers have too much work. Having the developers work on automated testing does help the testers and decreases the bottleneck, thereby increasing flow of value.

Eliminating waste is a core principle of both the Kanban and the Lean methodologies. Kanban has the following principles:

- Eliminate waste
- Focus on lead time (the time it takes for work to go through one's process from conception to final delivery, also known as "concept to cash")

Lean also has a set of principles:

- Eliminate waste
- Build quality in
- Create knowledge
- Defer commitment
- Deliver fast
- Respect people
- Optimize the whole

■ **Note** This book doesn't contain a detailed explanation of all the principles. Instead it focuses on using the tools of VS Team Services and understanding the ideas behind them. If you want more information, you can start at http://www.lean.org.

This may all sound nice in theory, but how do you apply it to something complex as a software development project? How do you apply these principles and analysis in practice? To optimize the whole and eliminate waste, you need to find the bottleneck. To find the bottleneck in your situation, you first need to discover your process. What steps does your team take to go from an idea to production? A possible sequence of steps can be:

1. Analyze

2. Develop

3. Test

4. Deploy

And maybe you have intermediate steps, like a code review or additional forms of testing such as user acceptance testing or performance testing. Try to make sure that the steps you select are inside your realm of control. Maybe the process of coming up with the backlog is done by the marketing department and is not something you can fully measure or influence. If you have your steps you can start with creating what's called a *Kanban board*.

Kanban is a Japanese word meaning signboard or billboard. A Kanban board looks a lot like a Scrum board. A typical Scrum board has columns for To do, Doing, and Done. Items move from left to right to signal their state. The signal part is important. Since Scrum uses only three states, the amount of signals you can give is limited. If an item is in the Doing state, what does this mean? Is it being analyzed, developed, or tested? Where is the most time spent? Is the item waiting to picked up by someone else?

A Kanban board expands the columns to mimic the actual process the team follows. Looking back at the previous list, this would mean that you have four columns. This particular board can look like Figure 5-2.

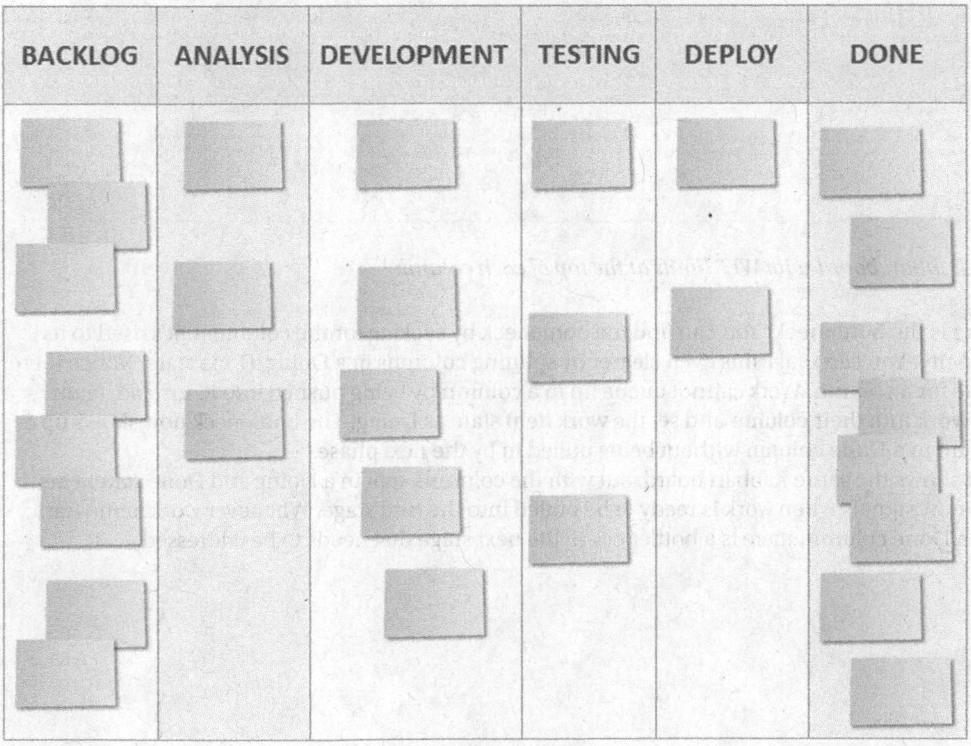

BACKLOG	ANALYSIS	DEVELOPMENT	TESTING	DEPLOY	DONE

Figure 5-2. *A sample Kanban board with columns that map to the team's process*

And now comes a very simple trick that will show you where your bottleneck is: limiting work in progress. Setting a work in progress limit (WIP limit) limits the amount of work a team member is doing in parallel. People are not allowed to pull a new task into their column when they are at their WIP limit. Switching between tasks costs time and leads to tasks not being completely finished. A typical WIP limit is 1-2 tasks per person. Appling WIP limits to a Kanban board can be as simple as putting the number on top of your column contrasted with the current number of tasks, as shown in Figure 5-3.

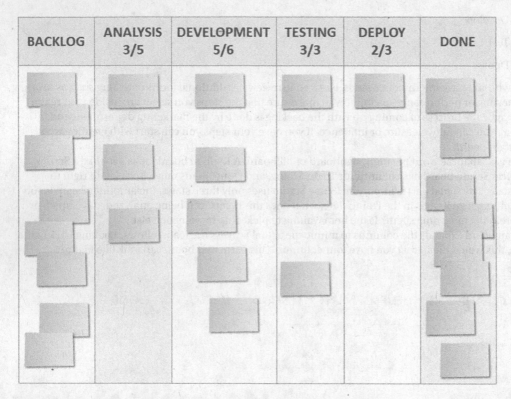

Figure 5-3. *A Kanban board with WIT limits at the top of each column*

Now where is the bottleneck? You can find the bottleneck by seeking for the column that's used to its maximum capacity. You can make this even clearer by splitting columns in a Doing/Done state. Notice there is no To do state for a column. Work cannot queue up in a column by being pushed into it. Instead, team members pull work into their column and set the work item state as Doing. The bottleneck now shows up as items queuing up in a Done column without being pulled in by the next phase.

Figure 5-4 shows the same Kanban board, but with the columns split in a Doing and Done state. The Kanban board now signals when work is ready to be pulled into the next stage. Whenever work items start queuing up in a Done column, there is a bottleneck in the next stage that needs to be addressed.

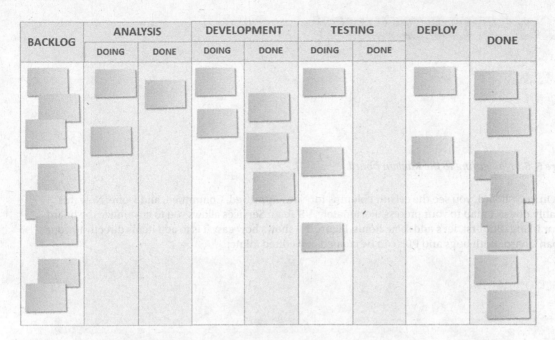

Figure 5-4. *A Kanban board with columns split into Doing and Done*

Kanban and Lean are about optimizing the flow of value through your process. Eliminate wait times and other forms of waste that might happen. Kanban is a natural addition to a Scrum process. If you use Scrum, map your process and apply WIP limits to start improving your flow. You could argue that this is a *ScrumBut* because you're no longer using sprints and are depending on the flow of items. As I see it, ScrumButs are reasons for a company to ignore certain well established rules for internal reasons. Kanban is not about ignoring rules and doing something like Scrum in a way you prefer. Instead, Kanban offers you a way to view your Scrum process in a different way. Lots of things don't change but it's true that you do change some things.

■ **Note**   This was just a short introduction to Kanban and Lean and there is much more to learn about them. There are very good books completely dedicated to this subject. Two that I want to recommend are *The Phoenix Project* by Kevin Behr, George Spafford, and Gene Kim and *Kanban: Successful Evolutionary Change for Your Technology Business,* by David J. Anderson and Donald G. Reinertsen.

The remainder of this part focuses on how to use VS Team Services to use a Kanban board and configure it for your team. When you create a new project, you automatically get access to a Kanban board. If you navigate to the Work hub, you see the link to your board at the top of your backlog (see Figure 5-5). You can also use the shortcuts that are available in VS Team Services: *g w* to go to the Work hub and then *b* to go to the Kanban board. You can press ? anywhere in VS Team Services to show a popup with the currently available shortcuts.

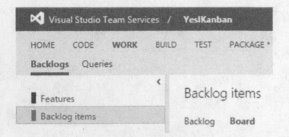

Figure 5-5. *Navigating to the Kanban board*

On your board, you see the default columns for New, Approved, Committed, and Done. Now this probably doesn't map to your process. Fortunately, VS Team Services allows you to customize the board to your liking. But first, let's add some items. Figure 5-6 shows how easy it is to add items directly to your Kanban board. Both bugs and PBIs can be created and edited inline.

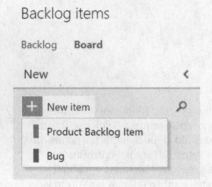

Figure 5-6. *Adding items to the Kanban board*

Once you have a PBI, you can add tasks to it. By clicking on the ellipses, you open a simple drop-down that lets you edit the title and add a task (Figure 5-7). Each task's status can also be changed from the Kanban board.

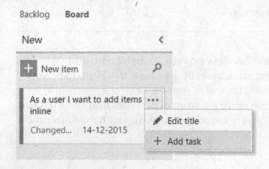

Figure 5-7. *Adding tasks to your PBI directly on the Kanban board*

Having the ability to create a task directly on the Kanban board gives your teams a lot of freedom. I see teams adopting a hybrid approach where they split PBIs into tasks when the item is complex and keep simpler items as just a PBI. The same freedom applies to bugs. Moving bugs and tasks across your Kanban board is easy. You can use drag and drop or you can open the work item and change its state. As you will see when configuring your columns, a state maps to a particular column.

If you open the Settings pane for your Kanban board (the gear icon at the top right of the board), you see a lot of options. You can configure fields shown on your cards, set rules for changing the background color of cards, and set specific colors for tags. You can also configure the board itself. Columns and swimlanes and the order of items on the board are all configurable.

Let's first look at styling your cards. Adding a field to a PBI (or a bug) is easy. A couple of default fields can be shown (or hidden) with a checkbox such as ID, Assigned To, Effort, and Tags. Any additional fields can be added by clicking on the green plus sign before the field. Figure 5-8 shows how to add the Changed Date field to your card.

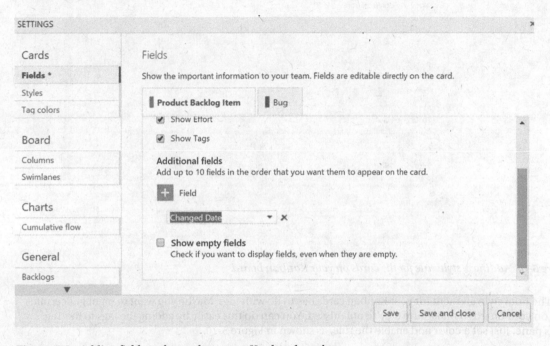

Figure 5-8. *Adding fields to the cards on your Kanban board*

You can also change the card style based on a simple rule system. A styling rule can change the background color of your task and the style of the title (bold, italic, underlined, and the color). A rule follows the format Field ➤ Operator ➤ Value. So for example: Effort > 50. This would apply the styling rule to all work items with an effort larger than 50. Figure 5-9 shows the configuration for this rule. I chose to change the card color to yellow and do nothing to the title. You can choose any style combination that is clear to your team.

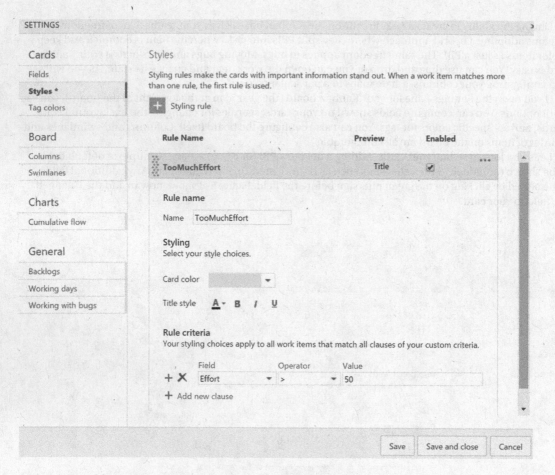

Figure 5-9. Adding a style rule for the cards on your Kanban board

The final style element for your Kanban cards has to do with tags. Maybe you want to highlight certain tasks on your board to make sure they're not missed. You can do this easily by adding the tags to the Tag colors pane. Just set a color and enable the rule, as shown in Figure 5-10.

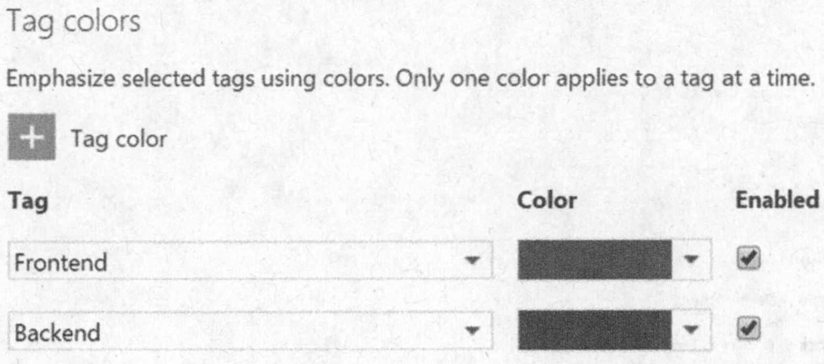

Tag colors

Emphasize selected tags using colors. Only one color applies to a tag at a time.

➕ Tag color

Tag	Color	Enabled
Frontend ▼	▼	☑
Backend ▼	▼	☑

Figure 5-10. *Configuring tag colors for the cards on your Kanban board*

Now if you take the Changed Date field, the Effort rule, and the tag colors and you have a PBI with an Effort of 51 and a Backend Tag, you get what's shown in Figure 5-11.

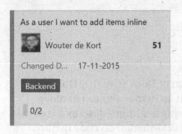

Figure 5-11. *A styled Kanban card*

Cards are not the only configurable thing on your board. You can also configure the board itself, namely the columns, swimlanes, and card ordering. To map the columns of your Kanban board to your process, you can add, remove, and reorder columns in the settings pane. For each column (except the columns that map to done and new), you can also choose to split the column in Doing and Done. And of course you can set a WIP limit. This limit is not strictly enforced. Instead, the WIP limit turns red the moment you have to many items in a column. Figure 5-12 shows the Development column with a WIP limit of 2 and the option to split into Doing and Done.

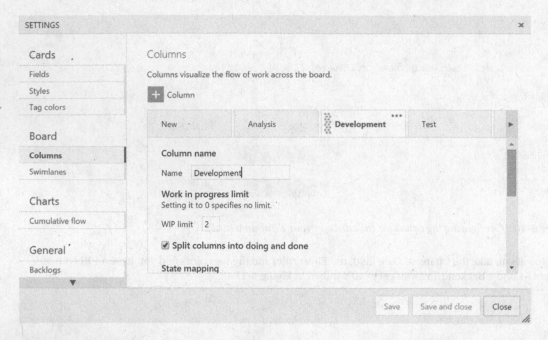

Figure 5-12. *Configuring a column on the Kanban board*

Finally, there is one more important step for each column: the Definition of Done (DoD). A DoD is an agreement between all members of your development team that states when an item is allowed to move to the next column. For the Analysis column, this could mean things like having a title and description, a storyboard, and acceptance criteria. For development, the DoD can contain information on code quality, unit tests, review requirements, or anything else that matters to your team. Having a good DoD is important to streamline your process. You can enter the DoD at the bottom of each column configuration. The field supports markdown so you can also add some style (like a bulleted list or highlighting certain words). Figure 5-13 shows this. You can see the *i* icon showing up next to the column title. Clicking it shows the DoD.

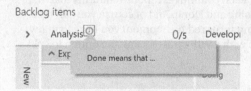

Figure 5-13. *A Definition of Done for the Analysis column*

Swimlanes are another important aspect of your Kanban board. Your Kanban board currently has only one swimlane. This means that there is one single path from left to right. Items in each column are equally important and move one by one through the lane. This is the default behavior and it's what you want most of the time. In some cases, however, you want specific items to move with a higher priority such as a hotfix. To allow this, you can add swimlanes to your Kanban board.

A swimlane on your board is nothing more than a name. Figure 5-14 shows how you can add an Expedite swimlane to your Kanban board. This is a swimlane that I find is often being added by teams. They use this swimlane for bugs and other hotfixes that have a high priority. Of course you should try to use an Expedite swimlane as little as possible. You want to keep a nice and steady flow of items. Putting items through your Expedite swimlane will cause regular items to be placed on hold. This decreases predictability of your flow and will impact stakeholder satisfaction.

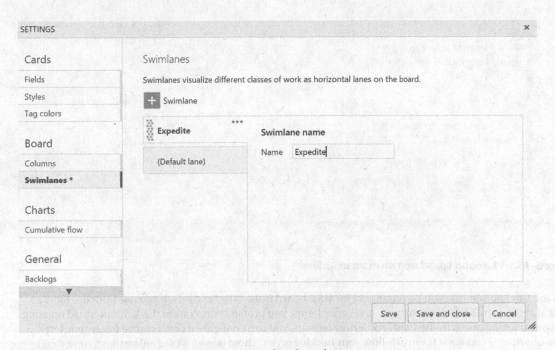

Figure 5-14. *Adding extra swimlanes to your Kanban board*

Having an extra swimlane gives you something like Figure 5-15. You can collapse a swimlane when you don't need it. The lanes are stacked on top of each other. They do have a shared WIP limit. If you want to rush a bug fix, this doesn't mean your team suddenly has more capacity.

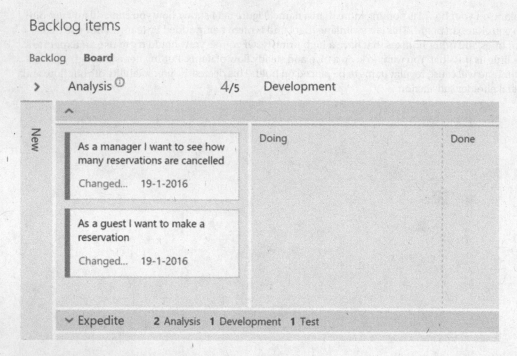

Figure 5-15. *A Kanban board with an extra swimlane*

One final option that you can configure for your board is the order of cards. If you use both the Kanban board and the regular backlog to create and order items, you probably don't want the Kanban board messing with your backlog order. In the Card reordering settings, you can configure if cards can be freely reordered on the board or if you want them to follow your backlog order. There is even a cool animation that you can play directly in VS Team Services to show the differences! Figure 5-16 shows a screenshot of the animation.

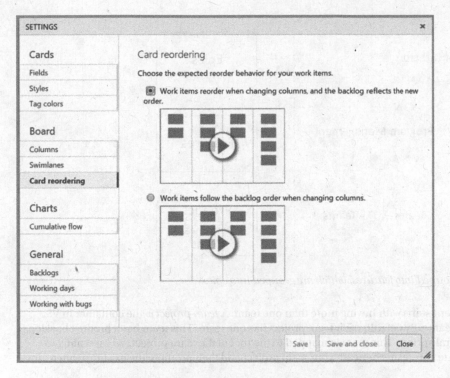

Figure 5-16. *Configuring the reordering of cards on the Kanban board*

Portfolio Management

The Agile tools that you looked at until now work great for a single team. You order a backlog, plan sprints, and run your team. The team then uses the Kanban board for their particular processes. Scrum states that the best team size is between six and nine people. But what if a single team is not enough? What if you want to run multiple teams and need a way to manage all those teams from a single location?

That's where the portfolio management capabilities of VS Team Services help you. Portfolio management allows you to create multiple teams that all have their own backlog, Kanban board, and capacity planning per sprint. All these teams roll up into other teams. This allows you to create a hierarchical backlog at different levels of granularity.

For example, the board of directors wants a new mobile strategy. The program managers split this into a cross-platform mobile app and a supporting backend. The individual teams then deal with the work at their level, such as building a universal Windows app. In the end, this will lead to a large amount of tasks linked to product backlog items. The product backlog items are grouped into features and the features are linked to an epic. Figure 5-17 shows the hierarchy you'll create.

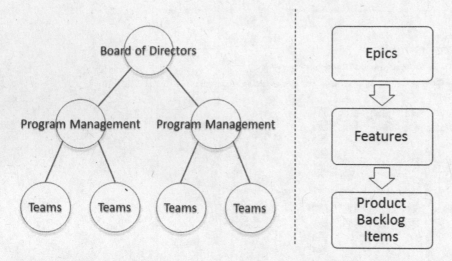

Figure 5-17. *PBIs are grouped into features, which are grouped into epics*

Portfolio management starts with having more than one team. A *team project* is the container in VS Team Services for your teams. By default, each team project has one team. This team has a product backlog, Kanban board, and several sprints. This team is mapped to the root of the team project. When scaling to multiple teams, you create sub-teams beneath your team project and then promote the existing team to an overview team.

Teams all control an area. *Areas* are the containers for the work that a team does. Multiple teams mean having multiple areas. You create a hierarchy of areas with teams functioning at the epic or feature level and on the level of product backlog items. This way, you can roll up the individual teams' work into the management teams.

Before you start adding teams, you should enable support for epics on your backlogs. In the Settings window that you used for your Kanban board, you can also configure the backlog levels you want to use. Figure 5-18 shows the Settings window with all navigation levels enabled.

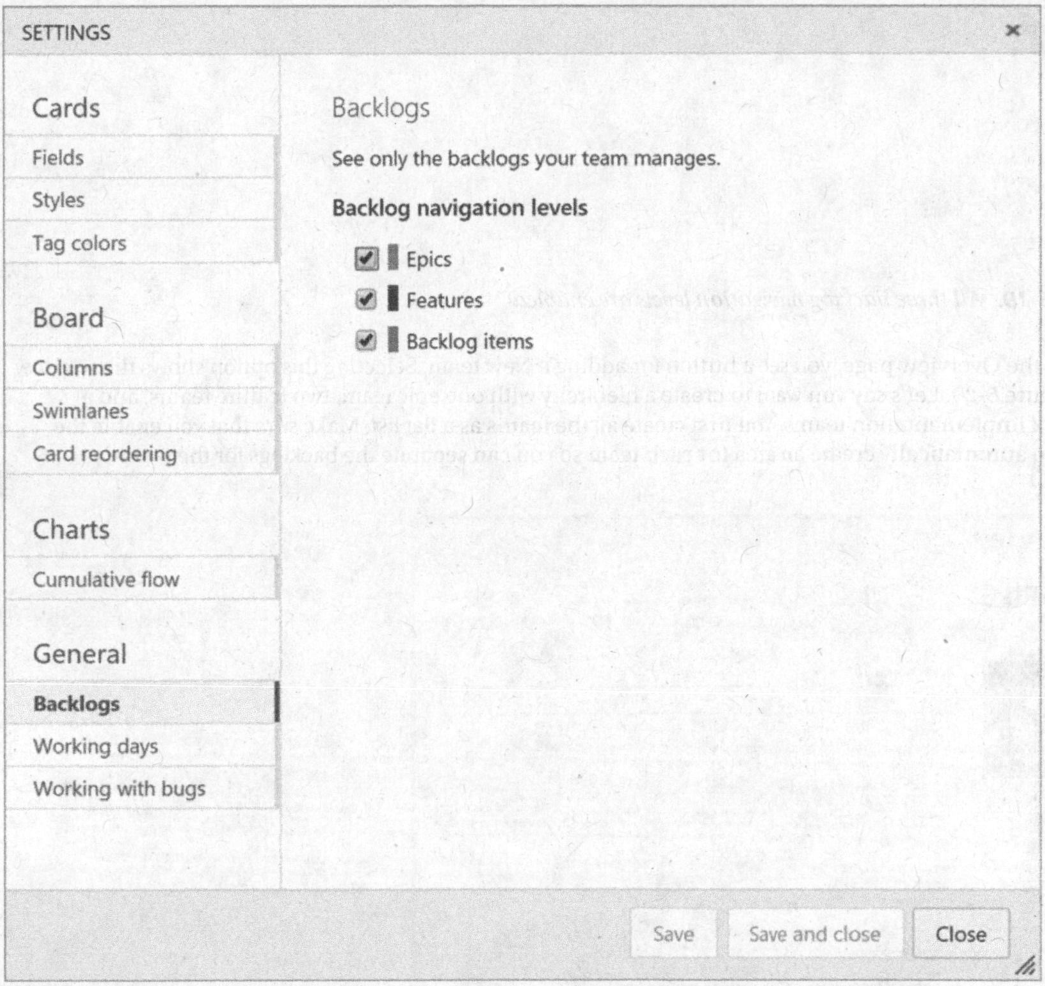

Figure 5-18. *Enabling backlog navigation levels in the Settings window*

If you navigate back to your backlogs, you will see that you have three levels enabled: epics, features, and "regular" product backlog items (see Figure 5-19). Adding teams to your team project is done in the Project Settings of VS Team Services. You open these settings by selecting the gear icon at the top right of VS Team Services. (Or you navigate to https://<youraccount>.visualstudio.com/defaultcollection/ <yourteamproject>/_admin).

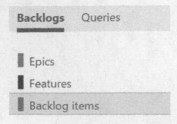

Figure 5-19. *All three backlog navigation levels are enabled*

On the Overview page, you see a button for adding a New team. Selecting this option shows the window from Figure 5-20. Let's say you want to create a hierarchy with one epic team, two feature teams, and a couple of implementation teams. You first create all the teams as a flat list. Make sure that you enable the option to automatically create an area for each team so you can separate the backlogs for the teams.

Figure 5-20. *Adding a new team*

Now you want to configure the hierarchy for the teams. You do this in the Area section of your team project's configuration screen. An area can have one parent and zero or more children. This allows you to set up a hierarchy. Figure 5-21 shows a hierarchy of areas. You have one top area, two management level areas, and six implementation teams.

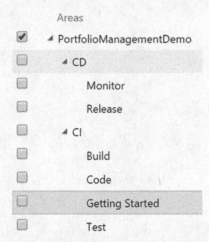

Figure 5-21. A hierarchical area configuration

By default, each area is configured to exclude sub-areas. This is good for the individual teams, but the management teams want to see everything that's beneath their level. You can toggle this behavior by right-clicking an area and selecting Include Sub-Areas. This will show all work items from the child areas in the PortfolioManagementDemo project (see Figure 5-22). You can do the same for your management level teams. The implementation teams don't have children in this example, so it's not required for them.

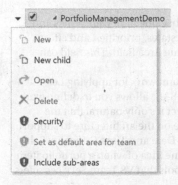

Figure 5-22. You can configure an area to include sub-areas

You want to make sure that all your teams follow the same sprint cadence, meaning they use sprints of the same length that start and end on similar dates. This allows you to align your efforts with multiple teams. You create one list of sprints and then link these sprints to your individual teams. By default, the top project has six sprints defined. Of course you can change the number of sprints, their start and end dates, and their name. What's important is that you navigate to each team and select the sprints that they can see in their work hub. Figure 5-23 shows how this looks for the Build team.

Figure 5-23. *You can configure the visible iterations per team*

Now that you've created your teams, you can assign team members to each team just as you previously did when you only had one team. Be aware that when navigating to the teams through the VS Team Services interface, the teams are shown as a flat, alphabetically sorted list. The hierarchy is only visible when working with work items.

The epic and feature are work item types, just as task, bug, and product backlog item were. Epics and features can be assigned to someone who is responsible for them. They have states, priorities, and efforts, just like regular work items. A field that's new for epics and features is the Value Area field. This field can have a value of Business or Architectural.

These terms come from the Scaled Agile Framework (SAFe). SAFe is a framework for applying Lean and Agile practices not only at the team level but also at the Enterprise level. SAFe allows you to define work items that target the business or architectural side of things. In an Agile project it's only natural that the architecture of the system evolves and that sometimes work needs to be done on the architecture to support further business epics. In addition to these fields, you also have a new Target Date and Time Criticality field. Especially in larger projects with more moving parts, it's essential to have some idea of when a portfolio item needs to be finished. Understanding how to use the portfolio management tools that VS Team Services offers is essential if you want to use SAFe or another scaling Agile framework.

■ **Note** SAFe is outside the scope of this book. You can find more information at the official SAFe site: `http://scaledagileframework.com/`. You can also have a look at `https://msdn.microsoft.com/Library/ vs/alm/work/scale/scaled-agile-framework` to see how SAFe is implemented in VS Team Services.

Creating an epic or a feature is the same as creating a product backlog item. You navigate to the backlog of your choice and use the Quick Add panel to add an item. Figure 5-24 shows the details of an epic. An important field is the Area field, since this allows you to assign work to a particular team.

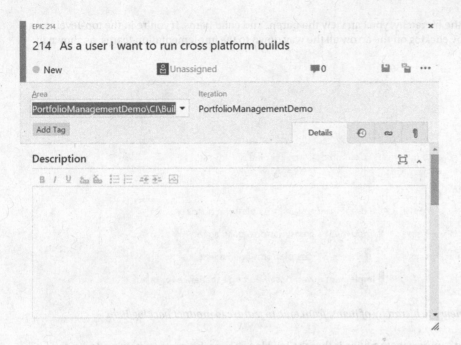

Figure 5-24. *The Details view of an epic work item*

Using this process, you can create a couple of features and product backlog items. These items aren't linked yet. You can use the Details tab of each work item to establish parent and child links, but there is an easier way. If you turn the Mapping pane on, you can then easily use drag and drop to establish relationships (see Figure 5-25).

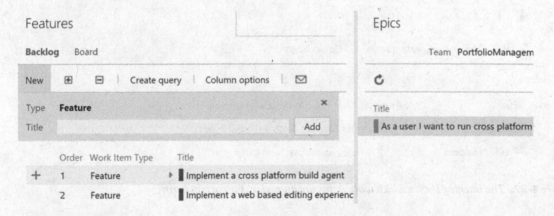

Figure 5-25. *Using the mapping panel to establish parent/child relations*

After establishing the hierarchy, you can view the parent and child items. If you're in the top-level team, you can expand items by clicking on the arrow all the way down to the implementation teams, as shown in Figure 5-26.

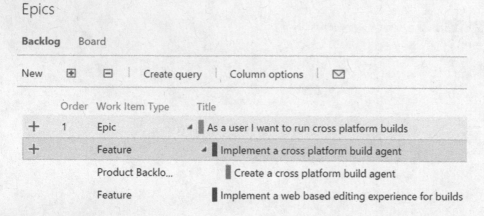

Figure 5-26. *You can view the hierarchy of items, from epic to feature to product backlog item*

One final thing that's important to notice is that the backlog shows who owns an item and who can manipulate it. In Figure 5-26, you view the work items starting at the top level. The rectangles in front of the work items are a solid color. In Figure 5-27, you see the same view from one of the child teams. As you can see, the epic and feature rectangles are only outlines. This means that they are owned by another team.

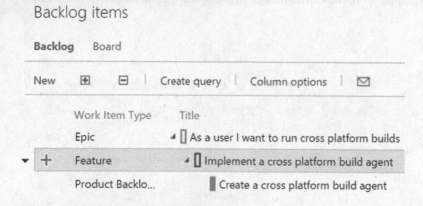

Figure 5-27. *The backlog shows which work items are owned by the current team*

If you also want to separate the locations that your team uses in source control, you can do so easily by creating multiple folders according to the teams' names (when using Git for version control, you can also create multiple repositories). The same is true for the Test and Release features.

Summary

In this chapter you first looked at the Kanban tools in VS Team Services. By using the Kanban board and configuring it with columns and work-in-progress limits, you can create a continuous flow of value to your stakeholders. By customizing cards and adding swimlanes, styles, and other board settings, you can make sure that your team can use these tools hassle free.

You also looked at the portfolio management tools that VS Team Services has. By using multiple teams and specialized work items such as epics and features, you can distribute work and track progress in a single location. Especially for organizations that are scaling their Agile implementation, these tools are a must-have.

Now that you had a good introduction to the Agile tools, it's time to continue learning about the dashboards and reporting tools that VS Team Services offers in the next chapter.

CHAPTER 6

■ ■ ■

Dashboards and Reporting

When running your project, you will generate a lot of data. Data from the Agile tools—such as Scrum, Kanban, and portfolio management—and other data such as code, test, and release data. Fortunately, Visual Studio Team Services has a querying system built-in and the ability to create dashboards for an up-to-date overview of your project. This chapter discusses the dashboard, query, and notification functionality of VS Team Services. You will also look at how to search through your code.

You start with looking at queries. These queries are the foundation of the data you show on your dashboard and the notifications you send.

Queries

Queries are an important part of VS Team Services. Being able to find work items in all kinds of ways is an important part of your daily work. This can range from picking a work item to start working on to deciding if the current sprint has too many bugs to be released.

Using the Search Box

When you open your VS Team Services project, the search box is at the top right. When you are at the overview page or on the work page, this search box lets you search through your work items. (When you navigate to other tabs, you can use this box to search through your code. You will look at this at the end of this chapter.)

Imagine you have the work items shown in Figure 6-1 in your project. This backlog defines four product backlog items. One is assigned to someone and one contains a couple of tags.

Order	Work Item Type	Title	State	Assigned To
1	Product Backlo...	As a user I want to find work items by ID	New	
2	Product Backlo...	As a user I want to find work items that are assigned to a specific person	New	Wouter de Kort
3	Product Backlo...	As a user I want to find work items that have changed since a specific date	New	
4	Product Backlo...	As a user I want to find work items containing a certain keyword	New	

Figure 6-1. *An example backlog that you can search through*

Opening a product backlog item shows the ID of the work item in the upper-left corner (see Figure 6-2). This is a unique number that identifies your work item throughout your VS Team Services account. This means that work items in different team projects within your account will have unique IDs. You can also change the column options to show the ID for each row. Enter the ID in the search box to immediately open the Work Item Detail page. Entering a non-existing work item ID or the ID of a work item that you don't have access to shows an error message stating 'TF401232: Work item xxx does not exist, or you do not have permissions to read it.'

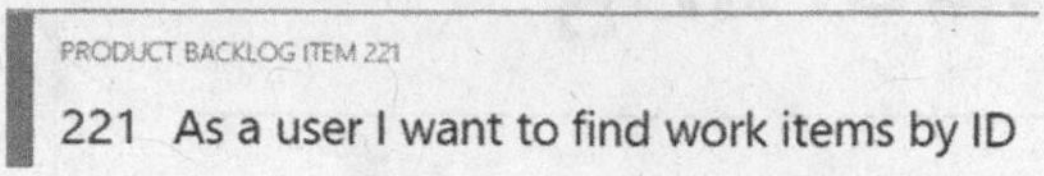

PRODUCT BACKLOG ITEM 221

221   As a user I want to find work items by ID

Figure 6-2. *The work item ID is shown on the Work Item Detail page*

You probably can't be expected to remember the ID number of every work item in your project. Fortunately, there are other ways you can search for work items. If you look at Figure 6-3, you see how VS Team Services has a couple of predefined filters that you can use (click on the arrow at the right side or place your cursor in the textbox and click the down arrow to show this popup).

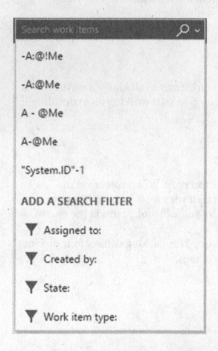

Figure 6-3. *The search filters for work items*

The Assigned To filter places the text a: "@Me" in the search box. If you then start the search (by pressing Enter or clicking on the magnifying glass), you launch a search for all work items that are assigned to you. Instead of @Me you can also enter the (partial) name of someone in your team. The Created By filter works in the same way, except you will now find all work items that were originally created by the person you search for.

The State filter lets you search for work items that are in a particular state. For example, a product backlog item can be in the New, Approved, Committed, Done, or Removed state (see Figure 6-4). These states are different per work item type.

Figure 6-4. *The States drop-down shows the possible states of a product backlog item*

Finally, you can directly search by work item type from the search box. You can enter the full or partial name of the work items you're looking for. So searching for *product* or for *product backlog item* will give you the same results.

You can combine these filters in one search by placing a space between them. So the search text S:New T:"product" searches for all product backlog items that are in the New state. Placing a : (colon) between your filter and the value allows you to run partial searches. Placing an = (equals sign) searches only for these values that exactly match what you specified. A third operator you can use is - (minus sign), which specifies a *not* operation. So searching for S-New finds any work items that are not in the New state.

Instead of using the predefined filters, you can also run a keyword search. VS Team Services then looks for work items that contain your keywords in the Title, Description, or Repro Steps (unique to the bug work item) fields. If you want to search for a (partial) sentence, you need to put quotation marks around your words like this: "certain keywords".

If you want to search for specific field values, you can enter the name of the field followed by a : (colon) or = (equals sign) and then the value you want to look for. So searching for T=Bug System.Reason= Duplicate will search for all bugs that are duplicates. When you want to query against fields containing a date, such as Changed Date and Created Date, you can use the @Today macro to specify the current date. You can then subtract a number from it to move back in time. So searching for ChangedDate=@Today-7 gives you the work items that were modified seven days ago.

Work Item Queries

The search box that you used until now is a quick way of defining a query. Queries are items that you create in VS Team Services (or Visual Studio) that you can share with others and that you can use as the basis of charts and dashboard widgets. Take the example search text -A:@!Me (searches for all work items that are not assigned to me). If you run this on some sample data, you get a result shown in Figure 6-5.

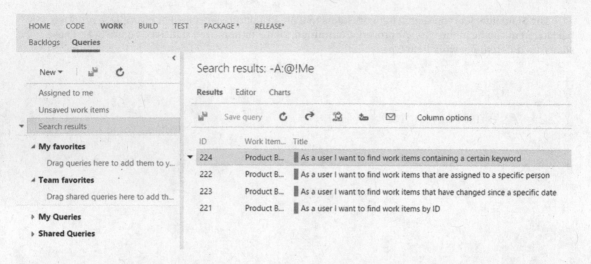

Figure 6-5. *The query results for a search*

What you see here is the Queries tab in the Work section of VS Team Services. You are immediately taken to a query called Search Results and shown the results. If you click on the Editor tab, you see the actual query that VS Team Services defined for your search. Figure 6-6 shows this query. In this case, there is only one clause in the query, namely a filter that makes sure that the Assigned To field does not contain your name.

Figure 6-6. *The query created by VS Team Services for a simple search*

Expanding this query is easy. You can add a new clause by clicking on the green plus icon. You then select a field or an operator and enter a value. If you scroll through the Field drop-down, you will see a whole lot of values. These fields are defined on all the different types of work items. One of these fields is the Work Item Type itself. You can use this field to limit your query to only certain types of work items.

The Operator drop-down lets you select operators that work with numbers (larger than, less than, etc.) and text and that let you compare one field to another. The Value field is a text field or a drop-down when you compare one field to another.

Clauses built upon fields, operators, and values are the basis of your queries. When you add multiple clauses, by default VS Team Services will search for items that match all your clauses. You can change the And/Or drop down to or if you want to return result if one of the two clauses is true or if both are true. If you want to compare groups of clauses, select clauses by checking the checkbox at the start of each clause and then clicking on the group icon at the top.

When searching for work items, you sometimes want to search for relationships between items. Maybe you want to find product backlog items that don't have a storyboard. Or you want to see if there are tasks created for certain bugs. You can search for work items and their direct links or for a whole tree of work items. Figure 6-7 shows a query that searches for all the product backlog items that are linked to an item that is assigned to you.

Type of query   ▦ Work items and direct links

Filters for top level work items

	And/Or	Field		Operator		Value
+ ✕ ▢		Work Item Type	▼	=	▼	Product Backlog Item

+ Add new clause

Filters for linked work items

	And/Or	Field		Operator		Value
+ ✕ ▢		Assigned To	▼	=	▼	@Me

+ Add new clause

Filter options

Only return items that have matching links   ▼

Types of links

◉ Return links of any type
◯ Return selected link types

  ▢ Affected By
  ▢ Affects
  ▢ Child
  ▢ Duplicate
  ▢ Duplicate Of

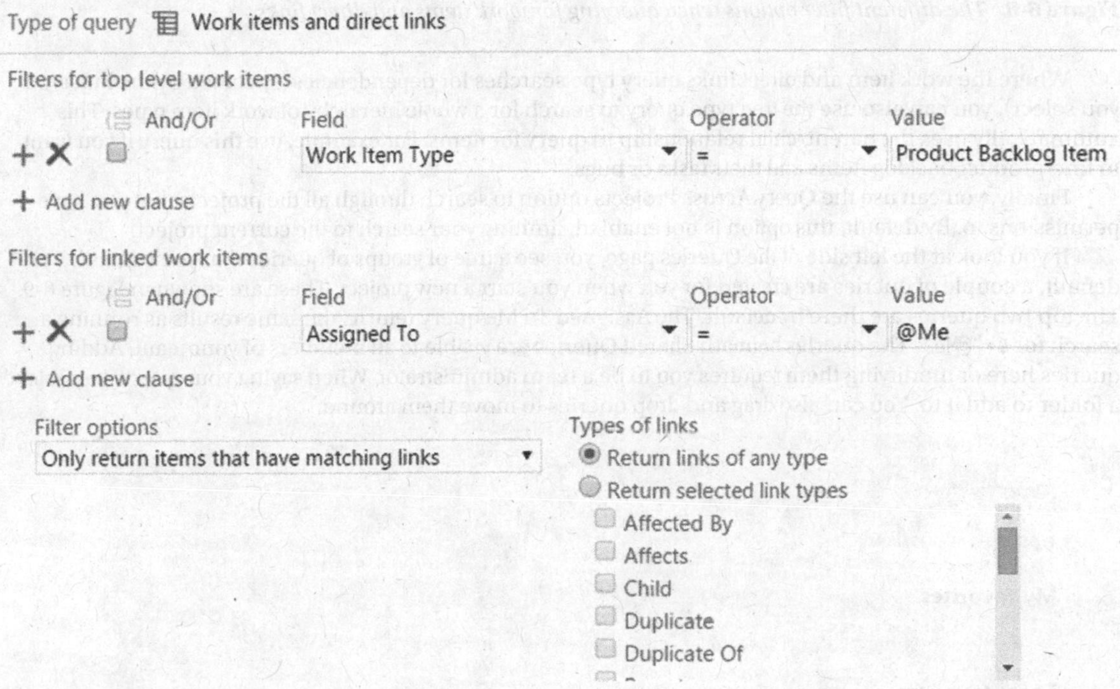

Figure 6-7. A query for work items and their direct links

A link in VS Team Services can mean a lot of different things. You have things like the parent or child of a work item but you also have links like Affected By or Referenced By. The previous query will find product backlog items with tasks that are assigned to you and product backlog items that are linked to a feature that is assigned to you. Product backlog items that are not linked to any item that is assigned to you won't be shown. If you want to change the type of link, you can do so by selecting the different link types (one or more) shown in the bottom-right corner of Figure 6-7. For example, selecting the Child link type will no longer return product backlog items linked to a feature that is assigned to you.

The Filter Options drop-down (Figure 6-8) is also interesting. When the option Only Return Items That Have Matching Links is selected, you won't get any results that match the top part of your query and not the bottom part. So, returning to the previous query as an example, you won't find all product backlog items even if they have no linked items that are assigned to you. If you select the second option, Return All Top Level Items, you will find all product backlog items. Items that have linked items that are assigned to you will be returned in the results. The final option, Only Return Items That Do Not Have Matching Links, negates the query. In the example, you will then find the product backlog items that do not have linked items that are assigned to you.

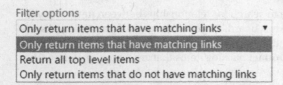

Figure 6-8. *The different filter options when querying for work items and direct links*

Where the work item and direct links query type searches for dependencies (specified by the link type you select), you can also use the tree type query to search for a whole hierarchy of work item types. This automatically uses the parent/child relationship to query for items. For example, use this query if you want to find product backlog items and their tasks or bugs.

Finally, you can use the Query Across Projects option to search through all the projects that you have permissions to. By default, this option is not enabled, limiting your search to the current project.

If you look at the left side of the Queries page, you see a tree of groups of queries that you can use. By default, a couple of queries are created for you when you start a new project. These are shown in Figure 6-9. The top two queries are there by default. The Assigned To Me query returns the same results as running a search for A="@Me". The queries beneath Shared Queries are visible to all members of your team. Adding queries here or modifying them requires you to be a team administrator. When saving your query, you select a folder to add it to. You can also drag and drop queries to move them around.

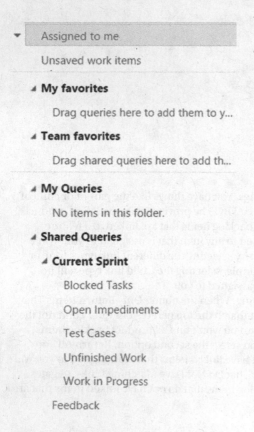

Figure 6-9. *The Query Explorer in VS Team Services*

Charts

Charts are graphical representations of your query. They can range from snapshots showing the state of bugs assigned to you to trend charts showing how your query is changing over time. Imagine you want to see in one glance how many items are assigned to you and what the state of those items is. Creating a chart for this is fairly easy. Figure 6-10 shows such a chart. The chart is based on the Assigned to Me query that's available out-of-the-box. The data is grouped by the State field and rendered as a Pie chart. In this case, there are two items committed—one is new and one is done. If you want to remove the Done work item from the chart, you need to edit the underlying query (or not, if you want to feel really good about yourself after a couple of sprints!).

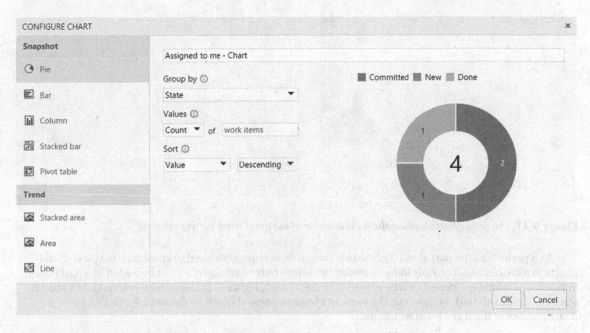

Figure 6-10. A pie chart showing the work items assigned to you, grouped by state

As you can see in Figure 6-10, there are a couple of charts you can use from. The snapshot charts look at the current state of your project. If you look at the pie chart example, you see that at this moment there are four items assigned to you. If you want to know when items were assigned to you during the last week, you can use a trend chart. Figure 6-11 shows an area chart, which is a type of trend chart, of the four items that are currently assigned to you. As you can see, all of them where created somewhere in the last two days.

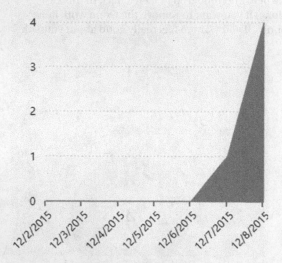

Figure 6-11. *An area chart showing the total number of assigned work items over time*

As a prelude to the part about dashboards later in this chapter, it's good to know how easy it is to add charts to a dashboard. The only thing to remember is that only shared queries can be added to a dashboard. Your own personal queries cannot be placed on a dashboard. Figure 6-12 shows how you can add a shared query to the dashboard. In this case, the Work in Progress query shows how the work for this sprint is distributed over the three team members.

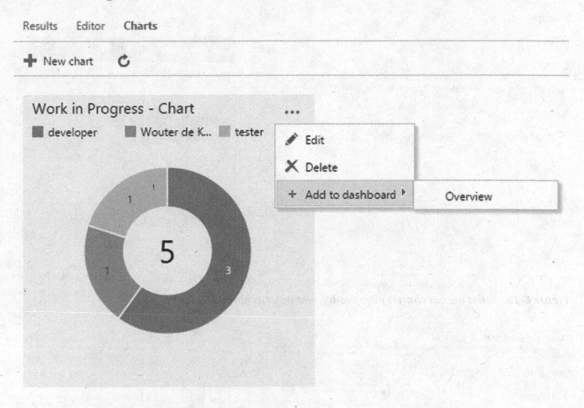

Figure 6-12. *Adding a chart based on a shared query to a dashboard*

■ **Note** Remember that only shared queries can be added to a dashboard. Your own personal queries cannot be placed on a dashboard.

Figures 6-13 through 6-19 show the different types of charts that you can create.

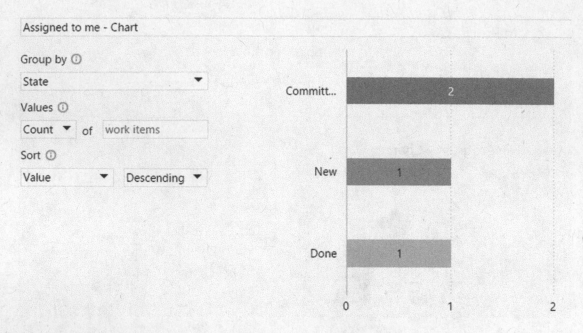

Figure 6-13. *Select the bar chart to view the different states as horizontal bars*

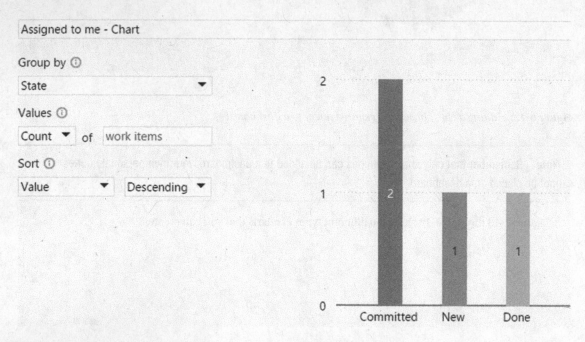

Figure 6-14. *Select the column chart to view the different states as vertical columns*

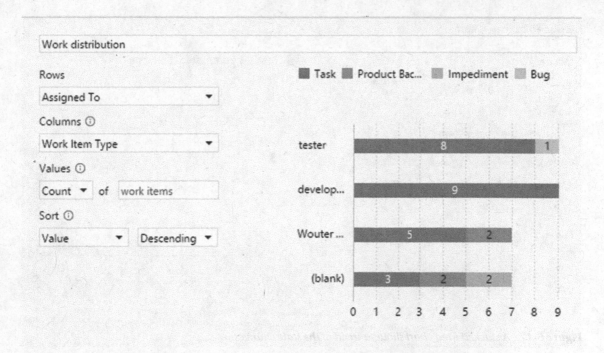

Figure 6-15. *A stacked bar graph showing the distribution of work across your team members*

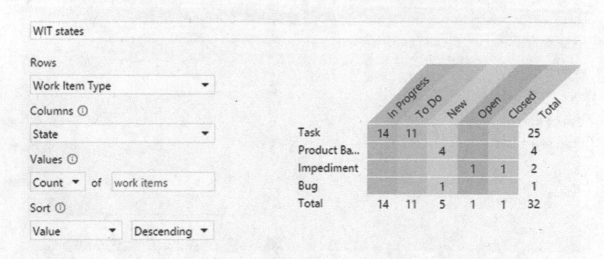

Figure 6-16. *A pivot table displays the different states set against work item types*

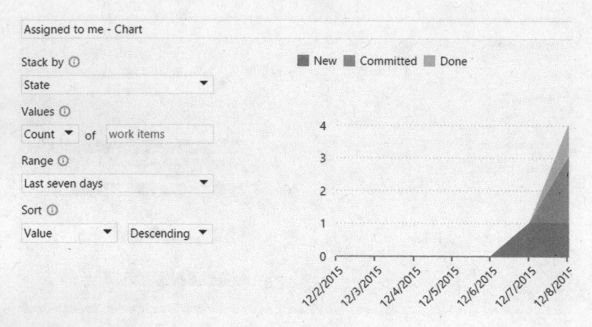

Figure 6-17. *A stacked area chart shows a trend of the state changes*

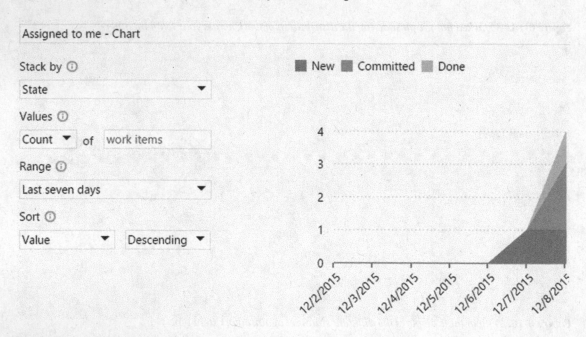

Figure 6-18. *A stacked area chart shows the total count of work items as a trend*

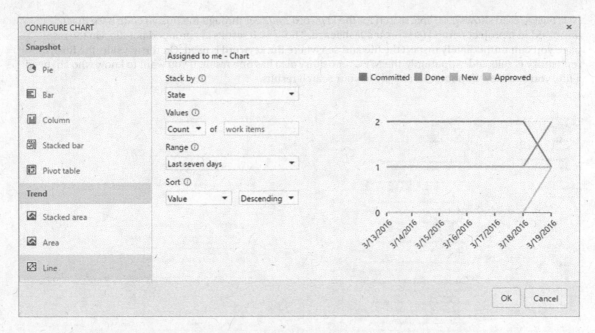

Figure 6-19. *A line chart shows a line for each state versus time*

Code Search

Do you search through your code? When inside Visual Studio, you've probably searched through files, projects, and solutions. You can use complex regex expressions or simple keyword searches. But what if you wanted to search through code in multiple team projects? That's where Code Search comes in.

Code Search is a feature of VS Team Services that allows you to search through multiple projects in multiple repositories in different languages. Why would you want to search through code? There are lots of scenarios when it would be helpful to do so. Imagine that your company has an extensive set of projects and you are tasked to build a new feature for your project. You want to know if someone else built something similar in the past. Running a search through your current project on your local drive is easy. But Code Search allows you to search through all the projects. The same is true when you're looking for examples of a particular API or library. Or what about searching for error messages that a customer reports in a bug? Doing a quick search will show you the error message not only in your project but also in projects you depend on.

I use Code Search quite often. I have a Samples Team Project in my VS Team Services account and it contains all kinds of projects that I use as references. This ranges from Roslyn (the C# and VB compiler) and ASP.NET MVC code to code snippets that I found useful. If I ever want to view the internals of a particular method or just find a certain snippet, I can use Code Search to go through both TFVC and Git repositories. And Code Search is not just a plain keyword search—it parses your files and understands the actual code. This allows you to filter your query to only include classes, methods, arguments, and other language types. This is what makes Code Search so powerful.

Microsoft implemented Code Search as an extension that you can freely install from the marketplace (see `https://marketplace.visualstudio.com/items/ms.vss-code-search`). After you have installed the extension, you can use the search box at the top of the VS Team Services page to search for code (except when you're on the Home or Work tab; then you search for work items).

Figure 6-20 shows a sample search for the keyword *analyzer* through the Roslyn code base that I imported in a project named `QueriesAndDashboard`. The search results are grouped per file. On the result page you can immediately inspect the file and see where the keyword is used. On the left side, the Roslyn repository is selected. Apparently, the MVC repository also has one result. If you want to know who changed a file, you can view annotations directly in your search results.

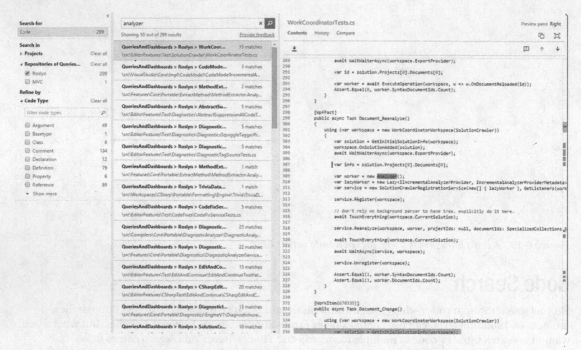

Figure 6-20. *The results of a basic keyword search*

Although a keyword search can be helpful, the real power of Code Search is shown when you start using built-in filters. Figure 6-21 shows which filters you can use. For example, searching for `class:Analyzer` limits the results to all places in the Roslyn code that a class called `Analyzer` is defined. Filtering the search with: `method:analyze*` limits your search to all methods that can be found that start with the word Analyze. The wildcard character * matches all characters, while ? matches only one character. So `method:analyze*` matches methods like `AnalyzerForLanguage` and `AnalyzeControlFlow`. A search for `arg:x?` matches arguments like `x1`, `x2`, or `xx` (all found in the Roslyn project!).

Search code   🔍

Filter by scope (e.g., Activity ext:cs)

ext:	With file extension	file:	Filename
path:	Under path	proj:	Inside project
repo:	Inside repository		

Filter by code type (e.g., func:ApiRoot)

arg:	Argument	basetype:	Basetype
caller:	Caller	class:	Class
classdecl:	Class Declaration	classdef:	Class Definition
comment:	Comment	ctor:	Constructor
decl:	Declaration	def:	Definition
dtor:	Destructor	enum:	Enumerator
extern:	Extern	field:	Field
friend:	Friend	func:	Function
funcdecl:	Function Declaration	funcdef:	Function Definition
global:	Global	header:	Header
interface:	Interface	macro:	Macro
macrodef:	Macro Definition	macroref:	Macro Reference
method:	Method	methoddecl:	Method Declaration
methoddef:	Method Definition	namespace:	Namespace
prop:	Property	ref:	Reference
strlit:	String Literal	struct:	Struct
structdecl:	Struct Declaration	structdef:	Struct Definition
tmplarg:	Template Argument	tmplspec:	Template Specification
type:	Type	typedef:	Type Definition
union:	Union		

▲ Show less

Operators (e.g., ToDo OR revisit)

AND   NOT   OR

For more ways to search, see the help page

Figure 6-21. *Available filters when searching through code*

In addition to filtering on code elements, you can also limit your search to a specific project or a file path. For example, searching for basetype:IDisposable path:*Test* finds all uses of the IDisposable interface limited to files that have Test somewhere in the path. You can also combine multiple statements by using the AND, OR, and NOT operators. Searching for basetype:IDisposable NOT path:*Test* excludes all results where the word Test is somewhere in the path. Instead of entering the filters in the textbox yourself, you can also use the checkboxes at the left side of your Code Search to gradually filter down to the results you want. For examples of all the different filter clauses, you can navigate to the help page shown at the bottom of Figure 6-21. You can also find a link to a Channel9 video that demonstrates Code Search use cases.

Code Search allows you to search through all repositories where you have read permissions. To make effective use of Code Search, you should have read permissions on as large a code base as possible. This is something you need to adapt to your company's regulatory rules.

Dashboards

Dashboards offer an easy way to create a view of the data in your project. By using the standard widgets and creating your own queries to fill widgets with data, you can quickly create a dashboard that fulfills your needs.

When you create a new team project, VS Team Services creates a standard Overview dashboard for you. This dashboard consists of widgets such as:

- Information on how to get started

- Data on work in progress

- How to create work items

- How to access different areas of the product

- How to manage team members

Figure 6-22 shows this default dashboard.

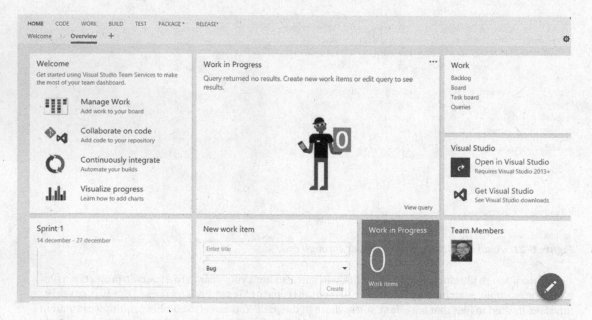

Figure 6-22. *The default Overview dashboard helps you get started and gives you a quick overview of your project*

Widgets on the dashboard can be rearranged by entering edit mode and dragging widgets to the desired location. Configurable widgets have an ellipsis at the top right that lets you edit them. Certain widgets, such as the Welcome and New Work Item widgets, don't have any settings. You can only add and remove these widgets from your dashboards. Other widgets can also be configured. For example, clicking on the Team Members widget opens a window where you can add and remove team members. The Query Results widget that's added by default is backed by a query that you can change from the configuration blade or by opening the query in the work hub (see Figure 6-23).

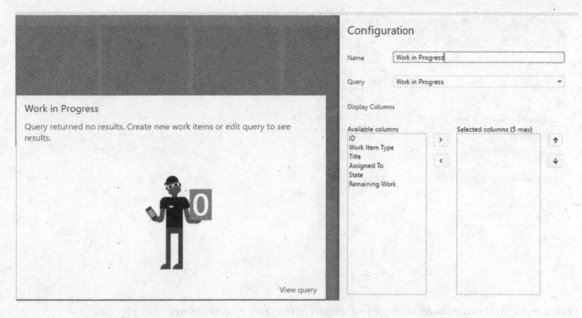

Figure 6-23. *Configuring a query widget on your dashboard*

What's nice about dashboards is that they can be made available to your team as well as to stakeholders who have access to VS Team Services. Since you can configure multiple dashboards, you can create dashboards targeting specific stakeholders and team members. By default, there is a selection of widgets provided; however, you can increase the selection by adding extensions or creating your own. Some of these widgets are pretty simple, like the Visual Studio widget that allows you to open your project in Visual Studio. The Welcome widget is a getting started guide for your team project that links to different parts of your projects. Other widgets offer more complex functionality like the Pull requests widget that shows active pull requests per Git repository.

Alerts and Notifications

Another feature of VS Team Services is the support for alerts and notifications. Imagine that you want to know when a build fails, a code review is assigned to you, or someone assigns a work item to you. Of course you can find all these in the VS Team Services Web Access interface, but having a system in place that notifies you by e-mail can speed things up.

This is all done by creating alerts for the team projects your interested in. An *alert* uses a filter that looks a lot like the queries that you already looked at in the beginning of this chapter. You manage your alerts in the Team Project settings. Figure 6-24 shows the Alerts tab in Web Access. As you can see, you set your own alerts and set alerts for the whole team.

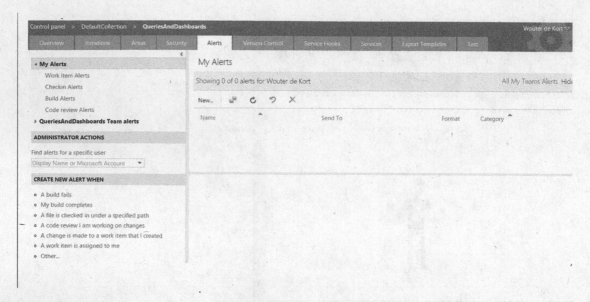

Figure 6-24. *You can manage alerts for your project in the Team Project settings*

Creating a new alert is simple. Let's say you want to get an e-mail whenever a code review is assigned to you. If you look in the Create New Alert When section, you see there is already a predefined alert for code reviews. If you select this alert, you can configure it as shown in Figure 6-25. As you can see, the Alert filter uses the same approach as regular queries.

A CODE REVIEW I AM WORKING ON CHANGES	✕

Name	A code review I am working on changes	Subscriber	Wouter de Kort ▾
Send to		Format	HTML ▾

Alert filters

	And/Or	Field	Operator	Value
✚ ✗ ☐		Changed by ˙ ▾	<> ▾	[Me] ▾
✚ ✗ ☐	And ▾	Requested by ▾	= ▾	[Me] ▾
✚ ✗ ☐	Or ▾	Reviewers ▾	Contains ▾	[Me] ▾

✚ Add new clause

	OK	Cancel

Figure 6-25. *Configuring an alert*

Aside from the query, you can also change the subscriber (if you're an admin) and the format of the message. When using HTML or plain text, you specify an e-mail address as the recipient. You can also choose SOAP. This allows you to specify an endpoint that's called whenever the alert triggers. So if you want to automate things, such as use a build monitor that changes color whenever a build fails, you can use a SOAP call for this.

You can view, remove, and edit your alerts. You can also find alerts for a specific user. This can be handy, especially when you are administering the VS Team Services environment. If a particular user complains that he gets to many e-mail alerts, you can quickly search for his name and see which alerts are configured.

If you want to create an alert that's not out-of-the-box available, you select the Other option in the Create An Alert When section. This shows a window where you can select an alert template. You have four categories of alerts: work item, code review, checkin, and build. This gives you a lot of freedom to set up your alerts and covers a broad spectrum of events.

There is one other type of event that will send an alert to your mailbox: mentions. A mention allows you to specify a team member by name, which will immediately send an e-mail to him. One place you can use this is in the discussion part of a work item, as shown in Figure 6-26. Other places, like adding reviewers to a Git pull request, also allow you to send mentions. Just type an @ and the first three characters of someone's name and see if the mention window pops up. The e-mail that the mentioned person receives looks like Figure 6-27.

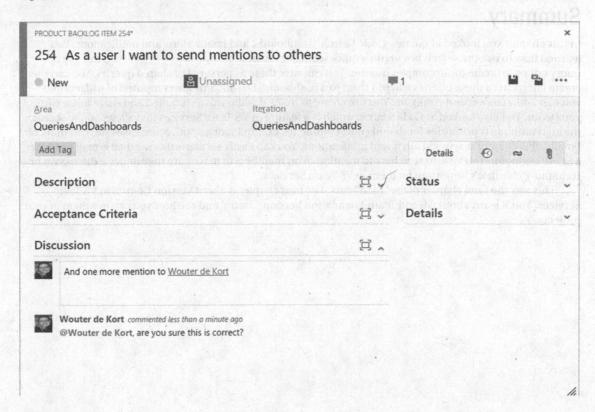

Figure 6-26. *Using mentions in a work item discussion*

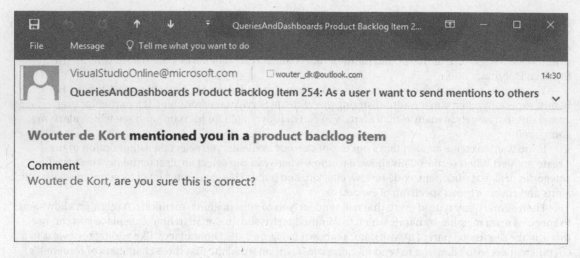

Figure 6-27. A mention sends out an e-mail to your target

Summary

In this chapter you looked at queries, Code Search, dashboards, and finally alerts and notifications. You learned how to use the search box to run a quick work item search. You've also seen how you can use the query editor to create more complex queries. You can save these as personal or shared queries. You can then create charts from these queries and pin them to a dashboard. Dashboards are composed of widgets that you can add, remove, and configure. You can create as many dashboards as required and share those with your team. You also looked at Code Search, which is a feature in VS Team Services that allows you to search through multiple repositories for shared code, comments, examples, or any other use cases you can think of. Finally, this chapter discussed alerts and notifications. You can easily set alerts that send an e-mail or trigger a SOAP endpoint. You've also seen how to mention team members to make sure they notice a discussion or something else that's important for them in VS Team Services.

This was the final chapter of the "Plan" part. The next chapter is about Version Control in VS Team Services. You'll learn about Git and Team Foundation Version Control and see how you can use them in your projects.

PART III

■ ■ ■

Code and Build

Code is essential to your application. Without code there is nothing to test, deploy, and use. Developers write code and are good at writing it. They can crank out as many lines as they want. However, writing code itself will not get you to a DevOps process. This part goes into the details of how to work together as a team by sharing code in an effective way. You will also learn what Visual Studio can offer you to fight bad quality code and how to set up a continuous integration process to monitor the state of your code.

CHAPTER 7

■■■

Setting Up Version Control

In this chapter you're going to learn what Visual Studio Team Services can do for you when it comes to storing your code in version control. You will learn what version control is and the two different flavors that VS Team Services offers: Team Foundation Version Control and Git. You will also learn some best practices for structuring your code through branches and how to take things a step further with feature toggles.

Introducing Version Control

Before I got into professional software development I did not know what version control was. I stored my code on my hard drive and made copies that I time stamped to take backups. This process quickly breaks down when working in a team. Sharing code and merging all the work that everyone does is a requirement for building software together. When I started working as an ALM consultant, I was extremely surprised to still find a company that used a shared network folder to share code within the team. As you can understand, this gave them quite some problems. They overwrote each other's changes, forgot to merge files, and sometimes completely missed changes. All this resulted in bugs and loss of time.

Version control is a basic need for development teams. Version control offers you a way of storing your code in such a way that you can easily share it with other team members. Changes are automatically tracked so that history is kept. Individual developers can get the latest changes downloaded to their computer and merged with their own changes. If you are in the unfortunate situation that your developers are not yet using version control, this is absolutely the very first thing you should adopt.

Two main flavors of version control are popular:

- Distributed Version Control
- Centralized Version Control

Centralized version control uses a centralized server that stores all the files and the history of the whole development team. Clients connect to the central server when they want to view the history of a file or want to undo their local changes (see Figure 7-1). The centralized server knows the state of each file and is capable of supporting operations like merging changes, rolling back to previous versions, and figuring out who made which change. Things go wrong when developers work on the same files for a long time and then try to merge those changes. This will always cost you time since you have to figure out which lines to keep and in which order.

© Wouter de Kort 2016
W. de Kort, *DevOps on the Microsoft Stack*, DOI 10.1007/978-1-4842-1446-6_7

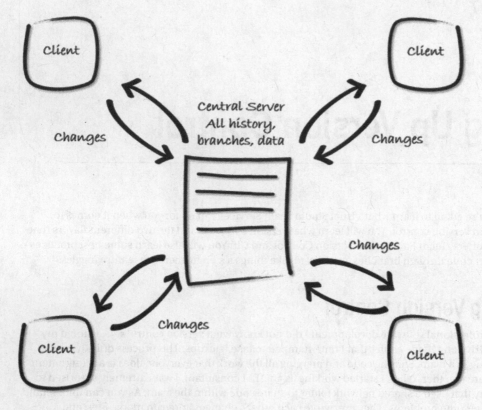

Figure 7-1. Centralized version control

Distributed version control does not require a centralized server. Instead, each client not only has a snapshot of the latest version of the files but also the complete history of them. This means that many tasks, like undoing changes or viewing history, can be done locally. This is more than just putting code on a file share. Git, the distributed version control system supported by VS Team Services, keeps track of everything that's happening in your repository. Each committed step is added to the history of the project, allowing you to switch very fast between versions, undo changes, and compare files. Whenever developers want to share some code with someone else, they share the whole repository, including all history (see Figure 7-2). Of course, these processes are supported by VS Team Services and this doesn't mean you have to manually copy folders between machines. The same issues as with centralized version control happen when developers work on the same files for a long time without merging their changes. Manually merging those changes takes time and is error prone.

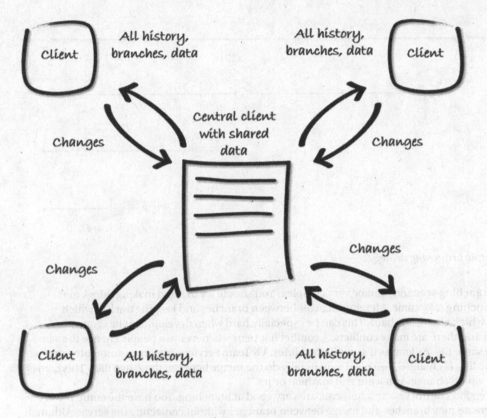

Figure 7-2. *Distributed version control*

One area where these two types of version control differ greatly is branching. Imagine that you want to work in parallel on different versions of your code. You have your application running in production and bugs come in. In the meantime, your team is working on a new version of your product. You can fix a bug in the current codebase your team is working on, but what do you ship? Do you ship a new version of your application with features that are not finished yet but that has the bug fixed? That's probably going to introduce some new bugs and unhappy customers. Preferably, you want to fix the bug in the codebase that is running in production. You could create a copy of your codebase each time you do a release and store it somewhere, but that is the scenario you are trying to avoid.

Instead, you can use a technique called *branching*. To understand branches, think about a tree. A tree has a trunk, which is the main code line. A branch is a fork of the trunk. This means that you create a separate path of code that diverges from the trunk. Now the difference with code is that you can merge the changes from a branch back into the trunk. If you take the previous example of having a version in production and doing new development, you would have your new development on the trunk. When you do your release, you create a branch at that point. Any bug fixes can be done on the branch and when successful, merged back into the trunk.

Figure 7-3 shows an example of a branching strategy. You have a main branch and then the servicing, hotfix, and release branches.

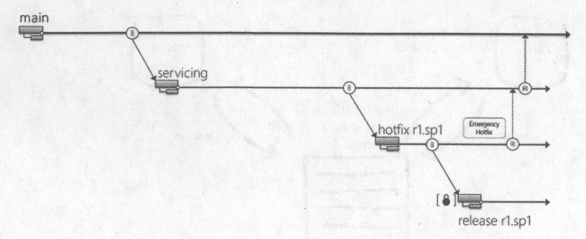

Figure 7-3. *A sample branching strategy*

As you see, branching scenarios can be very complex. You should try to avoid making things too complex since branching takes time. Merging changes between branches and keeping track of which branches contain which changes is hard. This can be especially hard when development has gone in a different direction and there are many conflicts. A conflict happens whenever two people change the same line of code in the same file. As long as it's on different lines, VS Team Services can do an automated merge. But when the same line is changed, you need to manually do the merge between these two files. This comes down to selecting which changes you want and in which order.

Distributed version control systems, however, are very good at branching. You have the entire history local, so you can create new branches and merge between branches without contacting the server. Although you don't contact the server, you still need to be aware of what your team is doing. Working on the same files can still create merge conflicts when you try to merge your repositories. Git, the distributed version control system that you'll work with when using VS Team Services, can determine the exact changes between two branches and make it even easier to branch. You can even create branches that you only have locally and never share them with anyone. It is not uncommon for developers used to distributed version control to create a new local branch for every feature they start working on. This does not mean they push all those branches to the server but locally it keeps things organized. Once done, they do a local merge (or a *rebase* when you're working with Git) and send the final result to a shared server.

With centralized version control, branching is a more complex operation. To create a branch, the server is contacted. The new branch is then created at the server and you get a local copy of it. This makes the branch visible to everyone on your team. Creating a quick branch and destroying it when you're done while keeping things locally is not supported in centralized version control. When submitting your changes to the branch located on the server, you can still get merge conflicts if someone else has submitted changes in the mean time.

Choosing your type of version control influences the way your team works. Because of the ease of branching, teams using distributed version control will create short-lived branches more easily, thus allowing them to quickly experiment and work in parallel. Centralized version control also supports branching but since it is a little more difficult, teams tend to use other ways of organizing their version control.

In addition to branching, a new method is gaining popularity that fits nicely with a DevOps strategy: *feature toggling*. Since branching has its shortcomings (time consuming, merge conflicts, etc.), wouldn't it be best to avoid branching? However, how then would you work on different parts of your project simultaneously without shipping unfinished features to your customer? The section called "Choosing a Branching Strategy," later in this chapter looks at feature toggling in more detail.

DISTRIBUTED VERSION CONTROL AND LARGE FILES

Since distributed version control systems share all history with all clients, storing large files becomes an issue. When I started a new application with a distributed version control system, in the first week a developer thought it would be nice to store a large video file in version control. The other developers tried to get the latest version of the code but all had a timeout because the file was too large to download. The original developer then removed the file, thinking this would solve the issue. However, since distributed systems share all history with all clients, the large file was still a part of the history and still needed to be downloaded by all team members. Fortunately, when you know what you're doing, you can rewrite history, effectively removing the large file completely. This is not an easy operation however and requires all the team members to synchronize and run some commands locally. Absolutely something you want to avoid! There is one solution, using Git-LFS (Large File Storage). This is an extension to Git that allows you to place large files on a shared server and only put a pointer to the file in your history. Although this works, it's still a best practice to avoid checking in large files when using Git.

VS Team Services has support for both distributed version control in the form of Git and centralized version control in Team Foundation Version Control (TFVC). Both can be used from within Visual Studio and through Web Access. If you want, you can also mix both types of version control in one team project. This allows you to have TFVC and Git repos side by side without having to create additional team projects. Feature toggling is something that is independent of your source control strategy because you implement it in your code. The following part discusses how to work with Git and TFVC. After that, you'll look at different branching strategies and how feature toggling can be implemented.

Using Team Foundation Version Control (TFVC)

Team Foundation Version Control (TFVC) has been a part of TFS since the very first version. Microsoft developed TFVC to help deal with the extremely large projects they were running internally. TFVC is a centralized version control system. TFVC can easily manage projects with more than 100,000 files. All those files are stored on the central server and clients only download the latest snapshot.

TFVC has a couple of key concepts that you need to know to work effectively with it:

- Workspace
- Get Latest and merge conflicts
- Checking in a changeset
- History and annotations
- Shelvesets and suspending your work
- Branches
- Check-in policies

Workspace

All files are stored on the server. When you want to work with the code on your own PC, you create what's called a *workspace*. A workspace is a mapping between a location on the server and a location on your hard drive. Each PC that you work on will have a unique workspace name that consists of your computer name and the path where you store the data locally.

■ **Note** I have seen this gone wrong with a team that used a virtual machine with the same machine name that they all worked on. TFVC got confused and this led to all kinds of errors.

Workspaces come in two flavors:

- Local workspaces
- Server workspaces

Figure 7-4 shows the configuration options for a workspace. The workspace has a name and a location on your hard drive. The Location option configures if your workspace is local or server.

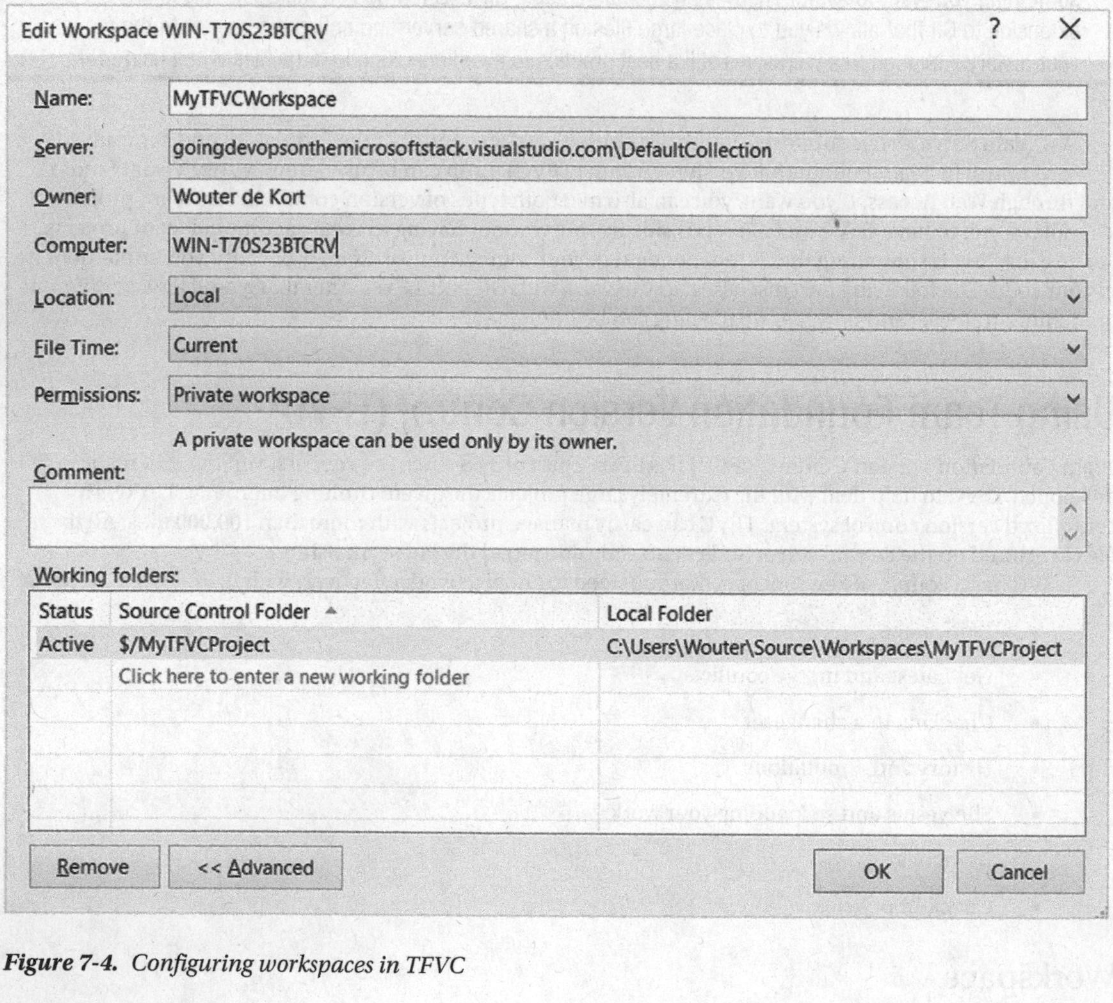

Edit Workspace WIN-T70S23BTCRV	? X

Name:	MyTFVCWorkspace
Server:	goingdevopsonthemicrosoftstack.visualstudio.com\DefaultCollection
Owner:	Wouter de Kort
Computer:	WIN-T70S23BTCRV
Location:	Local
File Time:	Current
Permissions:	Private workspace

A private workspace can be used only by its owner.

Comment:

Working folders:

Status	Source Control Folder ▲	Local Folder
Active	$/MyTFVCProject	C:\Users\Wouter\Source\Workspaces\MyTFVCProject
	Click here to enter a new working folder	

Remove	<< Advanced		OK	Cancel

Figure 7-4. Configuring workspaces in TFVC

Until Team Foundation Server 2012, only server workspaces where supported. A server workspace has an active connection to the TFVC server. Every time you change a file, Visual Studio contacts the server and signals that you are changing the file. This process is called *check-out*. Because of the connection to the server, you can always see which files are being edited by any of your team members. This also allows you to lock files and prevent others from checking out those files.

Having a permanent server connection, locking files and explicitly checking them out is a hindrance for many teams. You can't work offline and you slow down work because team members have to wait on each other. This is why Microsoft developed local workspaces, which is the current standard. In a local workspace, you can freely work on all files without having a server connection and you don't lock files anymore. This is the preferred option and you should only look at server workspaces when your project gets very big (more than 100,000 files).

With big projects there is another option. A workspace mapping is recursive. This means that if you map the root folder of your version control repository, you download all child folders and files to your computer. This can be a huge amount of data, possibly containing data that you won't need to do your work. To help you with this, you can *cloak* folders. This means that these folders and their children won't be downloaded to your PC. Figure 7-5 shows an example of a working folder that's cloaked. In this scenario, the BuildProcessTemplates folder won't be downloaded to my PC.

Figure 7-5. Cloaking a folder in a workspace

You choose the type of version control you want to use when starting a new team project. However, since you can combine TFVC and Git in a single team project, you can always add extra repositories. Once you've created a team project based on TFVC you are directed to the Overview dashboard. The easiest way to create a workspace mapping is to find the widget shown in Figure 7-6 and select Open in Visual Studio.

Visual Studio

Open in Visual Studio
Requires Visual Studio 2013+

Get Visual Studio
See Visual Studio downloads

Figure 7-6. The Visual Studio widget lets you open your project in Visual Studio

After launching Visual Studio, you can use Team Explorer (View ➤ Team Explorer) to map your workspace. Visual Studio is clever enough to know that you don't have a mapping yet and shows you an example mapping that you can change or accept. Figure 7-7 shows what this looks like. When you click Map & Get, the workspace mapping is created and the current versions of the files on VS Team Services are downloaded to your PC. Since this is an empty project, there are no files to download but the mapping is created.

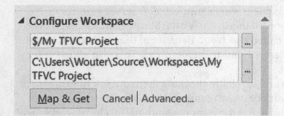

Figure 7-7. *Configuring a workspace mapping in Visual Studio*

Checking in a Changeset

Now that you have a local workspace, you can start adding files to it. Uploading the changes you made locally to the server is called a check-in in TFVC. When you change multiple files, those changes are grouped in a *changeset*. A check-in sends the changeset to the server. If there are merge conflicts, VS Team Services will try to solve those automatically. If this doesn't work, you get an error and you need to run a manual merge. It's a best practice to always run a Get Latest command before you do a check-in so you can be sure you've fixed all merge conflicts and validated that the code still works before checking in.

When checking in files, you can add a comment. This makes it easy for your teammates (and for you somewhere in the future!) to understand which changes are in this check-in. You can even make a comment required (see "Check-In Policies" later in this chapter). In Part II of this book, you've seen how you can pick up a work item through the My Work panel. When you've selected a work item and set it to in progress, your changeset will be automatically linked to the work item.

And that's where your traceability starts. By linking changesets and work items, you can easily see which code changes were made to implement a certain feature. Storyboards, code reviews, test cases, and finally deployments are all linked this way.

When you have an empty workspace, you probably want some code in it. After mapping your workspace, Team Explorer looks like the one shown in Figure 7-8. At the bottom, you see the option to create a new solution. You can use this option to create a new project and add it to your local workspace. This is nothing more than creating the solution in the folder on your local drive that's mapped to VS Team Services.

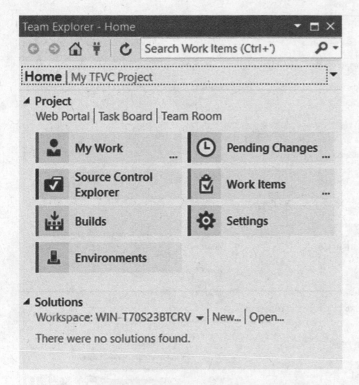

Figure 7-8. Team Explorer helps you create a new solution in your local workspace

While creating your project, you need to make sure the Add to Source Control button is checked, as shown in the bottom-right corner of Figure 7-9.

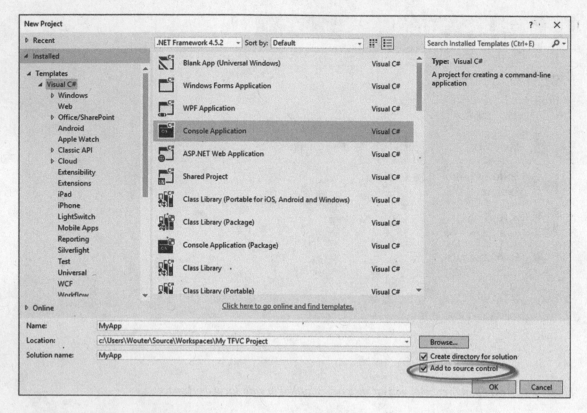

Figure 7-9. *Adding a newly created project to source control*

After the project is created, you can view the changes that are ready to be checked in through the Team Explorer ➤ Pending Changes. In Figure 7-10, you see how a check-in consists of a comment and one or more included files. Excluded changes are those changes you have locally but that you don't want to send to the server.

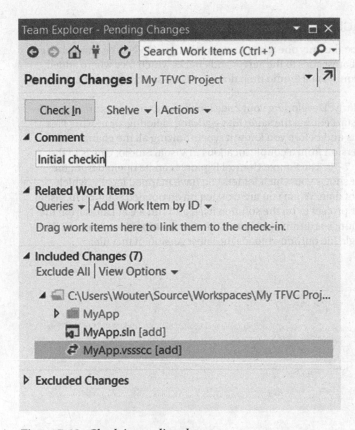

Figure 7-10. *Check-in pending changes*

After checking in your local changes, you can view the result in the Web Access of VS Team Services by navigating to the Code hub. As you can see in Figure 7-11, the Code hub allows you to explore your repository within your browser. You can also view the changesets and shelvesets (more on shelvesets later in this chapter).

Figure 7-11. *Exploring your repository through Web Access*

Get Latest and Merge Conflicts

When you're working in a team, you won't be the only one who checks in changes. To get the latest changes, you run a Get Latest command locally. Get Latest goes to the server and checks which files where added, deleted, or changed compared to your version. Visual Studio then downloads these changes and applies them to your local workspace.

You should run a Get Latest quite regularly. Developing your code locally without synchronizing with your teammates will lead to problems. You start editing the same files—adding, deleting, or moving files around—which then leads to merge conflicts and before you know it synchronizing all the changes takes a lot of time. You can execute a Get Latest version from a couple locations in Visual Studio. One is in the Source Control Explorer, as shown in Figure 7-12. The Source Control Explorer can be opened from the Team Explorer. The Source Control Explorer shows you which folders you have mapped locally, which files are downloaded, or which files are out of date. When you are working on an opened solution in Visual Studio, you can also right-click on any file or project or on the solution itself and run a Get Latest from the Solution Explorer. This is a recursive operation, so running Get Latest on your solution downloads all the changes in your project. Running it on a single file only downloads the latest version of that file.

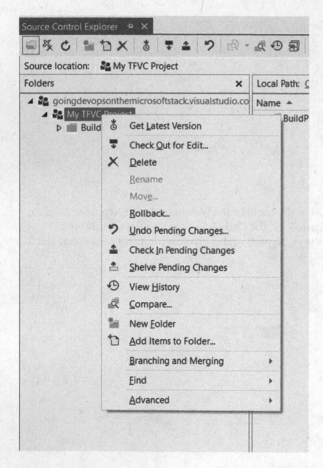

Figure 7-12. *Executing a Get Latest version from the Source Control Explorer*

A merge conflict happens when you and someone else on your team change the same line in a file. As long as your changes don't overlap, Visual Studio is smart enough to sort out the changes and merge them automatically for you. But whenever you change the same line, manual intervention is needed to sort things out. Merge conflicts can cost you a lot of time. Doing a regular Get Latest and communicating clearly on which part of the code you and your team members work helps avoid conflicts.

Figure 7-13 shows a merge conflict. Locally you've edited line 9, which is no problem. You've also edited line 13, which has been edited by another developer and already checked in. Visual Studio automatically merges line 9, but line 13 (14 locally) gives an error. You need to tell Visual Studio what you want it to do. Do you want to incorporate your local changes? The changes already on the server? Or a mix of both? You can use the checkboxes on the left and right to select the parts of your code to include. The result shows at the bottom. You can then manually edit the bottom part and save the result. After resolving the merge conflict, you can test your code locally and then check in your changes to share them with your team.

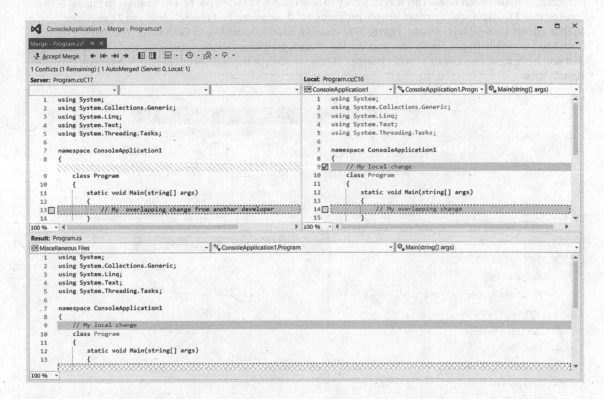

Figure 7-13. *Solving a merge conflict in Visual Studio*

History, Annotations, and CodeLens

When a developer checks in a changeset in TFVC, the latest version of the codebase is updated. The details of the changeset are also stored. This means that TFVC stores a detailed history of all the changes that ever happened to your codebase. This allows you to go back in time. You can view previous versions of your code and compare the changes that where made between two changesets. This can be handy when a new bug is introduced and you want to investigate the changes that were made to a file or when you want to know what changed on a project since you last worked on it.

History can be viewed at the file, folder, project, and solution level. When viewing a specific file, you can activate the Annotation feature. This allows you to see in one overview which changes were made and by whom. Of course, you need to avoid a culture where you start using this feature to blame people. Finding out who created a bug can be useful, but don't start using it as a weapon. Another way to keep track of what's happening with your code is CodeLens. CodeLens is an indicator that is shown directly in your code editor in Visual Studio and gives you information on your code. When connected to TFVC you will see if you have the latest version locally, who made changes, and what they did.

To view the history of a file, you can use the context menu and choose Source Control ➤ View History, as shown in Figure 7-14. This opens the History window, where you see a list of all changes that affected this file. You can open the individual changes to view the content of the file at that moment in time. You can also select two different changesets and choose Compare. This will open the window that you can see in Figure 7-15 and show both files side by side. When you select the Annotate option for a file, you see which person modified which lines. This way, it's easy to find out who made a particular change. In Figure 7-16 you see that I worked alone on this simple program. I did, however, first create a revision 21 and later 23 that added a single line. Finally, Figure 7-17 shows what this looks like in CodeLens. You can see that CodeLens is visible in your code editor at the top of each member. You can view who made the last change and you have direct access to a list of changes. If your version of the code is out of date, CodeLens also signals this.

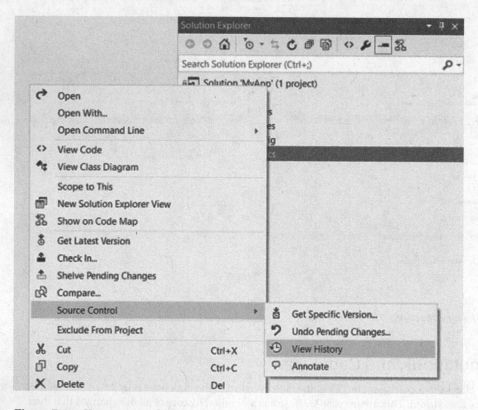

Figure 7-14. *You can view the history of a file, project, or solution*

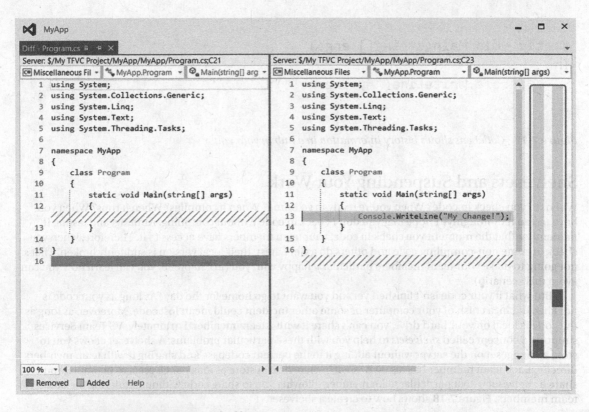

Figure 7-15. *Comparing two versions of a file*

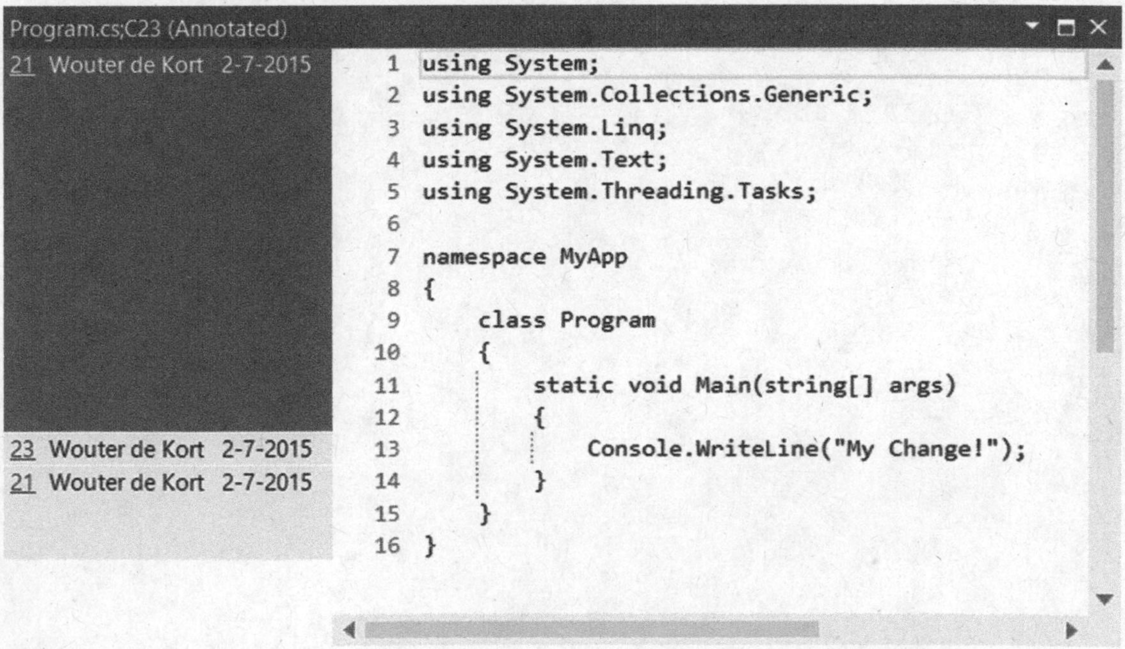

Figure 7-16. *The Annotate feature shows which changes were made, when they were made, and who made them*

113

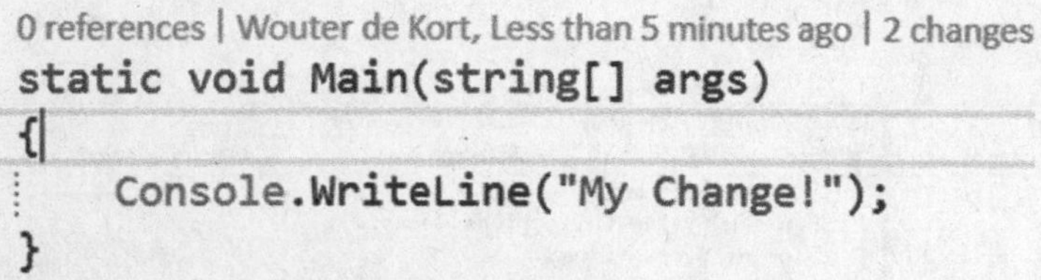

```
0 references | Wouter de Kort, Less than 5 minutes ago | 2 changes
static void Main(string[] args)
{
    Console.WriteLine("My Change!");
}
```

Figure 7-17. *CodeLens shows history information in a hub in your editor*

Shelvesets and Suspending Your Work

When do you check in code? When you're ready to go home? When it compiles? When it runs? When you have tested it thoroughly? I hope that you don't check in code without compiling, running, and testing it. Remember that the moment you check in code, your team members have access to it. Therefore, when you check in some non-compiling code and others do a Get Latest, their local version is suddenly broken. That's not going to make your team members particularly happy with you (in Chapter 9, you will learn how you can avoid this scenario).

But what if your code isn't finished yet and you want to go home for the day? As long as your code is not checked in, a crash of your computer or some other incident could mean lost code. Moreover, as long as the code is local on your hard drive, you can't share it with a team member. Fortunately, VS Team Services supports a concept called *shelvesets* to help you with these particular problems. A shelveset allows you to store a changeset on the server without adding it to the current codebase and sharing it with team members directly. Each team member has his own "shelf," where he can store as many shelvesets as he wants. You can share a shelveset with a particular team member, allowing you to share code without hindering the other team members. Figure 7-18 shows how to create a shelveset.

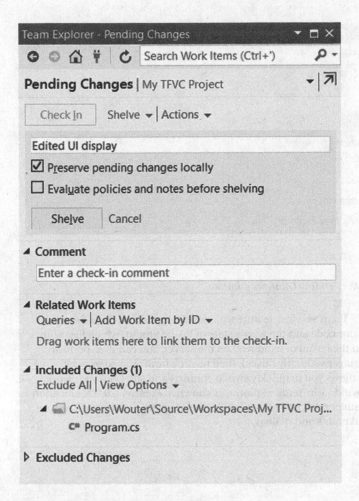

Figure 7-18. *Shelving pending changes*

You navigate to the Pending Changes window and choose for Shelve instead of Check-in. You then need to name the shelveset. You also select if you want to keep the changes you shelve locally. If you don't select this option, your changes will be rolled back and you need to restore your shelveset to continue working with your changes. Sometimes, this is exactly what you want because something else comes up and you want to put your changes away for a moment.

To restore a shelveset, you go to Pending Changes ➤ Actions ➤ Find Shelvesets (see Figure 7-19). This opens a window showing all your shelvesets. You can then simply select a shelveset and restore it. If you want to open a shelveset from someone else in your team, you need to search for their name.

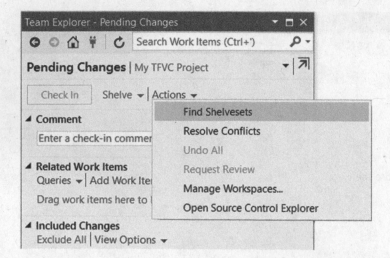

Figure 7-19. *You can find a shelveset from the Pending Changes window*

Shelvesets are also the basis of other VS Team Services features, namely Suspend and Code Review. Suspend lets you store the current state of your code and the whole state of Visual Studio (which files you have open, breakpoints you've set, and even the layout of windows) on the server. You can then perform some other work (like the bug that your manager suddenly raises), then resume from your suspended work and continue as if nothing happened. This allows you to quickly switch contexts and still keep your work. You suspend your work from the My Work window in Team Explorer, as shown in Figure 7-20. This location also shows you the work you've previously suspended and allows you to resume work. Resume will restore your code changes and other work like breakpoints and dialogs.

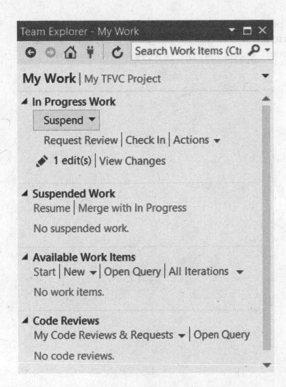

Figure 7-20. *You can suspend and resume work from the My Work panel*

Code reviews are also based on shelvesets. A code review allows you to ask a fellow team member (or a group of users) to look at your code. They can add comments and then send the review back to you. Code is shared through a shelveset, allowing the other users to see your code changes without having to check them in. You can request a code review in the My Work panel, as shown in Figure 7-21.

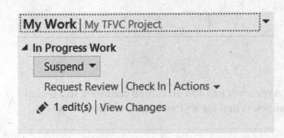

Figure 7-21. *You can request a code review from the My Work panel*

To start a code review, you need to add one or more people who you want to do the review. You also add a title and description. Optionally, you can add links to the work items that describe the feature you're working on. Once you have done this, you submit the request. Figure 7-22 shows a code review request.

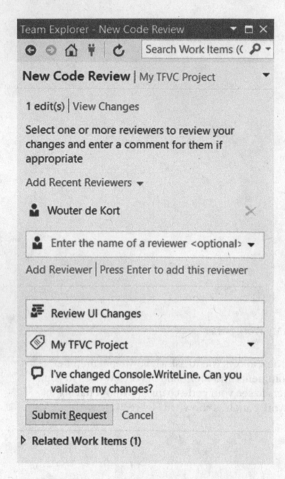

Figure 7-22. Requesting a code review

The reviewer sees the request in the My Work panel. A reviewer can add an overall comment to a review request. She can also add comments to the individual changes. When the reviewer is done, the review is submitted. Figure 7-23 shows a code review response.

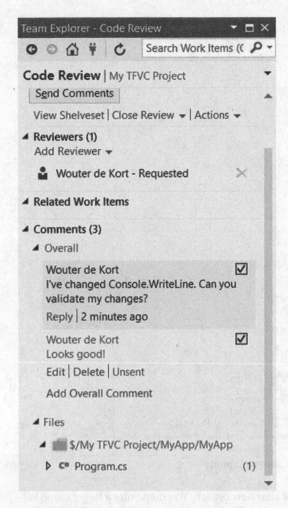

Figure 7-23. Responding to a code review

Branches

As discussed in the introduction, branching comes into play when working in parallel on different versions of the same codebase. Branching can be a powerful feature but it can also be dangerous (see the "Choosing a Branching Strategy" section later in this chapter). TFVC supports branching directly from Visual Studio. You can view visualizations of your structure and branch and merge from the Source Control Explorer. A best practice when starting a TFVC project is to add a single Main folder and add all your artifacts beneath that folder. If you ever need branches in the future, you can easily convert your Main folder to a branch and then create new branches based on Main.

If you view the context menu in Figure 7-24, you see the Branching and Merging submenu. You choose Branch to create a new branch and Merge to merge the changes of one branch into another.

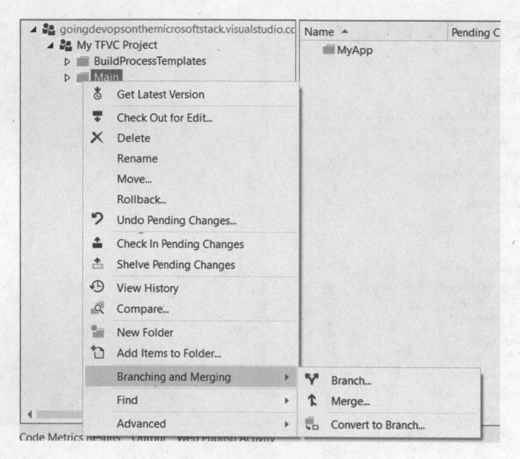

Figure 7-24. *You can branch and merge from the Source Control Explorer*

When creating a branch, you first select the source of your new branch. You then enter a target name for your branch. Figure 7-25 shows an example where you branch the Main branch to a Dev branch. The Branch from Version drop-down is interesting. By default, the latest version is selected. But if you want to, you can also branch from a specific changeset or a label. This allows you to create a branch from a point somewhere in the past. Finally, you select if you want to enable branch visualization and if you want to download the branch to your workspace. This means that when you're working with multiple branches in TFVC, you have several folders in your local workspace that contain these branches (as you'll see, this is different with Git). When working with branches, it's important to always make sure that you're in the correct branch before making a change.

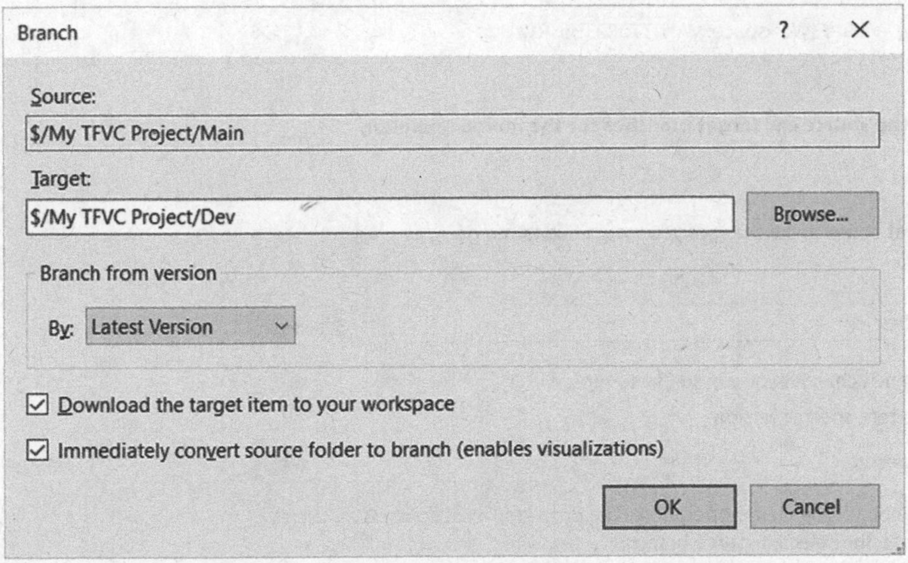

Figure 7-25. *Creating a new branch*

Now imagine that you have done some work in the Dev branch and you want to merge those changes to the Main branch. Figure 7-26 shows the Merge window. You select a source and a target branch. By default, you merge all changesets from the source to the target branch. You can also pick and choose which changesets to merge but that's something that goes wrong more often than right. Remember that it's easy to merge between Dev and Main because they have a direct link: you branched Dev from Main. If there is no direct link between two branches you can do what's called a *baseless merge*. Baseless merges are hard to execute. Since Visual Studio has no knowledge about the relationship between these branches, you need to do a lot of manual merges. It's best to avoid the baseless merge, but if you really need it, it's a powerful feature.

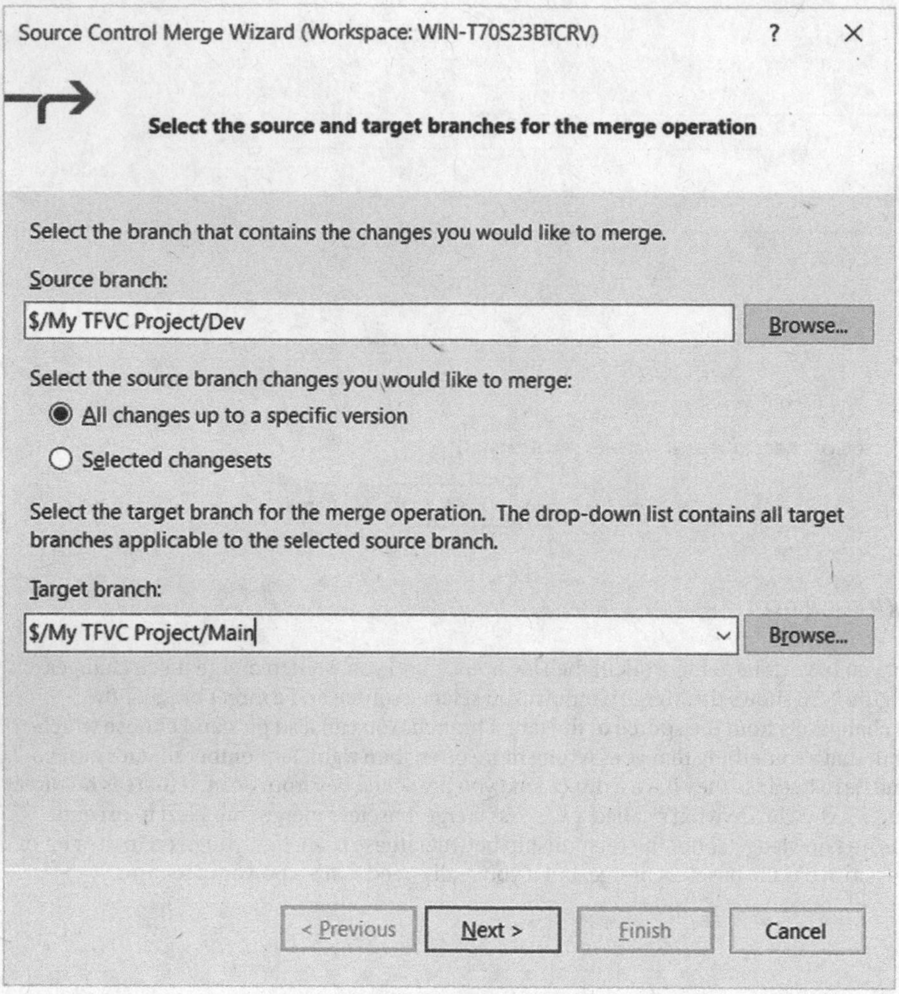

Figure 7-26. *Merging to branches*

Check-In Policies

Do you have a minimum quality gate for your code? For example, are developers allowed to check in code that doesn't compile? Are they required to add a comment to their check-ins? Ensuring that developers compile their code and run certain tests before they check it in to the server will help you improve quality throughout your whole process. Visual Studio and TFVC support this with check-in policies. A check-in policy runs each time the developers want to check in code. The policy can check certain things (Does the code compile? Is there a work item associated with this check-in?) and can deny the check-in if the policy fails. You can even create your own policies, distribute these among your team, and implement quality checks that are important to you.

You can configure a check-in policy from within Visual Studio. If you navigate to Team Project Settings ➤ Source Control ➤ Check-in Policy and then select Add, you see the window shown in Figure 7-27. These four check-in policies are available out of the box. The Builds policy makes sure that a developer runs a successful build of his code before checking-in. Changeset Comments Policy forces developers to add comments to their check-ins. The Code Analysis policy makes sure that developers run Code Analysis locally before a check-in. And finally, the Work Items policy makes sure that developers associate a work item with a check-in.

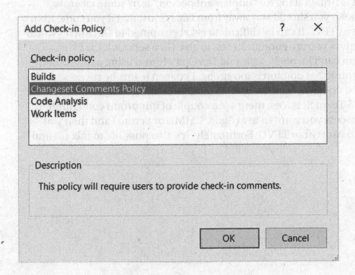

Figure 7-27. *Add a check-in policy for a team project*

Now imagine that you've selected the Changesets Comments Policy. If a developer now tries to check in some code without entering a comment, the warning in Figure 7-28 is shown. As you can see, there is an option to override the warning. You can set up an alert (see Chapter 6 for more info) to inform you whenever someone overrides the policy. Unfortunately, there is no option to disable overrides when using VS Team Services.

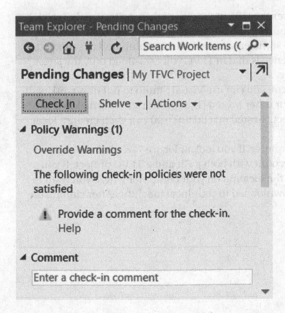

Figure 7-28. *A policy warning is shown when checking in changes*

Using the Git Version Control System

Git is a distributed version control system that's very popular. Git was created by Linus Torvalds for development on the Linux kernel. Git, which is British slang for "unpleasant person," is by some taken as a description of how Git works. That doesn't mean you should stay away from Git. It's just that if you come from a centralized version control background such as TFVC it can be difficult to get accustomed to Git. But it's worth it. The pure speed of Git and the flexibility it gives you are enough reason to give Git a serious look. I know of some ALM experts who even say that a team can't be really Agile and DevOps without using a distributed version control system like Git. Personally, I think that opinion is too strong. I've seen teams be successful with TFVC and I have seen them fail with Git. But it does give a clear signal as to how interesting Git is.

When creating a new team project in VS Team Services, there are a couple of important configuration options you set. First of all, you select the process you want to use (Agile, CMMI, or Scrum) and then you select the version control system you want to use: Git or TFVC. Fortunately, it's also possible to mix Git and TFVC in one team project.

Git is based on a couple of key actions:

- Clone
- Commit and Push
- Fetch and Pull
- Branch
- Fetch
- Pull Request

The following sections discuss each of these actions.

Clone

Working with a Git repository starts with a clone. You enter the URL of the external repository and then clone its content to your development machine. A clone gets you all the history of the repository and copies that to your machine. After the clone, you are completely self-sufficient. A clone can be compared to setting up your workspace mapping in TFVC. The significant difference is that in TFVC you download only the latest snapshot of the code, while Git gives you the whole history.

Since Visual Studio supports the standard Git protocol, you can use Visual Studio to not only work with a Git repository in VS Team Services but also on GitHub or other hosted Git repositories. This makes it very easy to use Visual Studio to work with Open Source projects hosted on GitHub. You can even create a local Git repository and never share it with anyone.

You clone a Git repository from within your Team Explorer. If you look at Figure 7-29, you see that my Team Explorer is connected to a VS Team Services account with both a Git and a TFVC project. If you select the Git project and choose Clone, you're asked for the location on your computer where you want to store the project. If you then click Clone, the project is downloaded to your local machine. After cloning the project, you can start working with it.

Figure 7-29. *Cloning a Git repository*

Commit and Push

I find commits one of the best features of Git. With TFVC, you make your changes locally, which forms a changeset, and you then upload this changeset as a whole to TFVC. Undoing local changes undoes all changes that you've made since your last check-in. If you want to work in small batches, you have to upload your code each time to TFVC. But what if your code isn't completely finished yet? You can't upload it to TFVC yet and you also lose the small batches that you can undo. Using shelvesets for this also isn't optimal since shelvesets don't contain history.

A local Git repository is truly local in the sense that you can commit changes to your local repository without uploading them to the server just yet. This means that while working you can commit your changes in small batches. These commits are stored locally and when you're done, you take your commits and push them to the server. You can undo local commits (before you pushed them) and so create a very flexible way of working. When you have multiple local commits, you can even squash them into one commit and send that to the server. This way, you can work very fine-grained on your development PC without flooding your team members with commits.

The most important change from a TFVC perspective is that you don't directly check in your changes. First you commit them locally, and then you push your local commits to the server.

■ **Note** At the time of writing, the Git tooling support in Visual Studio is still being worked on. Many of the Git commands are already supported from within the IDE. However, some commands, such as squash and amend, are not and you need to use the command line to execute those commands. For more info, see https://msdn.microsoft.com/en-us/library/dd286572.aspx.

Figure 7-30 shows the Changes panel that you can open while working with a Git repository. Here you see the changes that were made and if these changes are included or not. You are required to enter a commit message. You then choose Commit to add these changes to your local repository. This is not yet available on the server and others won't see your changes yet.

Figure 7-30. *You first commit your changes locally*

To share your changes with others, you run a Push command. Push takes your local repository and sends the changes to a remote Git repository. This two-phase commit and push is typical for Git. Committing is only locally, pushing is what sends your changes to the server. As long as changes are not pushed, you can undo them locally. You can even merge multiple commits together and push them as one to the server. Pushing is done from within the Synchronization panel in Team Explorer. If you look at Figure 7-31, you see one outgoing commit. This list contains all the commits you did locally since your last push (incoming commits are discussed in the next section). To send your commits to the server, you click Push.

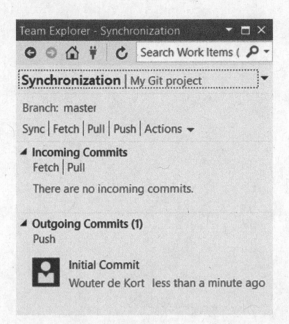

Figure 7-31. You can push local commits to a remote server

Fetch and Pull

When you want to update your local repository with changes made by your team members, it's time do a pull. Pull gets all the changes that where made since you got your latest version and downloads these to your PC. If there are conflicts, Pull will immediately start trying to merge them. Fetch, on the other hand, lets you first get a list of all the commits that you missed so you can inspect them before starting the merge. Figure 7-32 shows what happens when there are changes and you select Fetch. In this case, one remote change is not yet merged with your local repository.

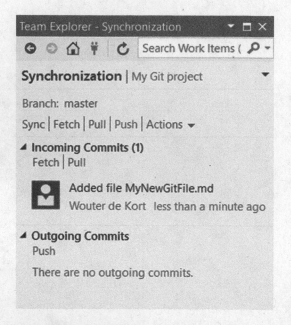

Figure 7-32. *You can fetch and pull changes from a remote repository to your local repository*

You also see an option called Sync. Sync runs first a pull and then automatically a push if there are no conflicts. I wouldn't recommend using this option. Sync sometimes has problems merging your changes. This will add an additional commit and mess up your history.

Branch

Branches are where Git really excels. In TFVC, you contact the server to create a branch. The branch is immediately visible to the whole team and the server controls merges between the different branches. Since Git has the concept of a local repository, you can also create branches locally. Say for example that there is a master branch at the server that all developers use to share code with each other. You work locally on a new feature and you want to keep this feature isolated from the other developers. Git allows you to create a local branch that exists only on your development PC. You make your changes in that branch and when you're done you merge the branches locally and push your changes. You can also choose to push the local branch, making it a public branch that others can see. It's not uncommon for experienced Git users to create and delete multiple branches during a day.

Git branches in Visual Studio are managed from the Team Explorer ➤ Branches panel. If you look at Figure 7-33 you see the branching structure of a newly cloned project. The remotes/origin point to your project on VS Team Services. The local branch is bold and is currently active.

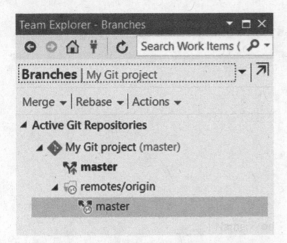

Figure 7-33. You can view the branches for your Git repository in Visual Studio

To create a new local branch, right-click the branch from which you want to branch and select New Local Branch From from the context menu, as shown in Figure 7-34. You then enter a name for your branch and run the create branch process locally.

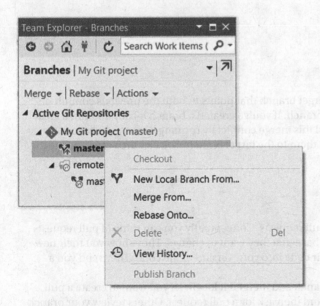

Figure 7-34. Creating a new local branch

Git stores branches differently than TFVC on your hard drive. Where TFVC creates a new folder for each branch, Git only needs one folder for your whole repository. When switching branches, Git applies the correct snapshot to your folder. One thing to remember is that uncommitted changes are not a part of the branch history. Merging a branch is also done from within Team Explorer. As you can see in Figure 7-35, you select a source and a target branch. Git will then execute the merge and ask for your help if there are any merge conflicts that you need to solve manually.

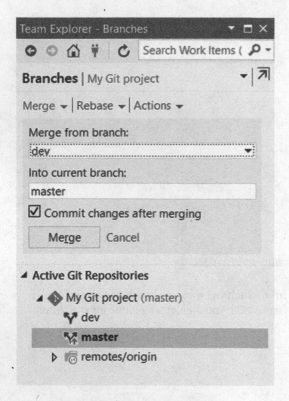

Figure 7-35. *Merging two Git branches*

Merging adds a new commit on top of your target branch that points to both the previous commit on that branch and to the last commit on the source branch. If you've created a branch locally and run a local merge before pushing your changes, you can avoid this merge conflict by running a rebase. Rebase takes the commits from your source branch and applies them to the target branch. You can then safely delete the source branch; it is as if that branch never existed.

Pull Request

Git has native code review built-in in the form of pull requests. Conceptually you can think of pull requests as someone e-mailing you a small part of the codebase that they want to change. They show you their new code and if you approve it, you copy and paste their code into your version of the code. They send you a request to pull some changes they made.

In the previous section, you created a local branch and merged it locally. If you want to create a pull request, you push your local branch to the server and then ask for a pull request. Others review your branch and comment on any changes you made. If the changes are accepted, the branch is merged into the main branch. Pull requests are a very nice feature of Git that you should definitely be familiar with.

To publish a branch, you navigate to the Branches panel in Team Explorer, right-click your local branch, and choose Publish. After finishing the publish, you see a result like Figure 7-36. Here, I published a local Dev branch to VS Team Services. You then see that you have both a local Dev branch and a remote Dev branch.

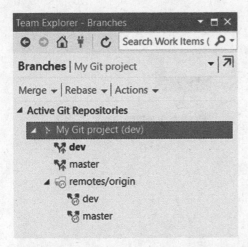

Figure 7-36. *A published local branch shows as a remote*

What's nice about Git is that there is a lot of support for operations in the Web Access. If you navigate to the Code hub of your project, you can switch branches as shown in Figure 7-37. You can then view the content of this branch directly in Web Access.

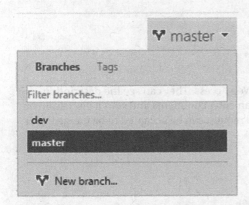

Figure 7-37. *Select a branch from the Code hub in Web Access*

After switching branches, you can select the option to create a pull request, as shown in Figure 7-38. You can then enter a name for your pull request (by default Merge <source branch> to <target branch>), include a description, and add reviewers (by default, your whole team). Instead of publishing the branch and then creating a pull request in two steps, you can also create a pull request directly from the Branches panel in Visual Studio. This will publish your branch and create a pull request in one step.

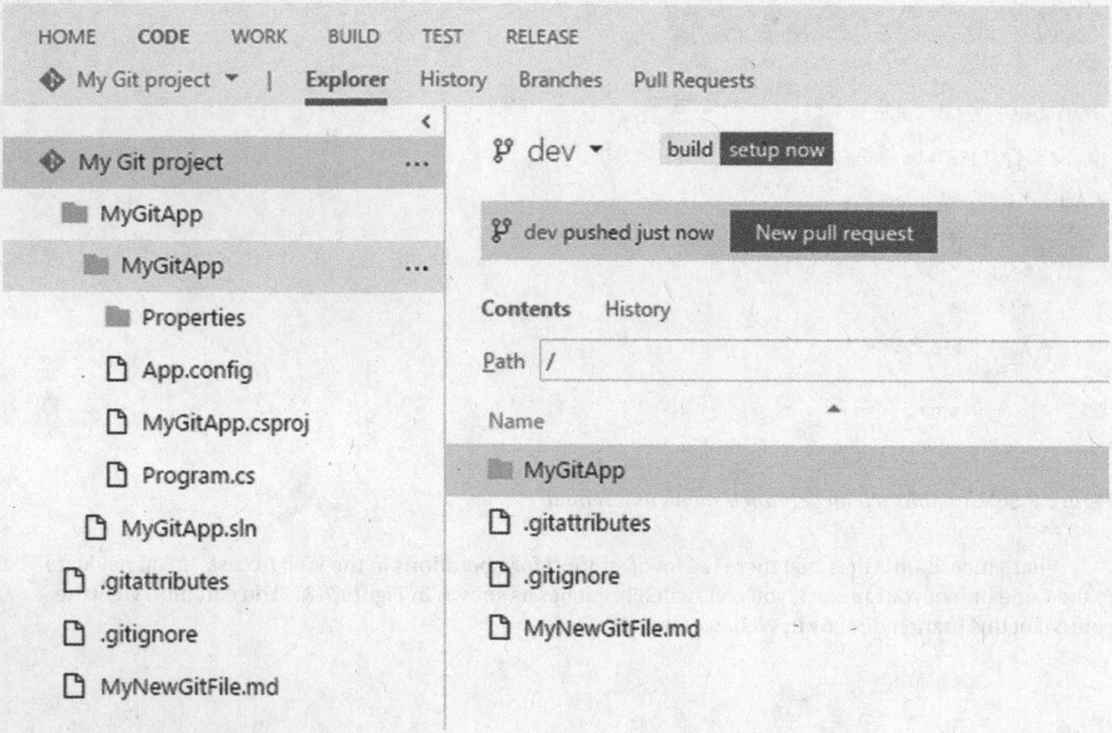

Figure 7-38. *Create a pull request from within Web Access*

Now your team members can view the pull request in the Web Access. They can see the description and the commits that you want to pull (see Figure 7-39). They can enter comments and start a discussion on certain changes (see Figure 7-40). Once you're finished, the pull request can be accepted to be merged with the target branch.

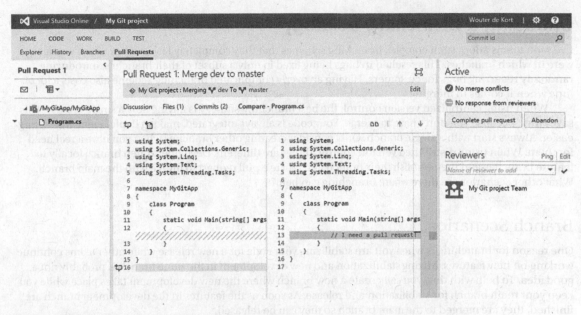

Figure 7-39. *In Web Access you can inspect the changes that a pull request introduces*

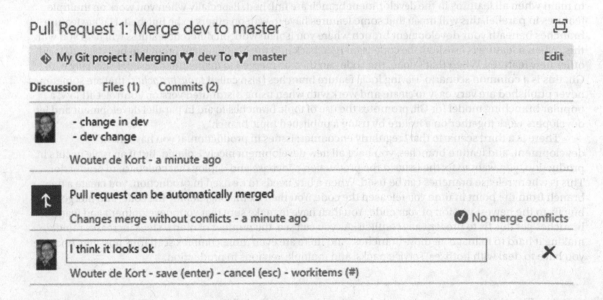

Figure 7-40. *You can comment on the changes of a pull request*

Choosing a Branching Strategy

I've seen teams adopt such complex branching schemes that they completely lose track of which changes were in which branches. This resulted in bugs being fixed in only a subset of their branches, introducing randomly recurring bugs for customers. Having an overly complicated branching scheme also costs a lot of time when it comes to merging.

When using centralized version control, the best branching strategy is having only a single branch. This saves time because you don't have to merge. Your code is always integrated, making deployment and testing easier. Always start with a single branch. Only consider creating other branches when you have a real need for them. When using distributed version control, things are different. Developers often branch locally to feature branches and then publish their branch and create a pull request to merge with the main branch. What other scenarios are there where branching can help?

Branch Scenarios

One reason for branching is when you are stabilizing your code for a new release while other teams continue working on new features. Mixing stabilization and new development in the same branch is probably not a good idea. To help with this, you can create a new branch where the new development takes place while you keep your main branch for stabilization and release. As soon as the features in the development branch are finished, they are merged to the main branch so they can be released.

Feature branches are sometimes used when a team works on multiple new features in parallel. If you start with a main and development branch scenario, you can only merge the development branch back to main when all features in the development branch are finished. Especially when you work on multiple features in parallel, this will mean that some features have to wait on others to be finished. Having feature branches beneath your development branch where you isolate work on different features will help you with this. When a feature is finished, the code is merged back into the development branch to be integrated with other new features. When that's done, the code can then be merged to main and released. Especially with Git, this is a common scenario. Having local feature branches (also called *topic branches*) that are sometimes never published are very easy to create and work with when using distributed version control. GitFlow, a popular branching model for Git, promotes the use of topic branches to aid in parallel development and let developers work together on a feature by using a published topic branch.

There is a third scenario that I regularly encounter: issues in production. If you have main, development, and feature branches, you have all new development nicely isolated. But if an issue occurs in production, you want to fix the issue in the production codebase and deploy that codebase to production. This is where release branches can be used. When a bug needs to be fixed in production, you create a new branch from the point in time you released the code. You then fix the bug, deploy the code, and merge the bug fix to the newest version of your code. You then have to make sure that your development and feature branches get this fix to prevent any conflicts. As you can see, the number of merge steps increases rapidly, making it hard to manage all those branches. And there are even more complex scenarios possible. Imagine you have to deal with hotfixes, service packs, and multiple versions in production.

■ **Note** The ALM Rangers have provided great guidance detailing all those scenarios. They can help you choose the best branching strategy for your situation. See `https://vsarbranchingguide.codeplex.com/` for more information.

Feature Toggles

What if you want to stick to as few branches as possible while still working on new features? How do you combine bug fixes, new development, and overall stability in your product? You already learned about feature toggles, but how do you actually implement them?

The basic idea behind feature toggles is extremely simple. You develop a new feature and hide the code that accesses it behind a simple *if* statement. If the feature toggle is true, the feature is shown. If it's false, it stays hidden. When the feature is finished, the toggle is removed to keep the code clean. You can create the toggle system as simple or as complex as you want. You can store the toggles in a database or in a simple configuration file. A toggle can be a simple true or false. But what about basing your toggle on a specific timestamp? If the date and time passes, the feature toggle is activated. This way, you can do timed releases of your new features. The feature is already in the production code. You can test it extensively and then release it to the world.

You can activate a toggle for only specific users or groups of users. This way, you can have beta testers or other early adopter programs. You can also use this to do A/B testing. A/B testing is all about running multiple versions of your product at the same time in production and measuring how users respond. So if you have two versions of a new feature, you can easily activate them for a part of your user base. By then measuring how they use your app, you suddenly have a way of steering your development process in the right direction.

There are a couple of Open Source feature toggle libraries that you can use. Of course you could build your own but it's always a good idea to see if there is something that's widely supported by the community. A popular feature toggle framework is Feature Toggle from Jason Roberts. You can find it at GitHub (https://github.com/jason-roberts/FeatureToggle) and install it through NuGet (https://www.nuget.org/packages/FeatureToggle/).

A simple example uses the following code to define a feature toggle:

```
class ShowMessageToggle : SimpleFeatureToggle { }
```

You can check if the toggle is enabled with the following code:

```
var toggle = new ShowMessageToggle();
if (toggle.FeatureEnabled)
{
  Console.WriteLine("This feature is enabled");
}
```

You configure the state of the toggle by adding a setting to your appSettings in the configuration file:

```
<appSettings>
  <add key="FeatureToggle.ShowMessageToggle" value="true"/>
</appSettings>
```

What's nice about this framework is that the toggles are implemented as typed classes. Removing a toggle is as simple as removing the class definition and then fixing all compile errors where the toggle is still referenced.

Feature toggles can be used in Greenfield and Brownfield projects. It just means that when you start building a new feature you hide it behind a toggle. This can be as easy as hiding a new option in your menu or another part of your user interface. It takes somewhat more planning when you want to replace an existing part of your code with a newer version. The easiest strategy is to add a feature toggle at a high enough level in your code that you can completely switch out the old feature for the new one. If you want to implement a true DevOps process, think of feature toggles before you start creating branches.

■ **Note**   Martin Fowler has published an excellent article on feature toggles written by Pete Hodgson that you can find at `http://martinfowler.com/articles/feature-toggles.html`. If you want more information on feature toggles, that's a good article to start with.

Summary

This chapter introduced you to version control and you learned about the two flavors that VS Team Services offers: TFVC and Git.

TFVC is a form of centralized version control. You create a mapping between your development environment and a central server. You then download only a snapshot of the code and work with it locally. You check in your changes and update your local repository by doing a Get Latest. You can use shelvesets, suspend your work, and ask for code reviews. You can also create branches and use check-in policies.

Git is a form of distributed version control. You start by cloning a repository that downloads not only the latest code but also the whole history. You can view the history locally without contacting a server. You can also create branches and switch between them. You update your repository by running a pull and you share code by pushing to a remote such as VS Team Services. You can create pull requests as a form of code review.

You also looked at a couple of branching strategies. One branch is absolutely the simplest solution if you can get away with it. Multiple branches are often used for feature isolation, stabilization, and bug fixes. Using feature toggles, you can avoid a lot of branching complexities while opening up new possibilities.

The following chapter discusses how to manage *technical debt* to make sure that your project is in a perfect state.

CHAPTER 8

■ ■ ■

Managing Technical Debt

If you have worked long enough as a software developer, you have definitely wished that you could start a project totally from scratch. Throw away all the messy code and build it from scratch with all the knowledge you have now. But why is it that code becomes messy? We even have specific terms to describe it—code rot, big ball of mud, spaghetti code. These terms all describe that code will become a mess when not carefully controlled and monitored. But what's the definition of "a mess"? Can you monitor the quality of code and actively manage it? This chapter discusses *technical debt* and shows you how you can use Visual Studio to track and manage it.

Debt is a common term in finance. Whenever you take a loan, you need to pay it back with interest. The same is true for code. If you want to quickly create some code, you take a loan on quality. When you want to pay back your loan, you pay interest in the form of extra maintenance costs. But when technical debt skyrockets, the interest becomes so large that it can strangle your project. That's the point where developers want to start from scratch and rewrite everything. Taking a loan can sometimes be a good decision, for example, for a mortgage when you buy a new house. The same is true for technical debt. Sometimes you willingly acquire it. Maybe time-to-market is essential and you want to skip on code quality to be able to launch quickly. It stays important that you know where the technical debt is and how much it is. As long as this is an explicit decision and not something that you unknowingly do, having some amount of technical debt can be a good idea.

How can you measure technical debt? That's a difficult subject. A lot of scientific research has been done and all kinds of models have been developed. If your code quality is low and it would take someone three months to fix it, you have a technical debt of three months. You only know exactly how much technical debt there is after you've fixed it. So measuring the exact amount of debt you have based on time is hard. But what you can measure is the quality (or rather, the lack of quality) of your code. This gives you an indication of what you would need to do to fix it.

Solutions like SonarQube (discussed in the next chapter) follow a rule-based system to correlate code quality and the amount of time it would take to fix it. So, you can measure the quality of your code. There are standard metrics that are often used and that give you a clear indication of the state of your code. These metrics are also used by Visual Studio to measure code quality.

The following parts detail a number of strategies you can follow to manage your technical debt. You will also have a look at another proven technique: unit testing. This chapter ends with a look at Roslyn analyzers and what they can do for your code and your team.

Don't underestimate how important code quality is. When it comes to changing the culture in your organization toward DevOps, building trust is a fundamental step. Quality of code is something that you can influence yourself as a developer. Increasing quality will give you social credit with your upstream and downstream colleagues or customers. So take this chapter to heart and see it as a big step to your DevOps implementation. Because, if you get faster at shipping code but not at improving quality, are you not just shipping bugs more often?

© Wouter de Kort 2016

W. de Kort, *DevOps on the Microsoft Stack*, DOI 10.1007/978-1-4842-1446-6_8

Running Code Analysis

The first tool I want to look at is Code Analysis. Code Analysis is used to check the style of your code. *Style* is a broad concept. The rules that Code Analysis uses are based on the Microsoft .NET Framework Design Guidelines. These guidelines specify a multitude of helpful rules, ranging from how to name properties to implementing security and performance-critical pieces of your code.

Code Analysis is available for both C# and Visual Basic. The following code listing shows an example in C#:

```
namespace CodeAnalysis
{
    public class MysampleClass
    {
        public int calculate(int x)
        {
            int y = x;

            return x * 2;
        }
    }
}
```

As an example, this code is hopefully exaggerated over what you normally encounter in the field. How many errors do you spot? Code Analysis gives eight warnings. You can see them in Figure 8-1.

	Code	Description	Project	File	Line
⚠	CA2210	Sign 'CodeAnalysis.dll' with a strong name key.	CodeAnalysis		
⚠	CA1014	Mark 'CodeAnalysis.dll' with CLSCompliant(true) because it exposes externally visible types.	CodeAnalysis		
⚠	CA1704	Correct the spelling of 'Mysample' in type name 'MysampleClass'.	CodeAnalysis	Class1.cs	3
⚠	CA1709	Correct the casing of 'calculate' in member name 'MysampleClass.calculate(int)' by changing it to 'Calculate'.	CodeAnalysis	Class1.cs	6
⚠	CA1704	In method 'MysampleClass.calculate(int)', consider providing a more meaningful name than parameter name 'x'.	CodeAnalysis	Class1.cs	6
⚠	CA1822	The 'this' parameter (or 'Me' in Visual Basic) of 'MysampleClass.calculate(int)' is never used. Mark the member as static (or Shared in Visual Basic) or use 'this'/'Me' in the method body or at least one property accessor, if appropriate.	CodeAnalysis	Class1.cs	6
⚠	CA1804	'MysampleClass.calculate(int)' declares a variable, 'y', of type 'int', which is never used or is only assigned to. Use this variable or remove it.	CodeAnalysis	Class1.cs	7
⚠	CA2233	Correct the potential overflow in the operation 'x*2' in 'MysampleClass.calculate(int)'.	CodeAnalysis	Class1.cs	9

Error List ▾ □ ×

| ▼ ▾ | ⊗ 0 Errors | ⚠ 8 Warnings | ⓘ 0 Messages | Search Error List 🔎 ▾ |

Figure 8-1. *Code Analysis warnings*

In this case, there are some class-level warnings about naming conventions, marking your method as static, an unused variable, and potential overflow issues. For the whole assembly, Visual Studio recommends signing your assembly and marking it as CLS compliant. Of course you can find these errors manually. But having an automatic mechanism in place that detects these problems and suggests a way to fix them takes things a level further then running manual checks.

You can run Code Analysis from the Analyze ➤ Run Code Analysis menu or through the context menu of your solution or project. You can also configure Code Analysis in the properties of your project. If you look at Figure 8-2, you see the Code Analysis properties page. If you activate the first option, Enable Code Analysis on Build, and then build your project or solution, Code Analysis will automatically run. Especially while fixing Code Analysis warnings, having this quick feedback loop is easy. When your project becomes bigger, you maybe want to disable running Code Analysis when running a local build and instead run it manually. The second option, Suppress Results from Generated Code, is activated by default. Code that's automatically generated by Visual Studio doesn't follow the Code Analysis rules most of the time. This is not because the code is bad but because it's optimized for being automatically generated and updated, not for readability and style.

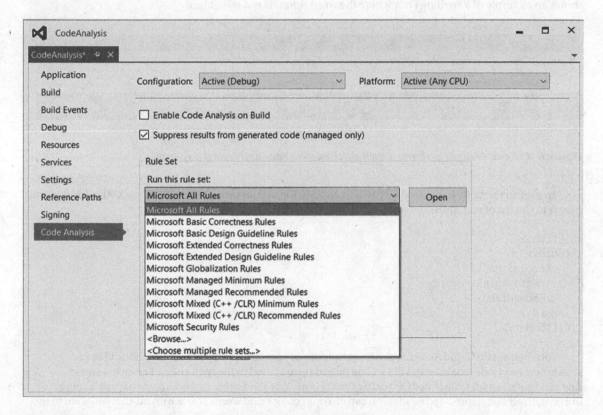

Figure 8-2. *You can configure Code Analysis on a per-project basis*

The third option, Rule Set, is an important one. As you can see from Figure 8-2, there are a couple of default rule sets that you can choose from. The Microsoft All Rules rule set is the biggest. The Microsoft Managed Recommended rule set is the default. When working on a project, you should experiment with the different sets and choose one that's best for your situation. Especially on an existing project, it doesn't make much sense to start with a very strict rule set because the amount of warnings can be overwhelming. Instead, you can start with a smaller rule set and gradually increase the rules as the project quality improves.

Not all of the warnings that are generated will be useful for you. You can decide to turn warnings off for your whole project or just ignore certain specific cases. You tell Code Analysis to ignore specific pieces of your code by adding the SuppressMessage attribute like this:

```
[System.Diagnosis.CodeAnalysis.SuppressMessage("Microsoft.Design",
"CA1039:ListsAreStrongTyped")]
Public class MyClass
{
    // code
}
```

One thing you probably want to configure for Code Analysis is the use of a dictionary file. Code Analysis performs a spell check on your code. If you use unknown words, like your company name or a product name, Code Analysis will report this as a violation. To help Code Analysis, you add a custom XML file that tells Code Analysis which additional words you want to allow, disallow, or mark as deprecated. Figure 8-3 shows an example of a spelling error where the word *Apress* is not recognized.

Figure 8-3. *Code Analysis performs a spell check on your code and reports any errors*

To extend the built-in dictionary, you add an XML file to your project. The following XML adds the word *Apress* to the list of recognized words.

```
<Dictionary>
  <Words>
    <Recognized>
      <Word>Apress</Word>
    </Recognized>
  </Words>
</Dictionary>
```

You then set the Build Action in the file properties of your XML file to CodeAnalysisDictionary. If you then run Code Analysis, this file will be picked up and used in the spell check. Figure 8-4 shows this configuration for a file called CustomDictionary.xml. You can further extend a dictionary by adding unrecognized and deprecated words. You can also add compound words and acronyms that you want to use.

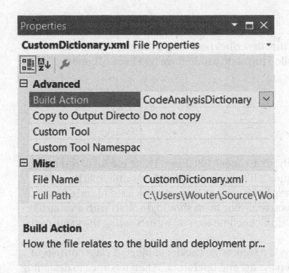

Figure 8-4. *Setting the build action to CodeAnalysisDictionary*

The techniques behind Code Analysis are changing. Have a look at the last part of this chapter for more information on how Roslyn can help you analyze your code and how Microsoft is using Roslyn to modernize Code Analysis.

Code Metrics

As developers, we develop a feeling for when code is good or bad. Consider an extremely long method, a class that seems to use all other classes in your project, or a method that has so many nested `if` statements that it almost looks like art. But as developers we are subjective. Making these observations in an objective way is what code metrics is all about.

Where Code Analysis touches topics like design, performance, and security and is somewhat subjective, code metrics are objectively calculated values based on your code.

Code metrics are based on the following concepts:

- Lines of code
- Cyclomatic Complexity
- Coupling
- Inheritance

Let's look into these values so that you understand what's behind them. This will help you interpret the results that the code metric calculations in Visual Studio give you.

Lines of Code

Lines of code is the easiest metric. This is just a number that describes how long a class or method is. Opening and closing brackets are not counted. So the following code would have two lines of code:

```
public int MyMethod()
{
    return 42;
}
```

What do you think is an acceptable length for a method? 10 lines? 100 lines? There is a lot of research going on in topics like these and people use different values. I like to keep my methods under 20 lines of code. But I know of companies that use an even lower threshold, even as low as seven lines of code for a single method. Deciding what's good is something that you and your team should do. Start with a value like 20 and evaluate regularly if this is reasonable. Of course, don't become too soft by increasing the value each time you find a difficult method.

What would be an acceptable length for a class? This is a somewhat trickier subject. A class consists of constructors, fields, properties, methods, and maybe even events and operators. When it comes to designing classes, there are good design principles that guide you. These principles are not hard rules. One such principle is SOLID, which is an acronym for:

- *Single Responsibility Pattern*: A class should have only one reason to change. Meaning that a class should have no more than one responsibility.

- *Open/Closed Principle*: Software entities should be open for extension but closed for modification

- *Liskov Substitution Principle*: Derived classes can be used everywhere a base class is expected

- *Interface Segregation Principle*: A client shouldn't be forced to depend on methods he doesn't use

- *Dependency Inversion Principle*: Depend upon abstractions, not implementations

If this is the first time you heard about SOLID, I can understand this makes your head spin. When code quality is a problem in your project, SOLID is a very good place to start your research. First focus on writing short methods, then start applying Single Responsibility Pattern (SRP) to break classes into smaller parts. After that, you can take on Open/Closed Principle (OCP) and finally the other three methods. Discussing SOLID in more detail is outside the scope of this book but there are some very good books written on this subject.

So how do you make a method shorter? By breaking the method in multiple, smaller parts. Take the following code:

```
public decimal Calculate(int id, Order order)
{
    Customer customer = _customerRepository.GetCustomerById(id);

    decimal shippingCosts = 0;
    if (customer.PostalArea != DefaultPostalArea)
    {
        shippingCosts = 10;
    }
```

```
decimal totalOrderCosts = 0;
foreach(OrderLine o in order.OrderLines)
{

    totalOrderCosts += o.Cost;
}

decimal totalCost = totalOrderCosts + shippingCosts;
return totalCost;
}
```

If you look through this method, you see several distinct parts. You can refactor the code to several smaller methods like this:

```
public decimal Calculate(int id, Order order)
{
    Customer customer = _customerRepository.GetCustomerById(id);

    decimal shippingCosts = CalculateShippingCosts(customer);
    decimal totalOrderCosts = CalculateOrderCosts(order);

    decimal totalCost = CalculateTotalCost(shippingCosts, totalOrderCosts);

    return totalCost;
}
```

A personal rule of thumb that I try to stick to is that whenever I feel the need to add comments to my code, I try to extract that piece of code and use a descriptive method name. This brakes the code in smaller parts and makes it easier to read.

When you start calculating code metrics through Visual Studio, you will see discrepancies between the lines of code on your screen and the number of lines reported by code metrics. This is because code metrics operates on the Intermediate Language (IL) that's generated by the compiler and not on the source code that you see on your screen. Take the following code:

```
interface IMyPointyInterface
{
    int X { get; set; }
    int Y { get; set; }
}
```

Since this interface doesn't result in any executable IL code, the code metrics calculation reports this interface as having zero lines. This won't result in any problems when you look at the statistics for a whole project but if you see any strange numbers, remember that it has to do with the compilation of source code to IL.

■ **Note**   SonarQube (discussed in Chapter 9) also calculates code metrics. SonarQube uses its own parsers and as a result gives different metrics than the code metrics implementation in Visual Studio.

Cyclomatic Complexity

Having short methods and classes will do a lot for the quality of your code. The following method is less than 20 lines. Do you find it easy to understand?

```
public int HighComplexity(int x, int y)
{
    if (x < 0 && y < 0)

        if (x < y)
            return y;
        else if (x > y)
            return x + y;
        else
            return x;
    else
        if (x * y > 100)
        if (x < y)
            return x;
    return y;
}
```

Cyclomatic complexity describes the number of paths that go through your code and correlates to the number of unit tests you have to write. A simple method that goes from top to bottom has a complexity of one. If you add an `if` statement, you get a cyclomatic complexity of two. Adding an `else` branch or a nested `if` increases the cyclomatic complexity even more. And not to mention `switch` statements with many options.

Cyclomatic complexity is required for our programs to work and it's no problem to use `if` or `switch` statements, but you have to think about how you use them. Nesting too many statements makes your code harder to understand and thus harder to extend and maintain. As a rule of thumb I try to stay within a range of 1-5 for cyclomatic complexity. With values between 6-10, I investigate the method and see if I can simplify it. With values above 10, the method is an absolute candidate for refactoring.

Coupling

What do you think is wrong with the class diagram shown in Figure 8-5?

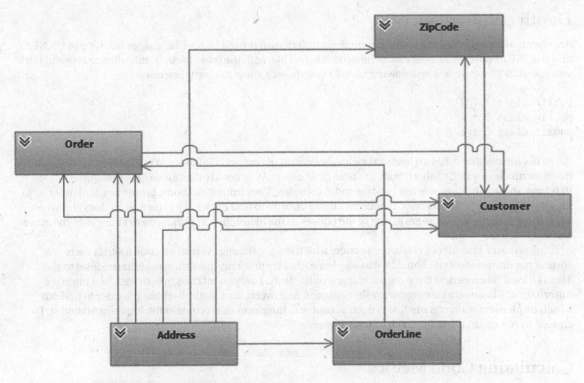

Figure 8-5. *A class diagram with high coupling*

Besides the fact that this particular example probably doesn't make sense to build, there are a lot of lines in this diagram! Each line between two classes means that the class uses the other class directly in code. This also means that if you change a class, all classes that depend on it probably have to change too. Code with too many dependencies between classes is often referred to as spaghetti code. There is no clear structure and maintaining and extending the code becomes very difficult. Coupling is a numeric value that describes the number of relationships between classes. Take the following class:

```
public class Customer
{
    public Address Address { get; private set; }
}
```

This class has a coupling of one, since it depends on one other class in your project. A coupling of zero or one probably doesn't make for a very interesting application. It's normal that classes depend on each other. So having some coupling is no problem. Having too much coupling will lead to problems. As a rule of thumb, try to keep coupling less than nine.

Depth of Inheritance

Another code metric has to do with inheritance. Inheritance is used in .NET languages like C# and VB.NET and the .NET Framework uses a lot of inheritance. Just like with the other metrics, inheritance is useful but you shouldn't overuse it. The following code listing shows a simple inheritance example:

```
public class A { }
public class B : A { }
public class C : B { }
```

This means that A has an inheritance level of one, B of two, and C of three. Why does A start with one? Because all classes in C# inherit from the base class object. Why could inheritance be a problem? Classes that have more inheritance levels become more complex. They inherit methods, properties, and other members from their base classes. It becomes more difficult to find out what a class exactly does and where everything is declared. Changes in one of the classes in the hierarchy can propagate to changes in the other classes.

Inheritance also allows you to reuse code, which is a good thing. As with all code metrics there is a certain maximum level you should try to stay beneath. I try to set my maximum inheritance level to six. This is based on empirical data, not on real scientific study. I only count class inheritance, not interface inheritance. Classes containing the implementation and overridden methods make it harder to find out which implementation of a method is used at runtime. Interfaces don't contain the implementation so I choose to not count those for depth of inheritance.

Calculating Code Metrics

You calculate code metrics through Analyze ➤ Calculate Code Metrics for solution or for project (see Figure 8-6). This is available for C# and VB.

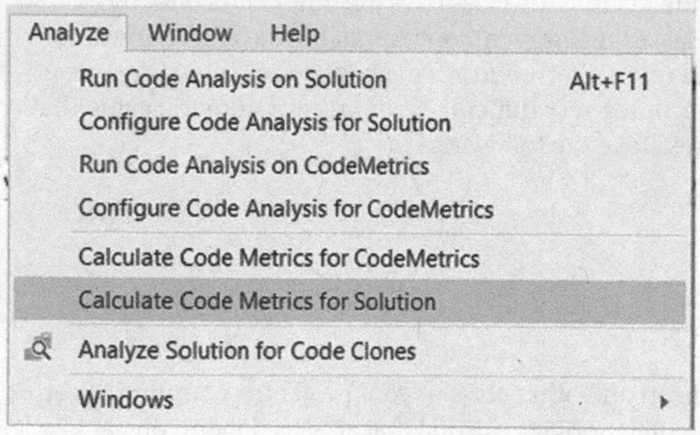

Figure 8-6. *Calculate code metrics for a project or for the whole solution*

The code metrics results are then displayed in a grid, as shown in Figure 8-7. You see a hierarchical tree of your project on the left. On the right you see the cyclomatic complexity, depth of inheritance, class coupling, and lines of code. The first value, Maintainability Index, is calculated based on the other four values. There are however strong objections in the community against the Maintainability Index. For example, the Maintainability Index turns yellow when the index drops below 20 and turns red when it's below 10. There is no clear explanation for these thresholds. Also, the formula that calculates the

Maintainability Index is based on research done on projects written in C and Pascal, which have different characteristics than an object-oriented language such as C#. So, take the Maintainability Index with a pinch of salt and pay attention to the individual metrics when reviewing code.

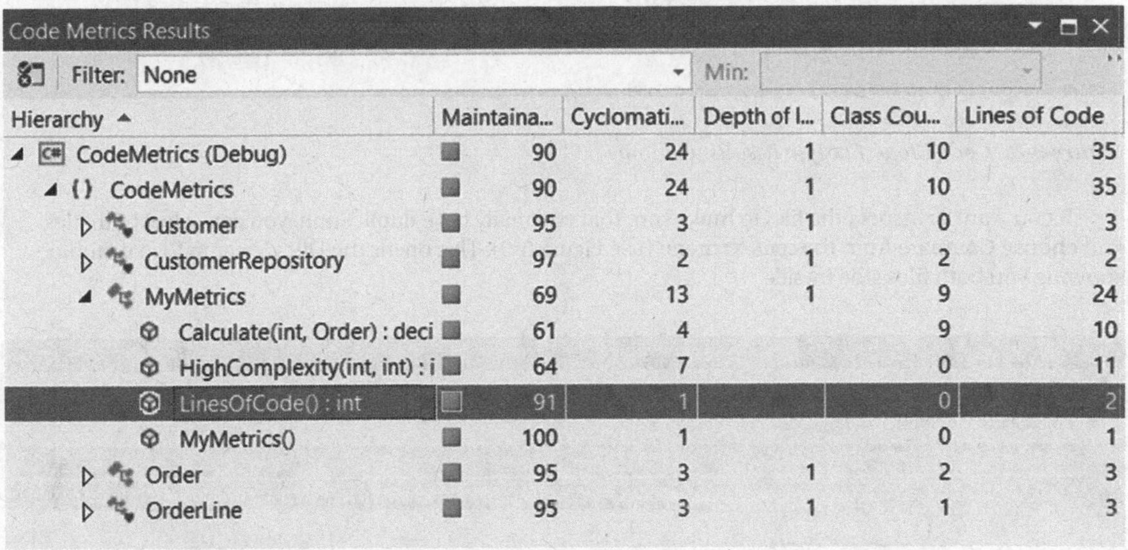

Hierarchy ▲	Maintaina...	Cyclomati...	Depth of I...	Class Cou...	Lines of Code
▲ C# CodeMetrics (Debug)	90	24	1	10	35
▲ { } CodeMetrics	90	24	1	10	35
▷ Customer	95	3	1	0	3
▷ CustomerRepository	97	2	1	2	2
▲ MyMetrics	69	13	1	9	24
Calculate(int, Order) : deci	61	4		9	10
HighComplexity(int, int) : i	64	7		0	11
LinesOfCode() : int	91	1		0	2
MyMetrics()	100	1		0	1
▷ Order	95	3	1	2	3
▷ OrderLine	95	3	1	1	3

Figure 8-7. Code Metrics Results window

The Code Metrics Results window has an option to export the result to Excel. I often use this because of the easy sorting and filtering that Excels offers over tabular data. Within Excel, for example, it's easy to find the largest method in your project, while in the Code Metrics Results window you have to expand each node and manually search for it. Excel also allows you to do other computations (such as the average of a metric) and visualizations (such as pivot tables and graphs).

Finding Duplications

Duplicate code is evil. Duplications cause your projects to become bigger (making it more difficult to find something) and make your code harder to maintain because you have to fix bugs in multiple places. Forgetting one location could introduce other subtle bugs that are hard to find. Visual Studio helps you find duplicate code with a very sophisticated algorithm. Code that is the same yet has renamed identifiers, rearranged statements, or small statements added or removed will still be detected.

The Code Clone Analysis tools in Visual Studio will report duplication in three groups:

- Exact
- Strong
- Medium

You can inspect the findings and compare the different locations. You start the analysis by choosing the Analyze ➤ Analyze Solution for Code Clones menu option. Figure 8-8 shows an example result of an exact match between two files.

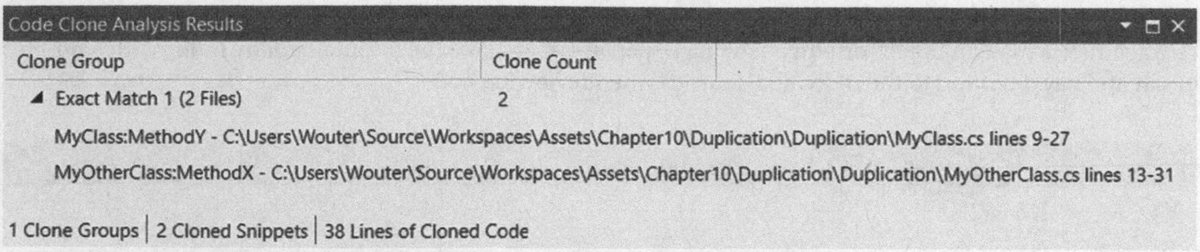

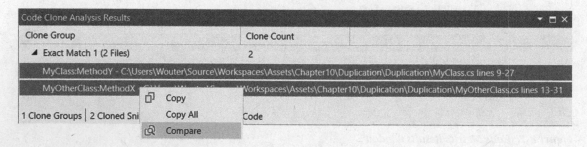

Figure 8-8. *Code Clone Analysis Results window*

If you want to inspect the files to make sure that you really have duplication, you can select both files and choose Compare from the context menu (see Figure 8-9). This opens the Diff viewer in Visual Studio showing you both files side by side.

Figure 8-9. *You can compare two files to inspect the duplication*

You can configure Code Clone Analysis by using a XML file with a `codeclonessettings` extension. This file lets you exclude certain parts of your code, such as generated code, from the analysis. For example, the following XML excludes a file named `MyClass.cs` from the duplication analysis. You can exclude files, types, methods, and namespaces. You can even use patterns (wildcards like *) to exclude files (see `https://msdn.microsoft.com/en-us/library/hh205279.aspx` for more information).

```xml
<CodeCloneSettings>
  <Exclusions>
    <File>MyClass.cs</File>
  </Exclusions>
</CodeCloneSettings>
```

Validating the Architecture

The metrics we've looked at until now focus on projects, classes, and methods. Visual Studio also helps you validate the relationships between different parts of your application as described in your architecture. This feature is called *layer validation*. Typically, your application consists of several projects all containing specific parts of your application. You may have user interface, business, and data layers in an architecture. As an architect, you want to disallow certain interactions between these layers. For example, your user interface should never directly contact the database. Instead this should go through the business layer.

You implement these kinds of rules with an architecture project in Visual Studio. This project allows you to create a graphical representation of your project and then validate your project against the architecture model. Whenever a developer on your team violates the architecture rules you get an error. Figure 8-10 shows the Modeling Project project type. Once you have such a project, you can add modeling items to it, as shown in Figure 8-11. This scenario concentrates on the layer diagram.

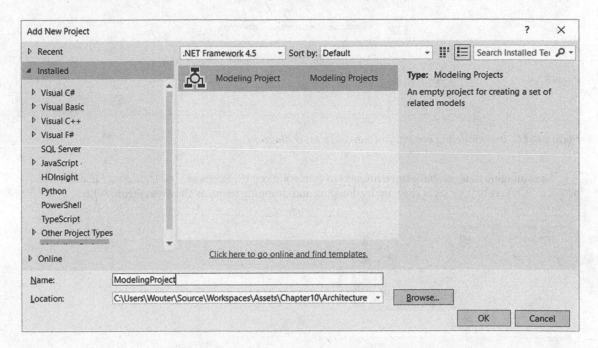

Figure 8-10. You can add a modeling project to your solution

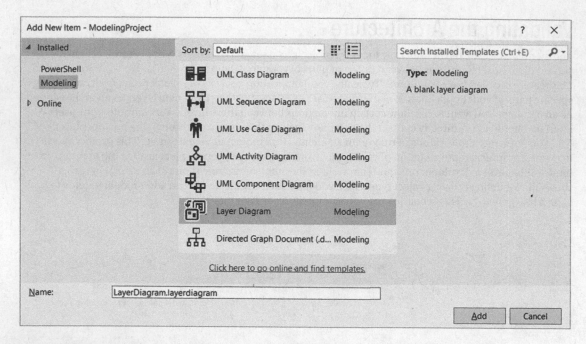

Figure 8-11. *In a modeling project, you can add a layer diagram*

Now imagine that you have three projects in your solution: UI, Business, and Data. You can add these projects as layers to your layer diagram by dragging and dropping them, as shown in Figure 8-12.

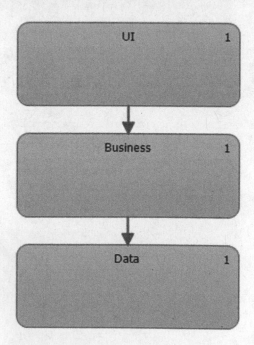

Figure 8-12. *A layer diagram of an architecture*

You can then manually run the architecture validation from the context menu of the modeling project, as Figure 8-13 shows.

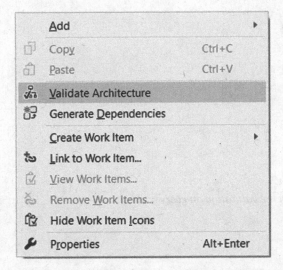

	Add	▶
⎘	**C**opy	Ctrl+C
⎗	**P**aste	Ctrl+V
⯒	**V**alidate Architecture	
⯒	**G**enerate **D**ependencies	
	Create Work Item	▶
⬿	**L**ink to Work Item...	
✓	V**i**ew Work Items...	
⬿	Remove **W**ork Items...	
⬿	Hide Work Item **I**cons	
🔧	**P**roperties	Alt+Enter

Figure 8-13. *You can validate the architecture with a layer diagram*

Now if your UI layer tries to use a class that's defined in the data layer, you get two errors, as shown in Figure 8-14.

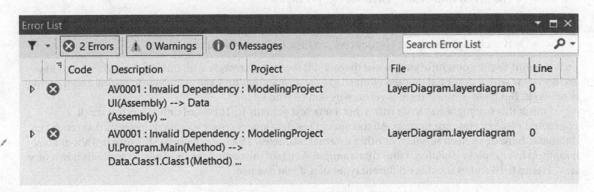

Figure 8-14. *Validation errors from the Architecture Validation*

You can configure the architecture validation to run automatically by editing the proper properties and setting Validate Architecture to true. When this option is true, Architecture Validation runs as a part of your build (see Figure 8-15).

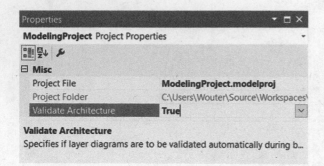

Figure 8-15. *Setting Validate Architecture to true will run the validation on every build*

Create and Run Unit Tests

Unit testing is a broad topic. Personally, I'm a big proponent of using unit tests. I would go as far to say that trying to move to a continuous delivery model without good unit tests is doomed to fail. Discussing unit testing is a book of its own. Fortunately, a couple of good books are already written on this subject. I particularly like these three books:

- *The Art Of Unit Testing, written by Roy Osherove*

- *xUnit Test Patterns, written by Gerard Meszaros*

- *Working effectively with legacy code, written by Michael Feathers*

Despite all the good information out there, I still see teams struggle with unit testing. Whenever I have an interview with a potential new developer, I get the answer that they see value in unit testing and that they don't do it. But if we all think there is value, why don't we do it?

I think this oversight has to do with what a unit test actually is. The word unit refers to a small, contained piece of your application. All too often, I see developers create so-called unit tests that touch the database, hard drive, web services, or other external resources. That's not a unit test! A unit test should test a method in complete isolation. I find that a simple sketch of the testing pyramid always explains it in a nice way. Figure 8-16 shows the three different types of test you can use.

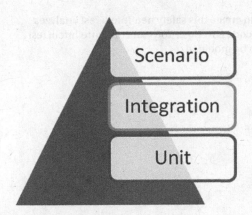

Figure 8-16. *The testing pyramid*

Compare this to creating and testing a new car. A car consists of a lot of parts like a motor, battery, and gear box. After you have fully assembled the car, you try to start it but it doesn't work. Any idea what's wrong? There could be a lot of different problems and without further examination it's pretty hard to fix. But what if you tested the different parts in isolation? You test the battery by attaching some measuring equipment. You could even place the battery in a fridge to check if it works under low temperatures. That's easier to do than place the whole car in the fridge. After having tested all the parts in isolation, you can start attaching them to each other. For example, if the dynamo runs, does it power the battery? After these integration tests, you start running scenario tests: you start the car and take it for a drive.

Unit tests are the broad bottom of the pyramid. You have a lot of them. Integration tests are less common. They test if parts work together. Scenario tests take the whole application and run specific user scenarios and are often done by actual testers. Unit and integration tests are created by developers and can easily be run automatically.

Creating integration tests and calling them unit tests often causes teams to totally abandon unit testing. Creating integration tests takes longer. They fail more often and are harder to maintain. Having lots of them makes your project more fragile. There is no hard rule for the ratio between unit, integration, and scenario tests. But be cautious that you keep your unit tests as actual unit tests. Use techniques like dependency injection to separate all parts of your application and make sure that you can run them in total isolation.

Another thing that goes wrong often is the coupling between test code and application code. Creating instances of a class in hundreds of test methods and then changing the constructor signature of the class leads to hundreds of compile errors. Sometimes teams see this as a reason to stop unit testing because the maintenance burden is too great. But writing unit tests in such a way is just a matter of bad coding practices. Why not refactor the creation of your class to a helper method? This way, you only have one point of change when you change the constructor signature of your class.

A lot of frameworks have been created that help you with writing good, maintainable unit tests. Some frameworks I personally like are xUnit, FluentAssertions, Moq, and AutoFixture. Invest time in solving the impediments that keep your team from unit testing. Train your team, search for or build frameworks that help your team, and understand that good unit tests are the basis of the quality of your system.

Microsoft understands that unit testing is difficult for many teams. This is why they introduced a tool to help you get started with a complete set of unit tests for your application: IntelliTest. These automatically generated unit tests won't find any bugs for you. They just test what you created. What they do however is give you a safety net for your application. Whenever someone makes a change that breaks one of your tests you're immediately informed of this. Having a good safety net in place allows you to start refactoring your code and adding new features without having to worry about breaking something somewhere in your application.

IntelliTest is an extremely useful feature in Visual Studio to create this safety net. IntelliTest analyzes your code and creates unit tests that will give you 100 percent code coverage. You can configure IntelliTest in how it analyzes your code. The generated unit tests can also be modified.

Take the following code listing:

```
public int Run(int x, int y)
{
    if (x > 0)
    {
        return x * y;
    }
    else
    {
        try
        {
            return x / y;
        }
        catch (DivideByZeroException)
        {
            return 0;
        }
    }
}
```

To get 100 percent code coverage, you need to create two unit tests for the if statement: one that has an x value of less than 50 and one with x more than 50. You also need to trigger the catch clause by creating a DivideByZero exception. IntelliTest will automatically find these scenarios and create the correct unit tests for you. Of course your code will often be more difficult than this. IntelliTest will try to create instances of all objects it finds in your code. After the unit tests are generated you can modify this code, for example, to mock certain objects.

You run IntelliTest by right-clicking inside a method and choosing IntelliTest. If you run IntelliTest on the previous code, you get the results shown in Figure 8-17. IntelliTest is smart enough to calculate the boundary values required to reach 100 percent code coverage. It uses values of 0 and 1 for x and y. It also uses a int.MinValue for x, resulting in an OverflowException that's not handled by the code.

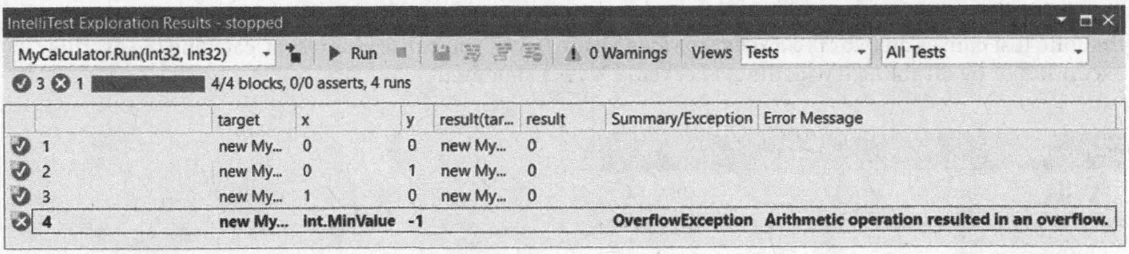

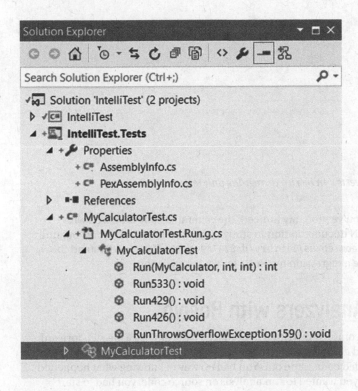

Figure 8-17. *IntelliTest results*

You can select the different tests in the IntelliTest window and let Visual Studio generate these tests as actual code. You then get something like Figure 8-18.

Figure 8-18. *Automatically created unit tests from IntelliTest*

If you run the unit tests in your project (Test ➤ Run ➤ All Tests), you see that three tests succeed and that one test causes an `OverflowException` (see Figure 8-19). You can fix this test by catching the overflow exception or by disabling it with the `unchecked { ... }` statement.

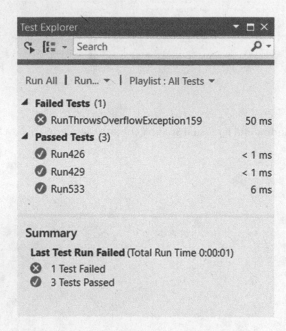

Figure 8-19. *The automatically generated tests can be run as regular unit tests*

IntelliTest is a very powerful tool. As you've probably noticed, the generated code is littered with attributes. I encourage you to use the MSDN documentation to study up on how IntelliTest works behind the scenes (see `https://msdn.microsoft.com/en-us/library/dn823749.aspx`). If you understand this powerful tool, it will help you quickly create a regression test suite for your application.

Creating Custom Code Analyzers with Roslyn

Roslyn is the new C# and VB compiler. It's completely written in managed code and it's a big step forward compared to the previous compiler. The old compiler was written in C++ and functioned more or less like a black box. Some code went in and compiled code came out. You had no way of knowing what happened inside the compiler. This meant that when you wanted to run analysis on source code, you had to start with building tools to parse the source code. You almost had to build your own compiler. That made it very difficult to create analytical tools for your code.

With Roslyn, this has become much easier. Roslyn offers you a whole set of APIs that you can plug in to. This means that you can very easily extend Visual Studio with new plugins that implement your specific rules for your code. A very good example of this is what the Azure team has done. They created a set of Roslyn analyzers that help users use the Azure API the correct way.

Take the following code:

```
SharedAccessBlobPolicy newBlobPolicy = new SharedAccessBlobPolicy
{
    Permissions = SharedAccessBlobPermissions.Write,
    SharedAccessStartTime = DateTime.UtcNow,
    SharedAccessExpiryTime = DateTimeOffset.UtcNow + TimeSpan.FromDays(1)
};
```

Do you see anything wrong with this code? Probably not if you're not familiar with the Azure APIs. But if you install the Azure Roslyn analyzers, you get a warning directly inside Visual Studio helping you with the correct use of this API. For this code, the Analyzer tells you that you can avoid setting `SharedAccessStartTime` since its default value is `UtcNow`.

What would you create if building these analyzers is extremely simple? Let's say you want to adhere to a specific naming convention for your namespaces. Every namespace should start with your company name and then the application name. Normally, you would just do some manual code reviews and make sure the namespace properties of your projects are configured correctly. With Roslyn, creating an analyzer for such a simple rule is very easy.

To create a Roslyn Analyzer, you first have to install a couple of prerequisites. You can find these in the Open Source GitHub repository of Roslyn at https://github.com/dotnet/roslyn/wiki/Getting-Started-on-Visual-Studio-2015. After you've installed these components, you can create a new code fix project, as shown in Figure 8-20.

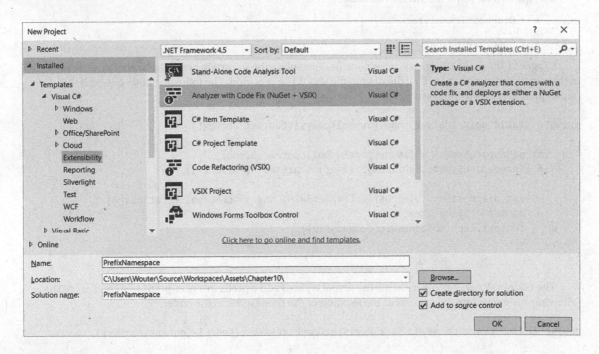

Figure 8-20. *Create a new code fix project*

If you run the project without changing anything, an experimental instance of Visual Studio is launched. In this instance you can test your extension. If you create a new console application, you can see the out-of-the-box quick fix at work in Figure 8-21. You see a green squiggly beneath the program class and a lightbulb icon in front of it. This is added by the code fix project you're running. The added quick fix lets you uppercase the class name. A nice preview is shown in the popup.

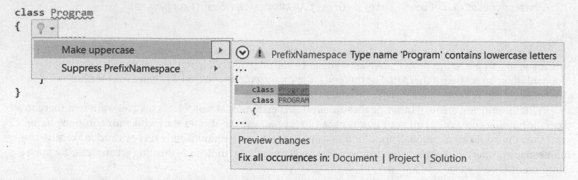

Figure 8-21. *A Roslyn quick fix that lets you uppercase class names*

The quick fix is implemented in two files:

- `DiagnosticAnalyzer`
- `CodeFixProvider`

`DiagnosticAnalyzer` registers your code fix. You subscribe to certain symbols (`SymbolKind.Namespace` in this scenario) and then verify if the diagnostic should be reported. The following code checks if the namespace is correctly prefixed:

```
private static void AnalyzeSymbol(SymbolAnalysisContext context)
{
    var namespaceSymbol = (INamespaceSymbol)context.Symbol;
    if (!namespaceSymbol.ToDisplayString().StartsWith("Apress"))
    {
        var diagnostic = Diagnostic.Create(Rule, namespaceSymbol.Locations[0],
        namespaceSymbol.Name);
        context.ReportDiagnostic(diagnostic);
    }
}
```

The `CodeFixProvider` file contains the actual logic to add a prefix to a non-prefixed namespace. The following code registers the code fix at the location of the namespace in the code:

```
public sealed override async Task RegisterCodeFixesAsync(CodeFixContext context)
{
    var root = await context.Document.GetSyntaxRootAsync(
                        context.CancellationToken).ConfigureAwait(false);

    var diagnostic = context.Diagnostics.First();
    var diagnosticSpan = diagnostic.Location.SourceSpan;
```

```
var declaration = root.FindToken(diagnosticSpan.Start).Parent
    .AncestorsAndSelf().OfType<NamespaceDeclarationSyntax>().First();

context.RegisterCodeFix(
    CodeAction.Create("Prefix namespace",
                    c => PrefixNamespaceAsync(context.Document, declaration, c)),
    diagnostic);
}
```

And finally, here's the code that runs when the user executes the code fix:

```
private async Task<Solution> PrefixNamespaceAsync(Document document,
            NamespaceDeclarationSyntax typeDecl, CancellationToken cancellationToken)
{
    var identifierToken = typeDecl.Name;

    var semanticModel = await document.GetSemanticModelAsync(cancellationToken);
    var typeSymbol = semanticModel.GetDeclaredSymbol(typeDecl, cancellationToken);

    var originalSolution = document.Project.Solution;
    var optionSet = originalSolution.Workspace.Options;
    var newSolution = await Renamer.RenameSymbolAsync(
        document.Project.Solution,
        typeSymbol,
        "Apress" + identifierToken.ToString(),
        optionSet,
        cancellationToken).ConfigureAwait(false);

    return newSolution;
}
```

Now when you run this code fix, you get the result shown in Figure 8-22. The full code is available as a download but the essence is what you read above. As you can see, a code fix isn't that hard to create. So next time you find yourself discussing coding guidelines with your team, think of a code fix and how you can help everyone on your team follow the same guidelines automatically.

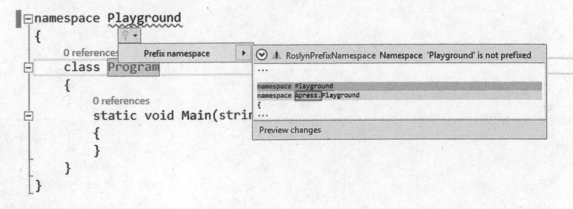

Figure 8-22. *The Prefix Namespace code fix at work*

Summary

This chapter showed you quite a lot of ways to improve the quality of your code. You've seen how you can use the Code Analysis tool to find all kinds of errors in your code, ranging from spelling mistakes to security and performance flaws. You've also worked with code metrics to objectively calculate grades for your code. Combining these two features will help you find a lot of problems in your code. Visual Studio has even more to offer. Analyzing your code for duplicates helps you increase maintainability. You can even strengthen your code at a higher level by using the architecture validation built in to the modeling projects. This way you validate your architectural constraints automatically on every build. Unit tests are another important aspect of increasing code quality. You've seen how you can run unit tests in Visual Studio and how IntelliTest helps you create a robust test harness. Finally, you've seen how Roslyn opens up a whole new world of code-analyzing tools.

In the next chapter you'll dive into the features of Visual Studio Team Services that help you automate all these code quality checks and more on each check-in by implementing continuous integration.

CHAPTER 9

■ ■ ■

Implementing Continuous Integration

If you've followed along until now, you have already accomplished quite a lot. You learned how to use the Agile Project Management tools, looked into increasing the quality of your code, and learned how Visual Studio and Visual Studio Team Services support you in these endeavors. On your road to DevOps and continuous delivery, the next step to take is setting up continuous integration. What is *continuous integration* and why do you need it? This chapter will show you what continuous integration is and how you can configure it for your projects. You will also learn about SonarQube, a specialized tool for measuring the quality of your code on a continuous basis.

Why do we talk about continuous integration? Well, you hope that developers check the quality of their code locally before sending changes to the central repository. But you can't guarantee this. If a developer is late to go home, he could decide to quickly check in his changes and leave. And what about deployments? Do you ask one of the developers to run a deployment from her local workstation? If these things sound familiar, you need a continuous integration build. Imagine that every time a developer uploads a change to version control, a process gets triggered that compiles the latest version of the code, runs unit tests, performs code analysis, and then delivers a package in a specified location ready to be released. That is continuous integration.

This means that whenever a developer checks in some malfunctioning code, the central continuous integration build fails. This increases the feedback loop for your developers. A failing build means that one of the checks failed and that the current version is not working correctly. Continuous integration is a process where you encourage developers to integrate as often as possible and where you continuously validate the integrated version of the code.

Implementing a continuous integration build is not hard. VS Team Services gives you some great tools and you can be up and running in minutes. The difficult part is making your team feel responsible for the build. When the build fails and team members keep checking in code without anyone fixing the broken build, having a continuous integration build adds absolutely no value. You need to work on making your team feel responsible for the build. One way to achieve this is to make the quality of the build easily visible to anyone. A simple monitor in your team room that shows the status of the latest build does wonders. Some teams even take this a step further. I once found a video showing a team that had built a rotating machine gun that fired tennis balls at the person who broke the build. Another company uses a giant teddy bear that gets placed on the desk of the person who broke the build and only moves on when someone else breaks the build. This is a process that has to grow but remember that instilling the importance of always fixing a broken build on your team is crucial.

© Wouter de Kort 2016

W. de Kort, *DevOps on the Microsoft Stack*, DOI 10.1007/978-1-4842-1446-6_9

Configuring a Continuous Integration Build

VS Team Services offers built-in capabilities for a continuous integration build. You create what's called a build definition in the web portal of VS Team Services. You then configure this build definition to trigger on every check-in, on a specific schedule, or manually. VS Team Services takes care of the rest. Of course, the builds that are triggered need to run somewhere. On your local environment, you have installed Visual Studio and probably a bunch of other tools and SDKs that are required to build your application.

When running a build in VS Team Services, these same tools need to be available. To help you with this, Microsoft runs what's called a *hosted build agent*. This is a preconfigured machine that has the most common tools already installed and is available on demand for your builds. Figure 9-1 shows the capabilities of the hosted agent. You can view these capabilities on your own VS Team Services account by navigating to the settings of your account and then choosing Agent Pools ➤ Hosted.

SYSTEM CAPABILITIES
Shows information about the capabilities provided by this host

Agent.Name	Hosted Agent
Agent.Version	1.85.1
AndroidSDK	C:\java\androidsdk\android-sdk
ant	C:\java\ant\apache-ant-1.9.4
AzurePS	0.8.16
bower	C:\NPM\Modules\bower.cmd
Cmd	C:\Windows\system32\cmd.exe
DotNetFramework	C:\Windows\Microsoft.NET\Framework64\v4.0.30319
grunt	C:\NPM\Modules\grunt.cmd
gulp	C:\NPM\Modules\gulp.cmd
java	C:\Program Files\Java\jre1.8.0_40
JDK	C:\Program Files\Java\jdk1.8.0_40
maven	C:\java\maven\apache-maven-3.2.2
MSBuild	C:\Program Files (x86)\MSBuild\12.0\bin
node	C:\Program Files\nodejs\node.exe
npm	C:\Program Files\nodejs\npm.cmd
VisualStudio	C:\Program Files (x86)\Microsoft Visual Studio 12.0
VSTest	C:\Program Files (x86)\Microsoft Visual Studio 12.0\Common7\IDE\CommonExte
Xamarin.Android	4.20.0.37

Figure 9-1. *Capabilities of the hosted build agent*

In the following section, you will look at installing a build server of your own if the hosted build agent doesn't meet your requirements. Whenever possible, I recommend that you use the hosted build agent since Microsoft keeps these servers up to date for you and does any other required maintenance work. This saves you a lot of time and energy.

A build server won't start running builds on itself. You need some kind of instruction set to tell the build server what to do. Figure 9-2 shows a default build template that ships out of the box with VS Team Services. This build template builds your code, runs unit tests, and then stores the build output in VS Team Services. These steps are executed on the build server.

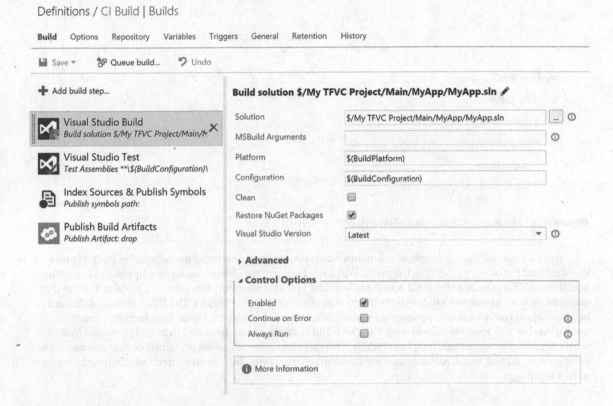

Figure 9-2. A build definition in VS Team Services

The build definition consists of a list of tasks that you want to execute. You can easily add build steps to your build and configure each step. For example, the Visual Studio Build step that's selected in Figure 9-2 lets you configure the solution you want to build, arguments you want to pass to MSBuild, the platform and configuration for your build, whether to start with a clean workspace on every new build, if NuGet packages need to be restored on build, and which version of Visual Studio you want to use to run the build.

The infrastructure behind the build system is cross-platform and easily extensible. The build steps are a combination of JavaScript and a platform-specific script that does the actual work. The build agent is a JavaScript, cross-platform application built in NodeJS that executes the build steps and keeps track of things like errors and logging. This means that the build system is not only capable of building .NET applications on Windows. It can also build and test cross-platform apps, like an iOS Xamarin-based mobile app on a Mac, a Core CLR-based ASP.NET application, or a Java application on Linux. These are all available out of the box. If you want, you can add your own tasks or use the default tasks that run a script of your own. In addition to the set of build steps, which forms the main part of your build definition, there are other options that you can configure.

You create a build through the Web Access portal of VS Team Services. Each team project has its own set of builds. If you open a team project, you see the Build hub in the top navigation bar. You can then select the green + icon to create a new build definition (see Figure 9-3).

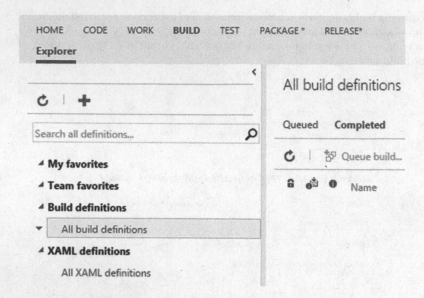

Figure 9-3. *The Build hub is a part of Web Access*

You can choose from a couple of templates when you create a new build definition. Figure 9-4 shows the standard list of templates. The Universal Windows Platform requires an agent that has both Visual Studio and the tools for creating Universal App installed. The Visual Studio template creates a build definition that requires only an installation of Visual Studio to compile and test your project. The Xamarin templates can be used when you are creating cross-platform mobile apps with Xamarin. These templates can compile an Android or iOS app. The Xcode template can build code on a Mac. You need to install your own Mac with a build agent to use this template. Finally, you can also start with an empty template that you can then configure by adding tasks. All templates are customizable and you don't limit yourself to anything by starting with a template.

Figure 9-4. Default definition templates for a build definition

After clicking next, you get the window shown in Figure 9-5. In this case, I've selected the Visual Studio Build Definition. You can then configure the repository source, the agent to run on, and whether or not this is a continuous integration build: a build that runs on every check-in. The Repository type lets you choose between Git and TFVC. You can also build externally hosted applications from GitHub (or another Git repository) or Subversion. Finally, you click the Create button to create your new build definition.

■ **Note**   For more information on building GitHub projects, see
https://msdn.microsoft.com/en-us/Library/vs/alm/Build/github/index.

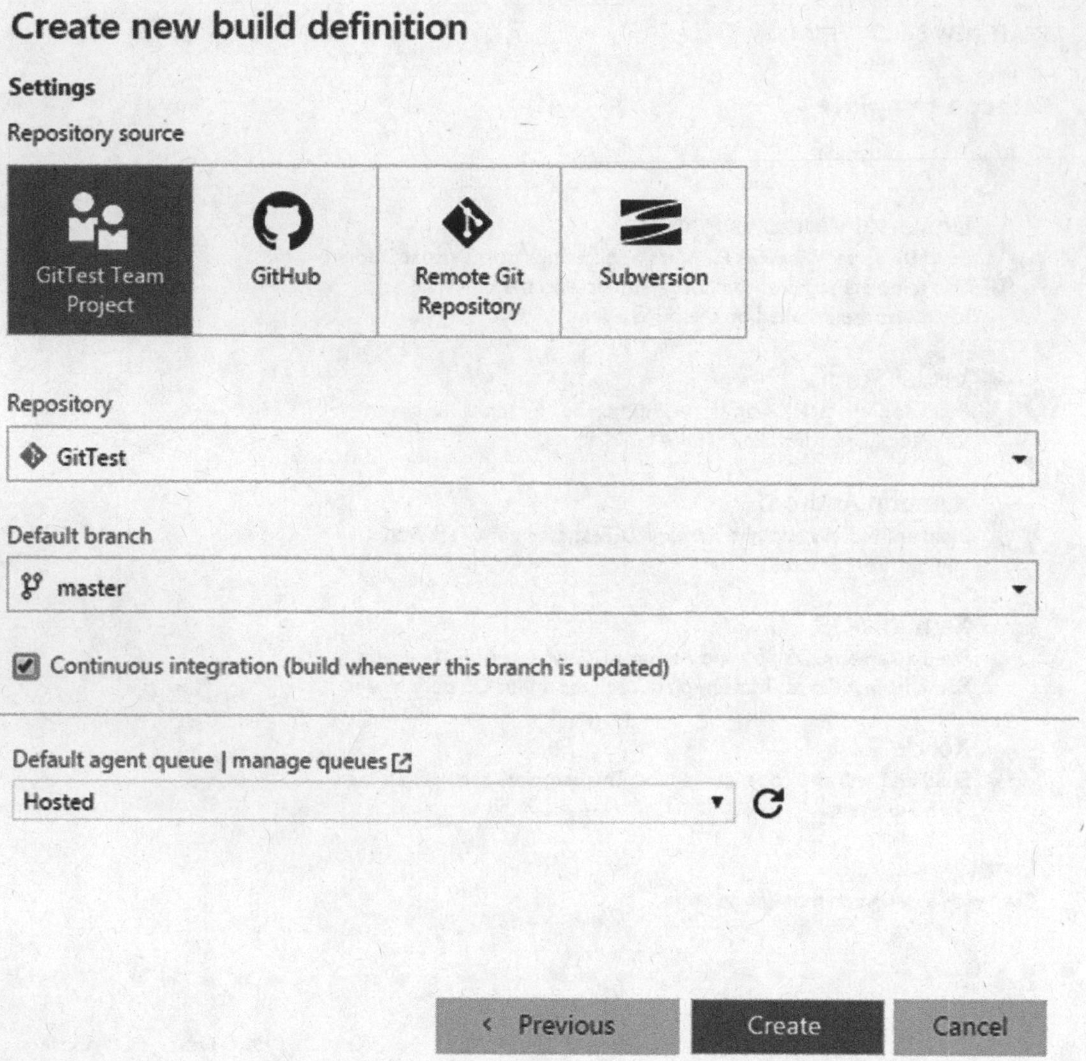

Create new build definition

Settings

Repository source

Repository

| ◇ GitTest | ▼ |

Default branch

| ⴹ master | ▼ |

☑ Continuous integration (build whenever this branch is updated)

Default agent queue | manage queues ⬚

| Hosted | ▼ | ↻ |

| ‹ Previous | Create | Cancel |

Figure 9-5. *Additional configuration options when creating a new build definition*

The Build tab of your new build definition lists the steps that compose your build, as you've seen in Figure 9-2. Here you can add new steps and configure each step to perform your build. The Options tab lets you run your build under one or more configurations (for example, you want to create both a Debug and a Release configuration). You can also choose to create a work item on failure. This makes sure that every broken build shows up as a work item assigned to the person who executed the build. You can choose what type of work item you want to create and whom to assign it to and then set any additional fields that are important to you. Finally, you can select if build scripts can interact with other parts of VS Team Services by using an authorization token.

You can see the Repository tab in Figure 9-4. Here you define how the build agent receives the sources of your project from version control. For TFVC, you can map and cloak folders just as you do on your own development PC. The Clean option lets you configure if the build agent should get all sources every time and start with a clean slate or if it can only get the updates that where made since the previous build. With large projects, cleaning your repository each time and downloading all the code takes sometimes too much time. In such scenarios, you can choose to disable the clean. Labeling sources means that each build gets assigned a label that you can later use to retrieve the exact set of files that were used in that build.

When you're working with a Git repository, you don't get the Mappings part of Figure 9-6. You do get the option to select which branch you want to build. You also get an option to check out submodules. A submodule in Git is a way to reuse code from another project without copying the code. Instead, a subfolder of your project points to another Git repository. As you can see, the build system is quite powerful.

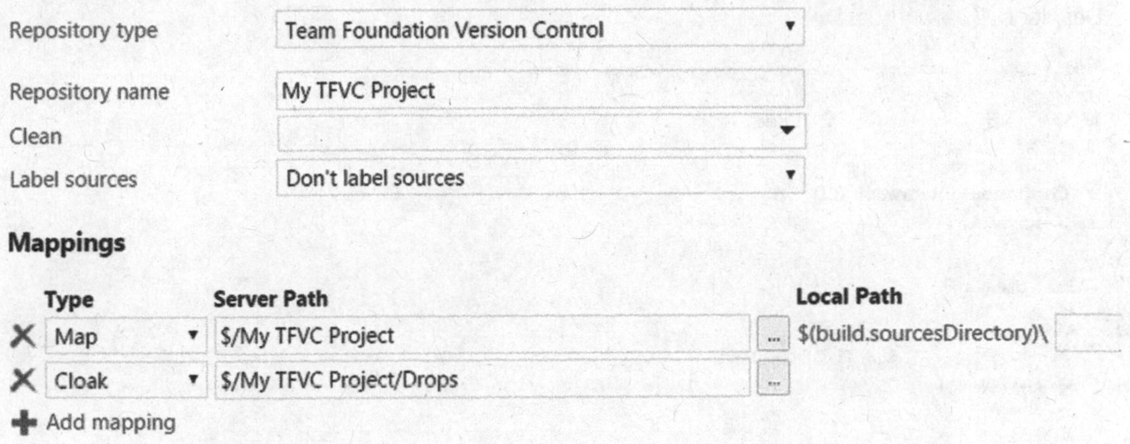

Repository type	Team Foundation Version Control ▼
Repository name	My TFVC Project
Clean	▼
Label sources	Don't label sources ▼

Mappings

Type	Server Path	Local Path
✕ Map ▼	$/My TFVC Project	... $(build.sourcesDirectory)\
✕ Cloak ▼	$/My TFVC Project/Drops	...

✚ Add mapping

Figure 9-6. Repository configuration for a build

The fourth tab, Variables (see Figure 9-7), lets you define name value pairs of properties that you can then use in your build definition. By default, you get properties that specify for what configuration and platform to build. You can use these variables with a $(VARIABLE_NAME) syntax. So, $(BuildPlatform) will be substituted with the value of that variable by the build agent. This a handy feature to avoid spreading all kinds of configuration options throughout your build template. Instead, you specify them and then use them in multiple places.

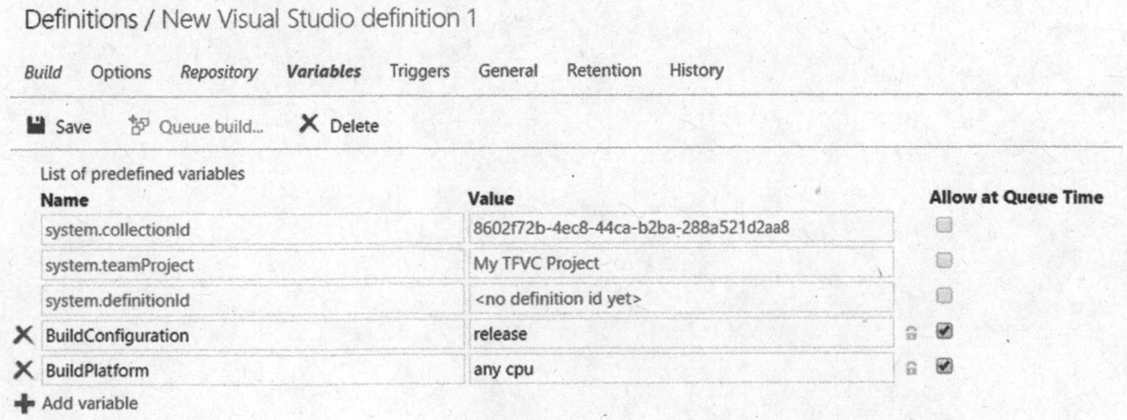

Definitions / New Visual Studio definition 1

Build Options *Repository* **Variables** Triggers General Retention History

💾 Save   Queue build...   ✕ Delete

List of predefined variables

Name	Value	Allow at Queue Time
system.collectionId	8602f72b-4ec8-44ca-b2ba-288a521d2aa8	☐
system.teamProject	My TFVC Project	☐
system.definitionId	<no definition id yet>	☐
✕ BuildConfiguration	release	🔒 ☑
✕ BuildPlatform	any cpu	🔒 ☑

✚ Add variable

Figure 9-7. Configuring variables for your build definition

The Triggers tab (Figure 9-8) allows you to specify when your build should run. If you don't configure any triggers, you can always start the build manually. You can also configure automated builds that run on a specific schedule or that run on every check-in. The option to batch changes can be important when you have a busy repository. Imagine that multiple users check in code while a build is still running. Without this option, every check-in would queue a build, thus creating a long waiting list. If you batch changes, all the check-ins that happen while a build is running are scheduled for the next build. If the build fails (which is hopefully rare), the builds are run separately so you know exactly which check-in caused the failure.

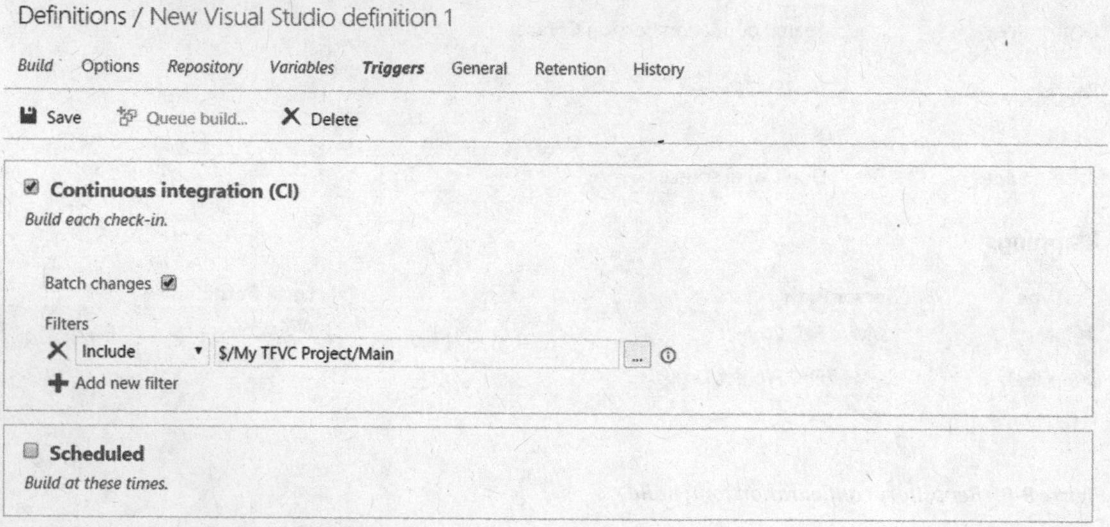

Definitions / New Visual Studio definition 1

Build Options *Repository* *Variables* **Triggers** General Retention History

💾 Save   🗐 Queue build...   ✕ Delete

☑ **Continuous integration (CI)**
Build each check-in.

Batch changes ☑

Filters
✕ | Include ▼ | $/My TFVC Project/Main | ... | ⓘ
➕ Add new filter

☐ **Scheduled**
Build at these times.

Figure 9-8. You can configure multiple triggers for your build definition

The General tab lets you configure a couple of options, as you can see in Figure 9-9, such as a description, build number format, and timeout. The agent queue determines where your build is going to run. You'll dive into this in the next part when you see how to configure your own agents. The Badge option lets you show the status of your build on an external web site. This is nice if you have an overview page or something where you want to have a simple image that shows your builds status. Beneath these options you see a list of demands. *Demands* are used by VS Team Services to figure out on which agent your build can run. Agents have capabilities and VS Team Services matches those to the demands of your build definition. In the example in Figure 9-9, the machine needs to have Visual Studio installed. This will automatically install MSBuild and VSTest so that all capabilities are matched.

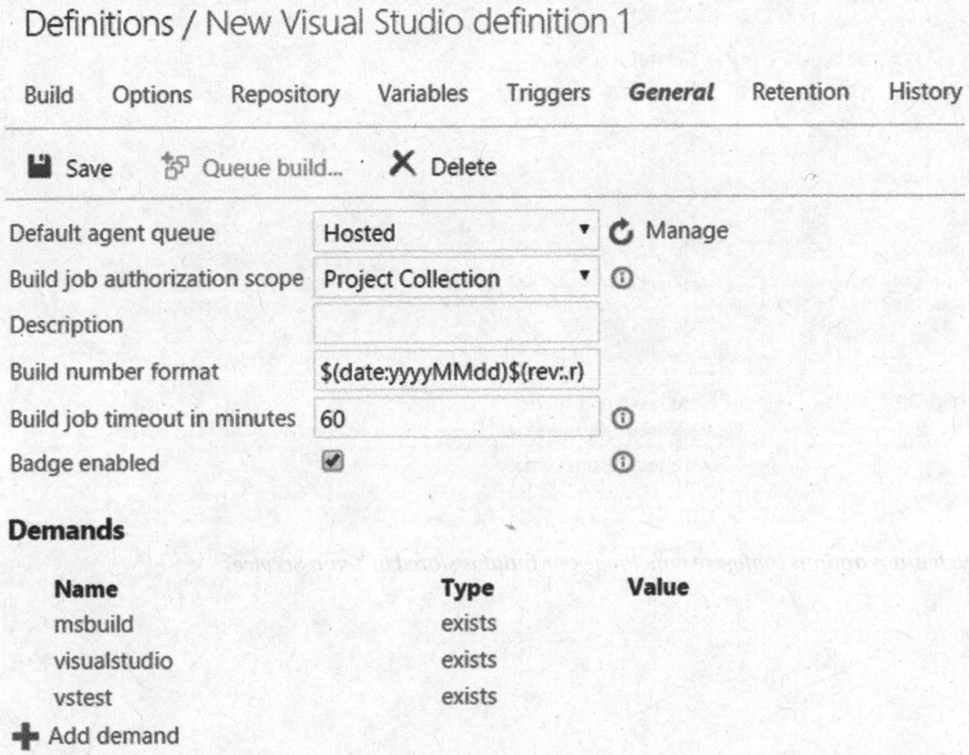

Definitions / New Visual Studio definition 1

Build   Options   Repository   Variables   Triggers   **General**   Retention   History

💾 Save   📋 Queue build...   ✗ Delete

Default agent queue	Hosted ▾ ↻ Manage
Build job authorization scope	Project Collection ▾ ⓘ
Description	
Build number format	$(date:yyyyMMdd)$(rev:.r)
Build job timeout in minutes	60 ⓘ
Badge enabled	☑ ⓘ

Demands

Name	Type	Value
msbuild	exists	
visualstudio	exists	
vstest	exists	

➕ Add demand

Figure 9-9. General options for a build definition

The Retention tab (Figure 9-10) determines how long your builds are kept once they're finished. When you have a busy team project, you will create a lot of builds. Keeping all those builds around clutters your environment and takes up a lot of space in VS Team Services. By default, there is a rule that deletes everything after 30 days. You can add rules and remove this default rule if you want. Finally, the History tab allows you to inspect previous versions of your build definition and roll back to them if you want to undo certain changes.

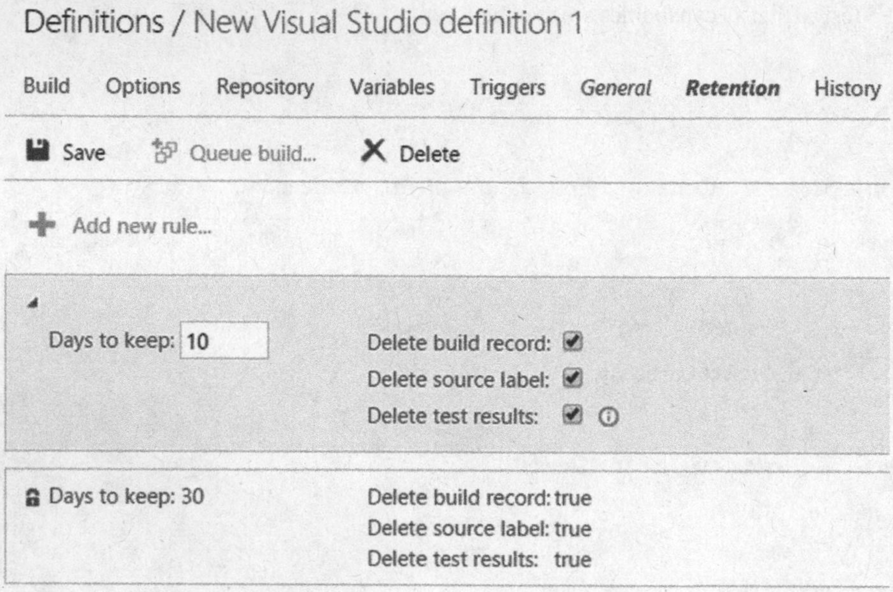

Definitions / New Visual Studio definition 1

Build   Options   Repository   Variables   Triggers   *General*   **Retention**   History

💾 Save   Queue build...   ✕ Delete

➕ Add new rule...

Days to keep: 10   Delete build record: ☑
                           Delete source label: ☑
                           Delete test results: ☑ ⓘ

🔒 Days to keep: 30   Delete build record: true
                           Delete source label: true
                           Delete test results: true

Figure 9-10. *Retention options configure how long your build is stored in Team Services*

Now that you have a build definition, you can use it to queue a new build. You can queue a new build directly from Web Access. When your build enters the queue, VS Team Services will launch a hosted build agent for you and start the build. While the build is running, you get a real-time log of the build output. This way, you can track progress and monitor for errors. After the build is finished, you can view the log files in your browser, or if they're too big, download them to your local machine to view them. Figure 9-11 shows how to queue a build.

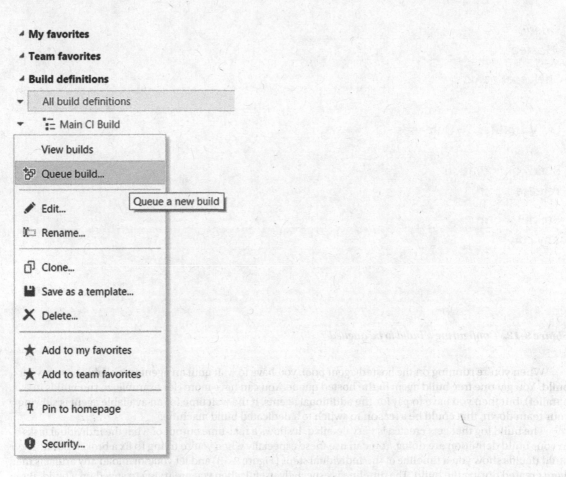

Figure 9-11. *Queue a new build*

When queuing a build manually, you configure the options shown in Figure 9-12. You select a queue and configure the variables and demands that are required. You can also select a shelveset if you want to run a build that uses the specific code in that shelveset.

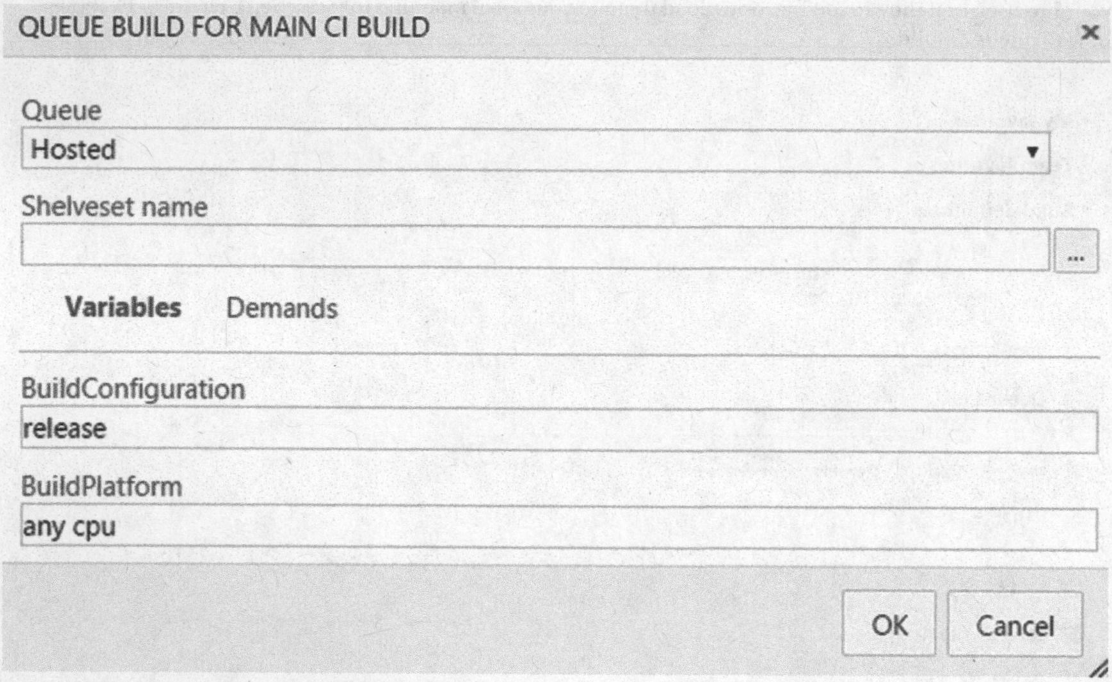

QUEUE BUILD FOR MAIN CI BUILD   ✕

Queue

Hosted   ▼

Shelveset name

_____   ...

Variables   Demands

BuildConfiguration
release

BuildPlatform
any cpu

OK   Cancel

Figure 9-12. *Configuring a build to be queued*

When you're running on the hosted agent pool, you have to wait until an agent is available to start your build. You get one free build agent in the hosted queue. You can have more (for example, to run builds in parallel), but then you have to pay for the additional agents. If the wait time for an available agent is slowing your team down, that could be a reason to switch to a dedicated build machine.

The build log that gets created is very detailed. It shows a real-time output of what the individual tasks in your build definition are doing. You can use these especially when you're trying to fix a broken build. The build details show you a timeline of the individual steps (Figure 9-13) and let you download any artifacts that were created during the build. The timeline is especially useful when you are trying to speed up a build. By checking the duration, you can easily see which step takes the most time and focus on speeding up the steps.

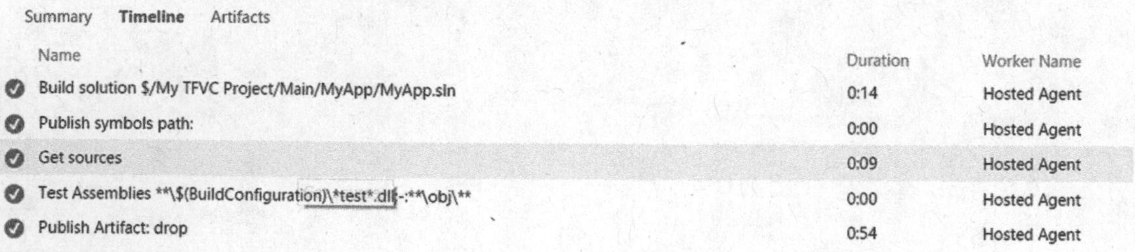

Summary   **Timeline**   Artifacts

Name	Duration	Worker Name
✔ Build solution $/My TFVC Project/Main/MyApp/MyApp.sln	0:14	Hosted Agent
✔ Publish symbols path:	0:00	Hosted Agent
✔ Get sources	0:09	Hosted Agent
✔ Test Assemblies **\$(BuildConfiguration)*test*.dll-:**\obj**	0:00	Hosted Agent
✔ Publish Artifact: drop	0:54	Hosted Agent

Figure 9-13. *The Timeline shows how long each individual step took in your build*

Installing and Configuring Build Agents

In the previous section, you looked at the default hosted build agent to run your builds. Microsoft maintains these hosted agents and they decide which software is available on the server. If you have specific requirements for the build server, be it security, installed software, or performance, you can run your own build servers and connect them to VS Team Services.

Build agents are grouped in pools. These *pools* are defined at the account level of your VS Team Services account. This means that the pools are available to all projects within your account. You can create as many pools as you want and each pool can contain a set of agents. An *agent* can exist in only one pool. The pools are linked to queues, which are defined at the collection level. A *queue* is what you select when you create a new build definition. This means that a new build is put in a queue. The queue is linked to a pool of agents and one of these agents will pick up your build. This allows you to put certain boundaries in place. By limiting the queues a project can use and placing your agents in separate pools, you control which build accesses which agent. Figure 9-14 visualizes this configuration.

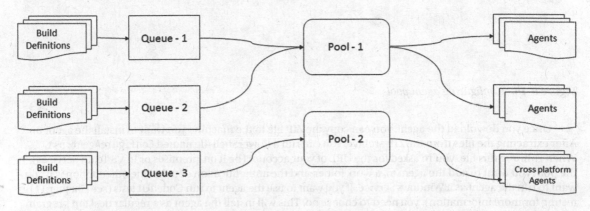

Figure 9-14. *The build infrastructure uses queues, pools, and agents*

In addition to the pools and queues, an agent is also selected based on his capabilities. System capabilities—such as environment variables and specific settings like the .NET Framework version or the installed editions of Visual Studio—are detected automatically. These capabilities are used to find the correct agent to run your build on. Capabilities are requested by the build definition based on the tasks you add. For example, adding the Visual Studio Build task requests a capability that Visual Studio is installed on the build machine. You can also add your own capabilities that are simple key/value pairs. This way, you can specify custom software that's installed on your build machine or other specific settings. By requesting those capabilities in your build definition, you make sure that your build runs on the correct agent.

If you want to install your own agent, you can navigate to the Account settings shown in Figure 9-15. Here you see the default pools that are available. You also see an option to download the agent.

Control panel

Control panel	Settings	Agent pools

New pool...   ↧ Download agent

Agents for pool Default

No agents are registered or you do not have permission to view the agents.

Agent pools permissions

▦ Agent Pool Administrators
▦ Agent Pool Service Accounts

Agent pools

▾ ▸ ⚙ Default
   ▸ ⚙ Hosted

Figure 9-15. *Configuring agent pools*

Once you download the agent, you can copy the ZIP file to the machine you want to install the agent on. After extracting the files from the ZIP archive, you can run a PowerShell file named ConfigureAgent.ps1. When running this file, you're asked for the URL of your account (be it on-premises or in VS Team Services), the pool you want to add the agent to, a work folder, and the authentication details. One other option is if you want to run the agent as a Windows Service. If you want to use the agent to run CodedUI tests (see Chapter 11 on testing for more information), you need to choose no. This will install the agent as a regular desktop program capable of launching and working with other programs. Figure 9-16 shows the configuration process when installing a new agent. Now that your agent is configured, it shows up under the pool you specified during configuration in VS Team Services. You can then start using this agent to run builds.

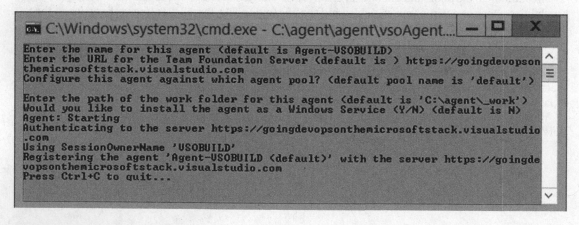

Figure 9-16. *Installing a new build agent*

Creating Custom Tasks

Out of the box, the build system ships with quite a lot of tasks. However, there will always be a time where you miss something. A simple extensibility point that you can use to run custom tasks is the task that executes a PowerShell script. You control the PowerShell script and you can let it do whatever you want. Figure 9-17 shows the PowerShell task and the configuration options. You can specify the script location and any arguments that you want to pass to the script. This allows for easy extensibility of your build system.

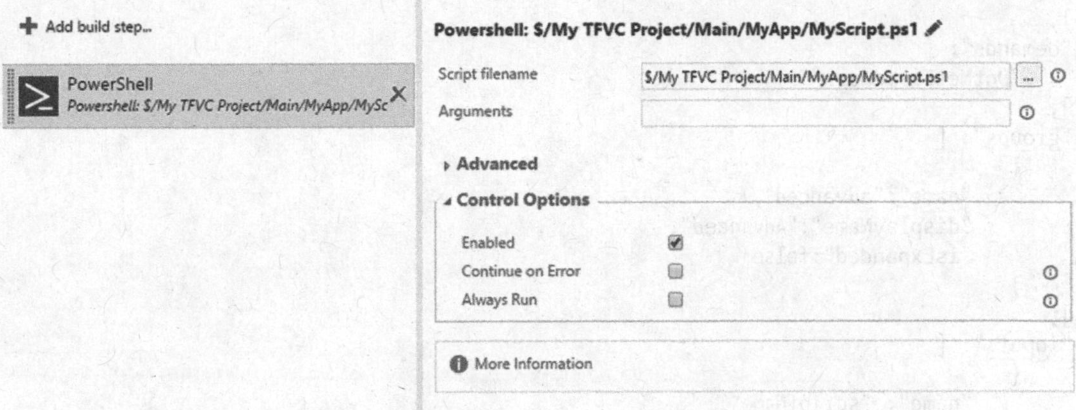

Figure 9-17. A PowerShell task

When passing arguments to your build task, be it PowerShell or another task, you have access to a number of variables inside the PowerShell script. These variables are created by the build system and contain information ranging from the current working directory to the account you're working on. You can find the complete list of variables at https://msdn.microsoft.com/en-us/Library/vs/alm/Build/scripts/variables.

If you find yourself using the same PowerShell script repeatedly, you can choose to encapsulate this script in a custom task. That way, you can just add your custom task with its own configuration options and you're done. All the build tasks are Open Source and you can inspect them to find out how they work. The basis of a task is the task.json file.

■ **Note**   You can find all the tasks at GitHub: https://github.com/Microsoft/vso-agent-tasks.

The following listing shows the task.json file for the PowerShell task from Figure 9-17.

```
{
    "id": "E213FF0F-5D5C-4791-802D-52EA3E7BE1F1",
    "name": "PowerShell",
    "friendlyName": "PowerShell",
    "description": "Run a PowerShell script",
    "helpMarkDown": "[More Information](http://go.microsoft.com/fwlink/?LinkID=613736)",
    "category": "Utility",
```

```json
    "visibility": [
                "Build",
                "Release"
                ],
    "author": "Microsoft Corporation",
    "version": {
        "Major": 1,
        "Minor": 0,
        "Patch": 5
    },
    "demands": [
        "DotNetFramework"
    ],
    "groups": [
        {
            "name":"advanced",
            "displayName":"Advanced",
            "isExpanded":false
        }
    ],
    "inputs": [
        {
            "name": "scriptName",
            "type": "filePath",
            "label": "Script filename",
            "defaultValue":"",
            "required":true,
            "helpMarkDown": "Path of the script to execute. Should be fully qualified path
            or relative to the default working directory."
        },
        {
            "name": "arguments",
            "type": "string",
            "label": "Arguments",
            "defaultValue":"",
            "required":false,
            "helpMarkDown": "Arguments passed to the PowerShell script. Either ordinal
            parameters or named parameters"
        },

        {
            "name": "workingFolder",
            "type": "filePath",
            "label": "Working folder",
            "defaultValue":"",
            "required":false,
            "helpMarkDown": "Current working directory when script is run. Defaults to the
            folder where the script is located.",
            "groupName":"advanced"
        }
    ],
```

```
"instanceNameFormat": "Powershell: $(scriptName)",
"execution": {
    "PowerShellExe": {
        "target": "$(scriptName)",
        "argumentFormat": "$(arguments)",
        "workingDirectory": "$(workingFolder)"
    }
}
}
```

This JSON file starts with metadata on the task such as the name, description, author, and version. The demands section requests the capabilities that need to be present on an agent. This allows the build system to match agents to build definitions and thus to individual tasks. The file then specifies the input parameters that users can supply through the interface. You see the script name, arguments, and working folder. The last part is execution. This node specifies what the task does when it runs on an agent. As you can see, the PowerShell task just executes PowerShell.exe and passes the input arguments to it.

More complex tasks use a similar JSON file but in the execution node call a PowerShell (or other type of script) that's included with the task. This script then does the actual work. For example, the VSBuild task has the following execution node:

```
"execution": {
    "PowerShell": {
        "target": "$(currentDirectory)\\VSBuild.ps1",
        "argumentFormat": "",
        "workingDirectory": "$(currentDirectory)"
    }
}
```

All it does is call VSBuild.ps1 and pass it the working directory. The VSBuild.ps1 script performs the actual work like NuGet restore, getting the sources, and running the build. The build system is cross-platform and JavaScript-based. You use gulp to compile the tasks and produce the output files. The gulp build step creates a tasks.loc.json file and an English strings file. You can use this to create localized versions of your task. You then package the output of the build and upload the package to VS Team Services.

■ **Note** Learning gulp is not required for creating build tasks. However, gulp is very powerful so learning it is definitely something you should look at. For more information on gulp, see http://gulpjs.com/.

To create a custom build task, you need a couple of tools. First, you need to have Node.js installed. This will install the Node Package Manager (npm) that you can then use to install the tools needed to create a build task: tfx-cli. As you can see in Figure 9-18, installing tfx-cli through npm downloads all the dependencies and makes sure you can run the package locally.

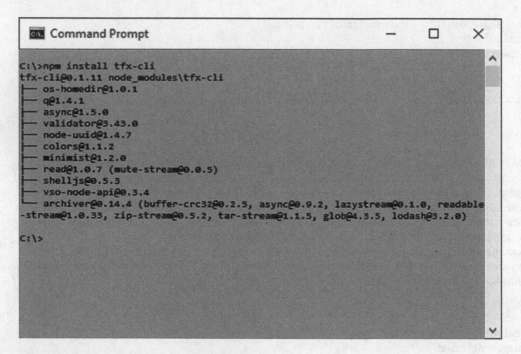

Figure 9-18. *You can use npm to install tfx-cli*

■ **Note**   Visual Studio looks at different places for your Node.js installation. If you get an error that states that you're not using the latest Node.js version, go to Options ➤ External Web Tools settings and make sure that your PATH environment variable is at the top.

Now that you have the tools, you can use the tfx command to create a skeleton of your new task. When running this command, you need to enter a value for the short task name, friendly name, description, and author, as shown in Figure 9-19. You execute the task by running:

```
tfx build tasks create
```

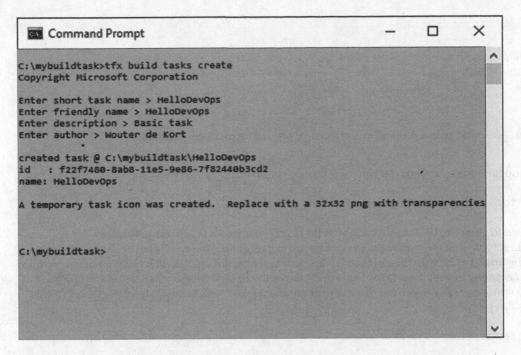

Figure 9-19. *Create a skeleton build task by running tfx build tasks create*

■ **Note** If you run into errors while creating the files for your task, make sure that you are running the correct version of Node.js. At the time of writing, the newest version of Node.js is not yet supported. Changing back to an older Node.js version fixes the problems. You can use a tool like nvm-windows (https://github.com/coreybutler/nvm-windows) to run multiple Node.js versions simultaneously.

This command creates a couple of files for you:

- icon.png: A sample icon for your extension
- sample.js: The JavaScript version of your task that can run cross platform
- sample.ps1: The PowerShell version of your task that can run on Windows
- task.json: The manifest file of your task that describes its settings and how to run it

You can the modify these files and create your task. Once finished, you need to upload the task to VS Team Services. To do this, you need a special token that you can use to authenticate from the command line. You can get such an access token by using the Web Access and navigating to your own profile properties. Figure 9-20 shows the Security tab of your profile. Here you can choose to create a new personal access token. You need to specify a name, a duration period, and the scope of your token. After creating the token, you see it only once. It's not stored in VS Team Services so you need to copy it and keep it safe.

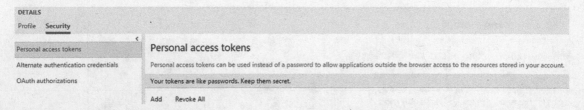

Figure 9-20. *You can create a personal access token for uploading your new build task*

After you have the token, you can run the following command to upload your task:

```
Tfx build tasks upload -task-path <path>
```

You need to enter the URL of your collection (`https://youraccount.visualstudio.com/defaultcollection`) and the personal access token you just received. (You won't see the characters appear. Just paste the token in and press Enter.) Figure 9-21 shows a successful upload. After this, you can verify your upload by navigating to your list of tasks. Figure 9-22 shows the Hello DevOps task I created and uploaded. If you want to remove a task you can run the following command. You can get this ID from the `task.json` file in your task directory.

```
tfx build tasks delete --id <id>
```

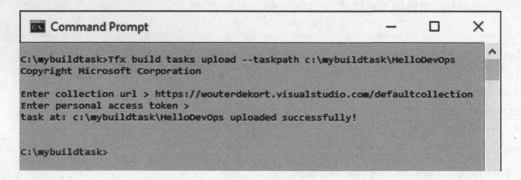

Figure 9-21. *Upload your build task to VS Team Services*

Figure 9-22. A newly uploaded task is visible in VS Team Services

Using SonarQube

As you've seen in the chapter on code quality, managing technical debt is important. Visual Studio offers some great features for this, such as Code Metrics, Code Analysis, and Unit Testing. These tools run on a developer's computer. When working on your continuous integration pipeline, an important step is to run these same quality checks at the central build server. This way, you start tracking your code quality on every check-in. You can then analyze trends and set minimum quality gates for allowing code to be checked in.

SonarQube is a product from SonarSource that helps you with this. Microsoft has partnered with SonarSource to make sure that VS Team Services and SonarQube work great together. There is now support for installing SonarQube on a Windows Server, analyzing C# code with the new Roslyn analyzers, and integrating this fully into the VS Team Services build system. To get a feeling of what SonarQube offers you, you can go to a free demo environment running at `http://nemo.sonarsource.org/`. Figure 9-23 shows you the dashboard of SonarQube Nemo.

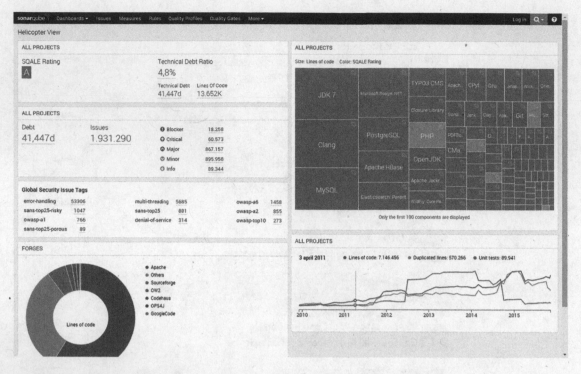

***Figure 9-23.** The SonarQube dashboard gives you a quick overview of the status of your projects*

To see more of what SonarQube can do, you can navigate to the analysis of the Roslyn compiler project by clicking on the icon in the top-right area of the Microsoft Roslyn .NET tile in the All Projects panel. See Figure 9-24.

ALL PROJECTS

Size: Lines of code   Color: SQALE Rating

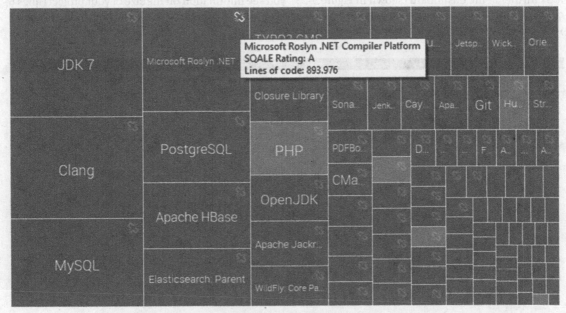

Figure 9-24. *The Roslyn project is also analyzed in this demo environment*

If you look at the resulting dashboard, you see something called a SQALE Rating. The SQALE method is implemented by SonarQube to evaluate the amount of technical debt you have in a project in an objective way. The result of this analysis is the amount of time it will take to fix all the technical debt in a project. These timing estimates are based on rules where each rule has a time attached to it that's based on the SQALE analysis model.

An SonarQube analysis of your project gives you a wealth of information. Not only do you see where the problem areas are, you also get immediate information on how much time it's going to cost you to fix your technical debt. This is a huge advantage to making decision on when to incur or pay technical debt. If you look further at the dashboard (shown in Figure 9-25), you see information on the size of your project (lines of code, number of files, classes, and functions). You also see information on code duplication, issues found in your code, and the amount of technical debt over time.

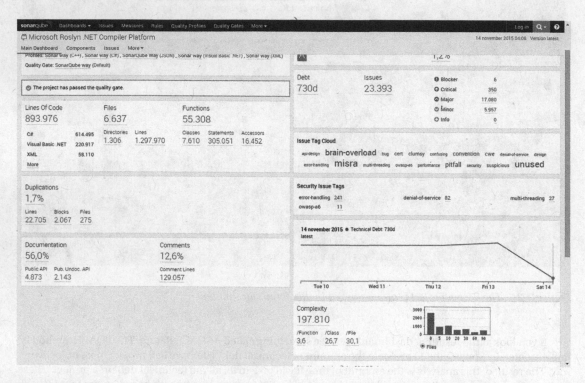

Figure 9-25. *The SonarQube dashboard for the Roslyn project shows a wealth of information*

The Issues list is what's most important. This is a complete list of issues detected by validating all the rules that SonarQube has installed. Issues have a severity and a full description of what the violation is all about and how to fix it. In every big project, there will be false positives so you can also mark items as something you won't fix. Figure 9-26 shows the Issues page for Roslyn.

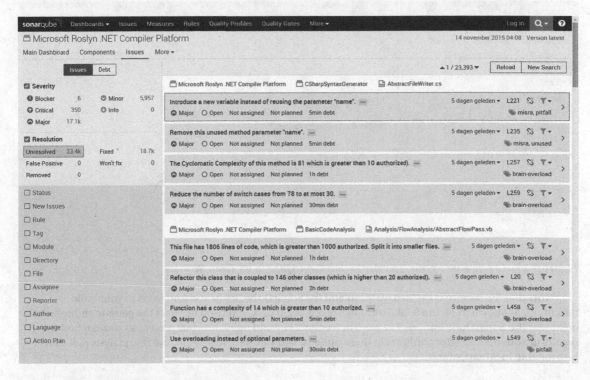

Figure 9-26. *The Issues page in SonarQube shows you all the technical debt in your code*

SonarQube integrates with .NET, Java, Objective-C, and Swift builds. Additional plugins are available from SonarSource. There is a free edition of SonarQube but it doesn't contain the SQALE rating. You can easily install SonarQube on a virtual machine that you create in Azure or that you host somewhere else. The ALM Rangers have a detailed installation guide that you can find on `http://aka.ms/vsartdsq`. After you have installed the server, you can start using it from within your builds.

When integrating with .NET builds, you use the SonarQube Runner for MSBuild. This runner needs to be started at the beginning of your build and stopped at the end. The Begin step contacts your SonarQube server and requests information on how you want to run your analyses (specifically, the quality profile and rulesets). When stopping the SonarQube runner, the results are published to SonarQube and you can view them in your dashboard.

The Begin step needs a couple of parameters:

- SonarQube endpoint: A configured service endpoint for your SonarQube server

- SonarQube project properties: The unique identifiers for the SonarQube project where you want to store the analysis results

The hosted agent can then run your build while communicating with your SonarQube installation for the analysis. The communication is done through a service that you define in VS Team Services, as shown in Figure 9-27. You create a new generic service with a name, endpoint, and credentials.

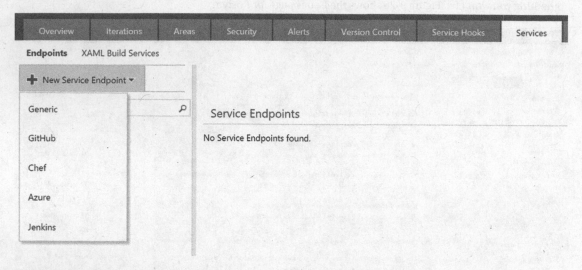

Figure 9-27. *Create a new generic service to link SonarQube to VS Team Services*

Now that the service is defined, you can add the SonarQube Begin and End steps to your build definition, as shown in Figure 9-28. To configure the Begin task, you need to select the generic endpoint you create for the SonarQube endpoint value. Then enter a key and name for your project so you can find the results in SonarQube. After configuring these options, you can start your build and the analysis details will be available in SonarQube.

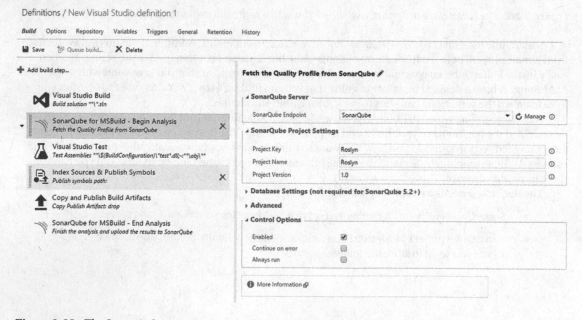

Figure 9-28. *The SonarQube steps for your build are available out of the box*

Summary

This chapter introduced you to the benefits of continuous integration. You learned how to create a continuous integration build running on VS Team Services. You've seen how easy it is to add your own build agents and create custom tasks that you can use in all your builds. You've also configured a SonarQube server and a build to use it. You've seen how easy it is to set up a build on VS Team Services that integrate with SonarQube. By using the correct plugins, you can now easily analyze your code. This helps you manage the quality of your code and avoid technical debt.

In the next chapter you're going to look at another exiting feature of VS Team Services: package management. You will see how you can use VS Team Services as a centralized repository to share code with others within your organization and how to keep track of the packages that are used.

CHAPTER 10

■ ■ ■

Creating and Sharing Packages

How many third-party packages do you regularly use in your projects? Packages like jQuery, Twitter Bootstrap, AngularJS, and NHibernate are very popular and come from a variety of third-party developers and companies. Microsoft is using more and more Open Source for its own projects. ASP.NET MVC, Web API, Roslyn, Entity Framework, and various extensions and utilities for Visual Studio Team Services are some of the projects that Microsoft hosts on GitHub. And of course you probably have some projects of your own that you reuse or share with other projects inside your organization. But how do you keep track of all these shared components? And what's the best way to be able to share code and use third-party components but still have an effective way of managing which packages you use? That's what this chapter is about. You will learn about the Package Management feature that VS Team Services offers. You'll create your own package and share it with your team using these features.

What Are Packages?

To get started, it's important to discuss what a package is and how packages are currently distributed. Take for example jQuery, a very popular library for web developers. If you go to http://jquery.com, you'll see a big Download jQuery button where you can apparently download two different versions (see Figure 10-1). If you then look at the list of packages you can download, you get to choose between a compressed, uncompressed, and map file for jQuery 1.x and 2.x. Do you know which one you need? If you have some experience using JavaScript libraries, you probably want all three! The compressed version is for production, the uncompressed version is for development, and the map file is used to map the compressed version to the uncompressed version.

Figure 10-1. *You can download jQuery from the jQuery web site*

© Wouter de Kort 2016

W. de Kort, *DevOps on the Microsoft Stack*, DOI 10.1007/978-1-4842-1446-6_10

If you download the uncompressed version, you get a single file named jquery-1-11.3 (for this version at least). Now if you want to use this JavaScript file, you'll probably copy it to the scripts folder of your web application and reference it from your HTML file to load it at runtime. An advantage of jQuery is that it doesn't have any dependencies. This makes it easy to download and include this single file. But imagine you want to use a package that does have dependencies. For example, bootstrap depends on jQuery being available. Downloading all these files separately and placing them in the correct location is doable, but you can see it breaking down quickly when your project becomes larger.

Fortunately, there is an easier way to work with packages. Package Manager allows you to install packages and their dependencies without manually going to their web site to download the files and put them in your project. This is best explained with an example. NuGet is a Package Manager that is frequently used in .NET projects to distribute packages. Say you want to add EntityFramework to a new project. If you open your empty project in Visual Studio, you can view the NuGet Package Manager by going to Tools ➤ NuGet Package Manager ➤ Manage NuGet Packages for Solution. This opens up the page shown in Figure 10-2.

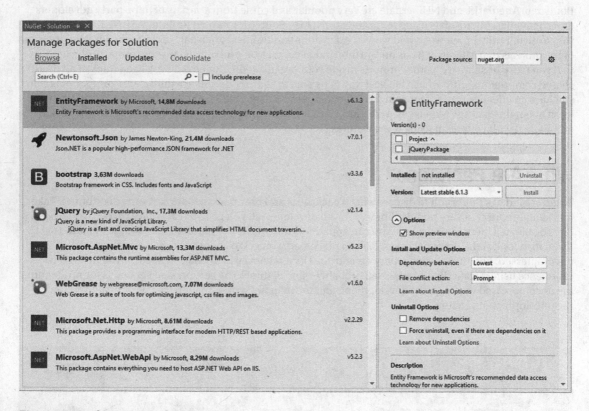

Figure 10-2. *The NuGet Package Manager in Visual Studio*

As you can see, the top package is EntityFramework. If you select your project and click on Install, the binaries for the EntityFramework are downloaded to your project and a configuration change is made. If you view this in Solution Explorer, you'll see that an App.config file (or Web.config if you're building a Web Project) is added with the following content:

```xml
<?xml version="1.0" encoding="utf-8"?>
<configuration>
  <configSections>
    <!-- For more information on Entity Framework configuration, visit http://go.microsoft.
    com/fwlink/?LinkID=237468 -->
    <section name="entityFramework" type="System.Data.Entity.Internal.ConfigFile.
    EntityFrameworkSection, EntityFramework, Version=6.0.0.0, Culture=neutral, PublicKeyToke
    n=b77a5c561934e089" requirePermission="false" />
  </configSections>
  <entityFramework>
    <defaultConnectionFactory type="System.Data.Entity.Infrastructure.
    LocalDbConnectionFactory, EntityFramework">
      <parameters>
        <parameter value="mssqllocaldb" />
      </parameters>
    </defaultConnectionFactory>
    <providers>
      <provider invariantName="System.Data.SqlClient" type="System.Data.Entity.SqlServer.
      SqlProviderServices, EntityFramework.SqlServer" />
    </providers>
  </entityFramework>
</configuration>
```

A new *configSection* is added that configures EntityFramework to use your localdb (a development version of SQL Server that comes installed with Visual Studio). Since the starting project was empty, the configuration file is added with the new content. If you already have a config file, NuGet is smart enough to append the new changes without completely overwriting your settings. In addition to the configuration settings, two references are also added: EntityFramework and EntityFramework.SqlServer. If you inspect the properties for these two references, you'll see that they point to a packages folder stored in your Solution folder. Figure 10-3 shows the file tree of the EntityFramework package that you installed. In the root, there is one file with a nupkg extension. This is the actual NuGet package that is copied to your solution. If you change the extension to .zip, you can open the file as a normal ZIP file. It contains the content, lib, and tools folders and the metadata files that describe the content and how the package can be installed. The content folder contains two transform files. These files contain the logic to update or create your *app* or *web config* file. The lib folder contains the required DLLs if you're targeting .NET 4.0 or .NET 4.5. Finally, the tools folder contains a set of scripts and executables that are used to first install EntityFramework and later work with it.

▲ content

    App.config.transform

    Web.config.transform

▲ lib

  ▲ net40

    EntityFramework.dll

    EntityFramework.xml

    EntityFramework.SqlServer.dll

    EntityFramework.SqlServer.xml

  ▲ net45

    EntityFramework.dll

    EntityFramework.xml

    EntityFramework.SqlServer.dll

    EntityFramework.SqlServer.xml

▲ tools

    about_EntityFramework.help.txt

    EntityFramework.psd1

    EntityFramework.psm1

    EntityFramework.PowerShell.dll

    EntityFramework.PowerShell.Utility.dll

    init.ps1

    install.ps1

    migrate.exe

  EntityFramework.6.1.3.nupkg

Figure 10-3. *The files copied to your solution when you install the EntityFramework package*

As you can see, a NuGet package is way more than just some DLLs that you downloaded manually. It's a set of instructions on how to add the files to your project and even configure it. But where does this package come from?

If you look back at Figure 10-2, you see a drop-down called Package Source in the upper-right corner. By default, you can select nuget.org or Microsoft and .NET. These package sources point to a URL. For example, nuget.org points to https://api.nuget.org/v3/index.json. If you open this URL in your browser, you'll get a JSON object that defines other URLs that can be used to query NuGet and that offer to autocomplete the search when you're searching for a package by name. Accessing https://api-v3search-0.nuget.org/query returns a large JSON object that contains information on the available packages. This is the data that's nicely displayed when you use the NuGet Package Manager in Visual Studio. How did these packages end up on NuGet? Somebody took the time to build the nupkg file that you saw in the EntityFramework example and then uploaded this package to NuGet. NuGet is public for everyone. You can freely create an account and then use your credentials to upload your own packages. These packages will then be available to you and others to consume.

If you don't want your packages to be freely available to everyone, you can use the Package Management features for VS Team Services to host your own feed. You can then add packages to this feed and only people with the correct URL and credentials will be able to connect to this feed and download the packages. This means that you can use Package Management to distribute shared components within your organization. You no longer have to store these on a network share or in a version control system. Instead, VS Team Services offers you a secure centralized location to manage packages.

This can also be used if you want to restrict the use of certain packages. Take for example software that's published with a so-called copyleft license. A strong copyleft license allows you to freely use some software and then requires that your product uses the same licensing and is published as Open Source. If you unknowingly use a component with a copyleft license, you are still required to Open Source your product. There are situations where that's no problem but if you would rather not Open Source your intellectual property, paying attention to which packages you use is pertinent. The same is true for security concerns. Open Source packages are not free of risk. Some packages have vulnerabilities that are sometimes fixed in later versions or that haven't been fixed yet. Restricting the use of packages to a good, known set eliminates these problems. Instead of using public package feeds like NuGet, you restrict your developers to use only an internal, managed feed. If a developer requires a new package that's not available on the internal feed, they can request this package to be added which allows you to validate the licensing structure and security of the new package.

Until now, we've looked at NuGet as a popular example of a Package Manager. But NuGet is not the only source of packages. For example, while creating a custom Build task in Chapter 9, you used something called *npm*: Node Package Manager. Node.js is a JavaScript runtime that can run your server-side JavaScript code. The Node.js package ecosystem allows you to install hundreds of thousands of packages. Where npm focuses on server-side frameworks, Bower is another Package Manager that focuses on client-side libraries. Bower, NPM, and NuGet are all used as Package Managers in ASP.NET MVC 5 applications. If you create a new ASP.NET MVC 5 application based on the Web Application template, you get a series of files, as shown in Figure 10-4 (make sure to select Show All Files). The references folder no longer contains references to individual DLLs but instead has references to NuGet packages. The bower.json file contains a list of all Bower packages you want to use, while package.json references all npm packages. These other Package Managers have similar capabilities as NuGet; they just have a different usage scenario.

Now that you know what a package is and which Package Managers are used in the .NET ecosystem, you can dive into the Package Management features that VS Team Services offers you.

■ **Note** Creating NuGet packages is outside the scope of this book. If you want to know how to create your own packages, you can look at http://docs.nuget.org/create for more information

---

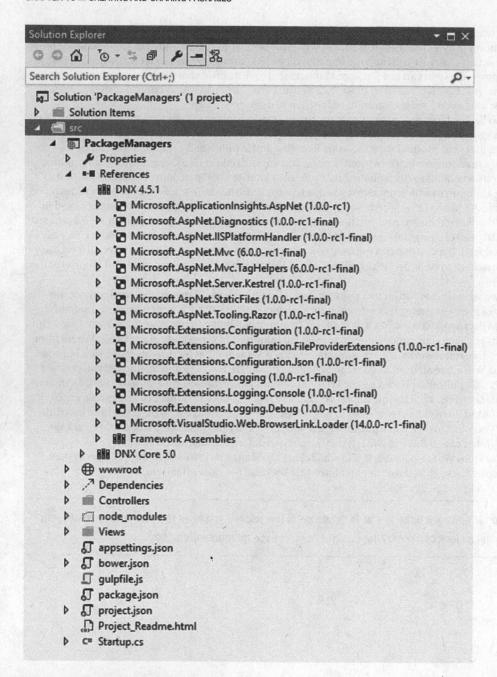

Figure 10-4. *An ASP.NET MVC application uses Package Management for all its references*

Package Management for Visual Studio Team Services

Microsoft delivers Package Management as an extension that you can install into your account. If you navigate to the marketplace at https://marketplace.visualstudio.com/#VSTS, you see the list of extensions available for VS Team Services. You can then navigate to Package Management (see Figure 10-5) and choose install to add the extension to your account.

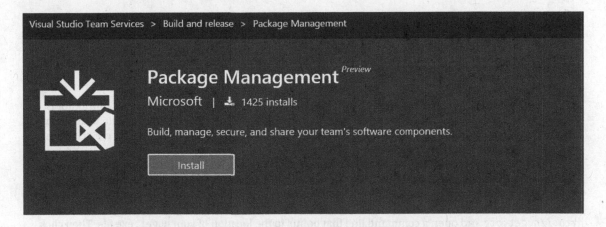

Visual Studio Team Services > Build and release > Package Management

Package Management *Preview*

Microsoft | ⬇ 1425 installs

Build, manage, secure, and share your team's software components.

Install

Package Management is currently supported in the US region only.

Share code with everyone in your organization by building and sharing packages of reusable components. The **Package Management** extension enables continuous delivery workflows by hosting your components/packages and making them available to your team, your builds, and your releases. If you're currently storing your NuGet packages on a NuGet server or on a file share that you manage yourself, you can move those packages to Team Services and enjoy deep integration with Team Build and Release Management. Package Management currently supports **NuGet** packages.

Figure 10-5. *You can find the Package Management extension at the marketplace*

Package Management is an extension that's installed at a global level for your whole account. You can access it by navigating to one of your team projects and selecting the Packages hub. As you can see in Figure 10-6, Package Management is based on feeds. A *feed* is a collection of packages that you can share with teams in your organization. You can set security permissions on the feed to allow people to read and contribute packages. To create a feed, just click on the green + icon shown in Figure 10-6. To create your feed, you enter a name, description, and permission settings.

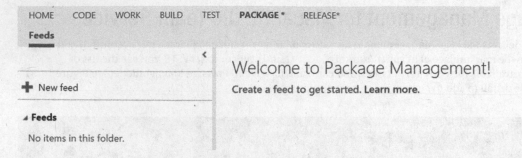

Figure 10-6. *Package Management is added as a hub to your account*

A feed has three access levels. As an Owner, you can rename and remove your feed. A Contributor is allowed to add packages to a feed and Readers can consume your feeds' packages. By default, your Team Build account is also added as a contributor. This allows you to automatically add packages created during your automatic builds and distribute these to your teams.

When you create a new feed, Package Management shows you a list of important steps for getting started using your new feed (see Figure 10-7). As an example, you can get the jQuery package from nuget. org and add it to a new feed named AllowedExternalPackages. When you switch the tool shown at the top of the page to NuGet 3.x, you see step-by-step instructions. First, you need to download nuget.exe from http://nuget.org and open a command line that points to the location of your nuget.exe file. Then click on Generate NuGet Credentials. This gives you a command that you can copy/paste into your command line. This command looks something like this:

```
nuget sources add -name "AllowedExternalPackages" -source https://<youraccount>.pkgs.
visualstudio.com/DefaultCollection/_packaging/AllowedExternalPackages/nuget/v3/index.json
-username "...." -password "..."
```

After running this command, the AllowedExternalPackages feed is added as package source to your global NuGet configuration. You can now test this by first downloading a package from NuGet.org and then uploading it to your own internal by running:

```
nuget install jQuery
nuget push jQuery.2.1.4\jQuery.2.1.4.nupkg -Source https://<youraccount>.pkgs.visualstudio.
com/DefaultCollection/_packaging/AllowedExternalPackages/nuget/v3/index.json -ApiKey VSTS
```

The first command downloads the jQuery package from NuGet.org. The jQuery package is installed in a subfolder of your current path. You then take the nupkg package of jQuery and add that to your own feed with the second command.

AllowedExternalPackages is empty. Connect and push a package!

First, pick your tool Visual Studio 2015 Update 1 RC ▾

Been here before? Jump right in.

NuGet package source URL

https://wouterdekort.pkgs.visualstudio.com/DefaultCollection/_packaging/AllowedExternalPackages/nuget/v3/index.json

You'll need credentials to authenticate. Follow the step-by-step instructions below, or learn more.

Or connect to this feed, step-by-step.

NuGet Package Manager (recommended) ▾   **Personal Access Tokens ▾**

Current releases of the NuGet Package Manager extension contain the VSTS Credential Provider, which enables Visual Studio to automatically acquire and refresh credentials as needed. Learn more.

1. Open Package Manager Settings (Tools > NuGet Package Manager)

2. Add this feed as an available package source

Figure 10-7. You can start by adding packages to your new, empty feed

If you now navigate to Package Management in VS Team Services, you see your new feed with the jQuery package, as shown in Figure 10-8. As you can see, not only the name of the package is listed but also a description and instructions on how to install the package. This information is contained in the jQuery nupkg package that you just pushed to your feed.

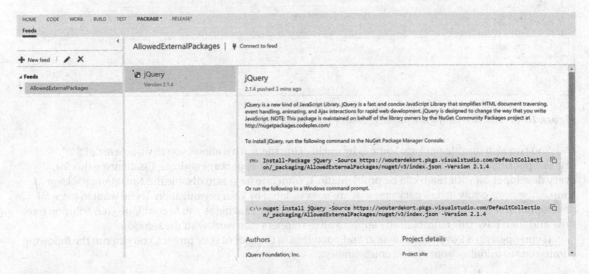

Figure 10-8. The jQuery package is now added to your AllowedExternalPackages feed

Most of the time you don't want to work with NuGet from the command line. Instead, you want to work with your feed from within Visual Studio. If you open Visual Studio and navigate to Tools ➤ Options ➤ NuGet Package Manager ➤ Package Sources, you can add new package sources, as shown in Figure 10-9. If you used the previous command-line command to add the package source, your new feed already shows up in the Package Sources window. If not, you can add it from this window by choosing the green + icon and entering the name and URL of your package source.

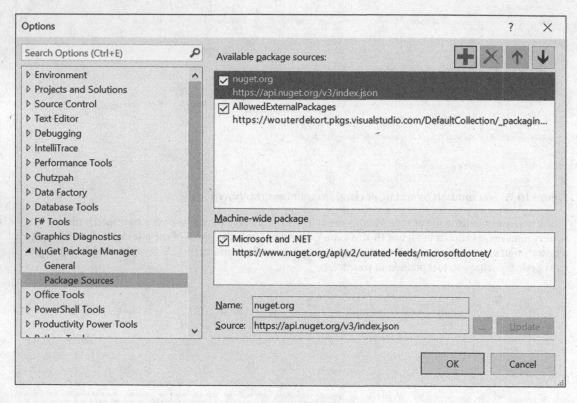

Figure 10-9. *You can configure package sources in Visual Studio*

You can also disable package sources by unchecking them. This allows you to disable NuGet. org as a package source and only use your own internal feeds as package sources. Configuring this for every developer on your team can be problematic. If someone forgets to disable the NuGet.org package source, they can easily install packages that are not validated by your organization. If you want to force all developers to use this configuration, there is a NuGet package that helps you to configure your solution one time and then have this automatically apply to all developers who work with the solution.

If you open up a PowerShell session and point that to the root of your project, you can run the following commands to initialize your NuGet configuration:

```
Invoke-WebRequest https://dist.nuget.org/win-x86-commandline/latest/nuget.exe -OutFile nuget.exe
.\nuget.exe install -OutputDirectory packages Microsoft.VisualStudio.Services.NuGet.Bootstrap
.\packages\Microsoft.VisualStudio.Services.NuGet.Bootstrap.*\tools\Bootstrap.ps1
rm .\NuGet.exe
```

The first command is an easy way to download NuGet.exe and store it in your working folder. The second command downloads the Microsoft.VisualStudio.Services.NuGet.Bootstrap package and stores this in the packages folder beneath your current location. As a part of this package, you get a bootstrap PowerShell script that initializes your environment. After running this file, you get a nuget.config file and an init PowerShell file. To initialize a developer's environment, you need to run the init PowerShell file. This downloads the latest NuGet tools and configures authentication. The nuget.config file contains the package sources you want to use in your project:

```xml
<?xml version="1.0" encoding="utf-8"?>
<configuration>
  <config>
    <clear />
    <add key="repositoryPath" value="packages" />
  </config>
  <packageSources>
    <!-- When <clear /> is present, previously defined sources are ignored -->
    <!-- Remove this tag or un-comment the nuget.org source below to restore packages from
    nuget.org -->
    <!-- For more info, see https://docs.nuget.org/consume/nuget-config-file -->
    <clear />
    <!-- Intentionally v2, as v3 doesn't yet support list which is used by Update-
    Environment.ps1 -->
    <add key="vss-package-management" value="https://www.myget.org/F/vss-package-management/
    api/v2" />
    <!-- <add key="nuget.org" value="https://api.nuget.org/v3/index.json" /> -->
  </packageSources>
  <activePackageSource>
    <add key="All" value="(Aggregate source)" />
  </activePackageSource>
</configuration>
```

You can add your own feeds hosted on VS Team Services (or at other locations) to this file by copying the line <add key="..." value="..." /> and setting the key to the name of your feed and value to the URL that you copy from Web Access. When running a VS Team Services build for a project that's configured this way, it's important that you add the NuGet Installer task (see Figure 10-10) to your build definition. You configure this task with the path to your nuget.config file. The NuGet Installer task then takes care of downloading your packages from the correct package sources.

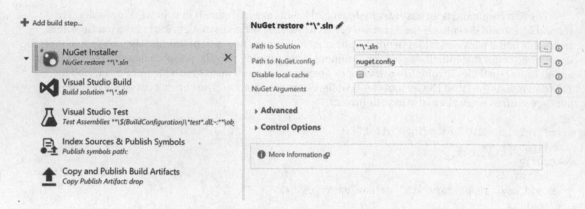

Figure 10-10. *The NuGet Installer task makes sure that your build knows where to find your packages*

An oft-used way to add packages to your feeds is from Team Build. This allows you to compile your project and automatically add packages to a feed. To help you with this, there are two packages available out of the box: NuGet Packager and NuGet Publisher (see Figure 10-11).

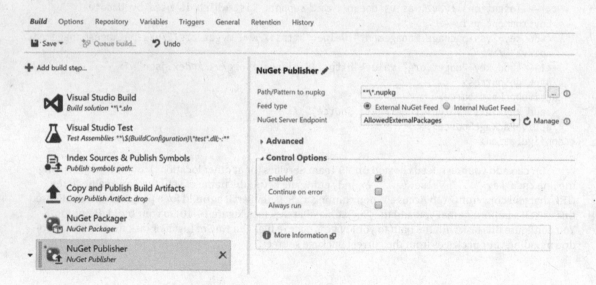

Figure 10-11. *Use the NuGet Packager and NuGet Publisher tasks to publish your packages*

The Packager task searches for all `nuspec` files in your repository and creates NuGet packages for these files. When you point the Publish task to an internal feed, you can just enter the URL of your feed to publish the packages to.

Currently Package Management only supports NuGet packages. In coming releases, Package Management will also support NPM and Maven. The overall idea will stay the same; you'll just be able to add feeds for other package types and use these in your projects.

Summary

Having an easy way to share third-party and internal components is an important step toward DevOps. VS Team Services Package Management helps you host your own feeds and use them in your projects. You can easily add existing NuGet packages or add your own packages to your feed. You can then bootstrap the developer environment to make sure that all your developers use these feeds. You can also integrate Package Management with your builds. You can install packages when running a build and create and publish packages to your feeds.

In the next chapter, you look at the extensive testing capabilities that are a part of VS Team Services.

PART IV

■ ■ ■

Test, Deploy, and Monitor

This part shows you how to integrate testers into your DevOps process. You'll learn the test features of Visual Studio Team Services and Microsoft Test Manager. You will also look at the possibilities of test automation. After this, you move on to Release Management to learn how you can set up automatic deployments. Finally, you'll learn about Application Insights and how that can help you monitor your application.

CHAPTER 11

■ ■ ■

Integrating Testers into DevOps

Testing is a crucial part of DevOps. When moving to continuous delivery, you don't want to optimize your process to ship bugs faster. You want to ship quality features as fast as possible. This means that in a DevOps process, there is no place for long stabilization phases where all development is halted. Instead testers work together with developers. This chapter details how testers can be the most effective by using the specific testing features of Visual Studio Team Services. You'll first look into *manual testing* and then explore the topic of *automated tests*.

Manual Testing Through Web Access

In addition to developers and other stakeholders, testers have a dedicated place in Web Access. The Test hub is the place where testers spend most of their time. In the Test hub, testers can create and run tests and track their overall progress. Figure 11-1 shows the Test hub for an empty project.

Figure 11-1. *The Test hub is a part of VS Team Services Web Access*

Tests are organized in a hierarchical structure. On the highest level, you work with a test plan. I often see teams creating a new test plan for every sprint they have (if they use Scrum). When going from sprint to sprint, they clone their test plan and then modify it to the needs of the new sprint. Other teams map their test plans to releases or another schema that makes sense for their project. Inside a test plan you have test suites. A *test suite* is a container for test cases. The individual *test cases* are where you specify what you want to test and what you expect. You can group these test cases in static suites, requirement-based suites, and query-based suites.

A static suite is just what the name says: a static collection of test cases that only changes when you change it. A requirement-based suite links your test cases to a specific item on your backlog. This relationship allows you to see which test cases are grouped under a product backlog item and use the results of the test cases to determine the state of the PBI. A query-based suite automatically contains all test cases that fulfill the query.

W. de Kort, *DevOps on the Microsoft Stack*, DOI 10.1007/978-1-4842-1446-6_11

Figure 11-2 shows the three types of suites grouped under a single plan. The first suite is a requirement-based suite pointing to a PBI with ID 261. The second one is a query-based suite that filters to test cases with a priority of 1 and the regression tests is a static suite. Static suites can also be used to group other suites.

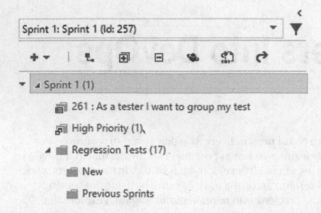

Figure 11-2. *A test plan groups test suites and a static test suite can group other suites*

■ **Note** The Test Case Explorer extension (`https://marketplace.visualstudio.com/items?itemName=ms-devlabs.TestCaseExplorer`) makes it easier to manage your test cases when you have a lot of them.

Creating this structure is easy. You use the green + icon to create new items. You first have to start with a test plan. You can then add child items and even create further nested items if you want. You then start adding test cases to the requirement-based or static test suites. Figure 11-3 shows a test case. Just as with other work items, you can set a title and state. The Assigned To field points to the person responsible for maintaining the test case. The tester assigned to execute the test case is assigned from within the suite that contains the test case. This separation allows you to make one person responsible for maintaining tests and others for actually running them. You can also add tags and have a discussion section. Unique for a test case are steps and tabs like Associated Automation.

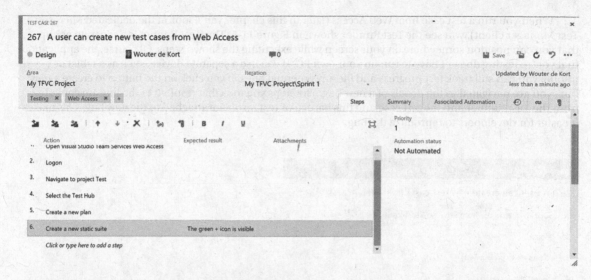

Figure 11-3. *A test case in VS Team Services Web Access*

The test steps are the heart of your test case. This is where you describe what a tester should do and which result to expect. For example, Figure 11-3 shows a list of steps that let users navigate to the Test hub, create a test plan and a static test suite and then check if the green + icon is available for the static suite to create test cases. If one of these steps fails or if the expected result fails, the tester marks the test case failed and files a bug. Running a test case can also be done through Web Access. Once you've designed a test case and set its status to Ready, you can choose the Run button from the toolbar in the Test hub, as shown in Figure 11-4.

Test suite: Regression Tests (Suite ID: 259)				No iteration dates
Tests Charts				Outcome All Tester All View List
+ New ▾ Add existing ✕ ⬚ ↻ ↪ ▶ Run ▾ 🗐 ⤴ ✓ ✕ ⊖ ⊘ Column options ▼ ⊟				
Outcome	ID	Title	Configurat...	Tester
● Active	267	A user can create new test cases from Web Access	Windows 8	Wouter de...

Figure 11-4. *The toolbar lets you run a test and change the test outcome*

When you run a test case from Web Access (later in this chapter you'll look at the dedicated Microsoft Test Manager client), you see the Test Runner shown in Figure 11-5. This Test Runner is a separate popup that you can position somewhere on your screen while executing the shown steps. Of course, the application that you're testing doesn't have to run on your own PC. If you use a separate device, such as a tablet or phone, you can still track test progress and file any potential bugs. If you click on the button to create a new bug, you are navigated to the details of a new bug. The steps you took that resulted to the bug are copied from the Test Runner and the test case and this particular test result are attached to the new bug. This makes it easier for developers to reproduce the bug.

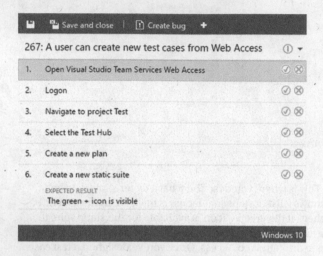

Figure 11-5. The Test Runner window

Another feature of test cases is the ability to add parameters. Let's say you're testing a registration form for your web application. Users need to enter their names and contact details and you want to make sure that your validation correctly reports invalid e-mail addresses or missing fields. You could create separate test cases that repeat the same series of steps but with different values for the specific fields but that's not very maintenance friendly. Instead you can add one single test case and then specify different rows of values that you want to run the test with. You create a parameter by using the @ sign in your test step. So the line Enter @firstname adds a new parameter named firstname. The parameters are listed as a grid at the bottom of your steps. Figure 11-6 shows an example of this.

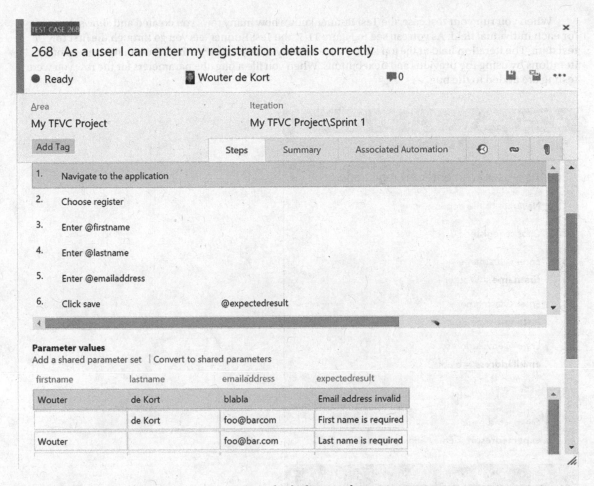

Figure 11-6. *You can use parameters to create multiple data sets for your test case*

When you run your test case, the Test Runner knows how many rows you created and shows the values for each individual field. As you can see in Figure 11-7, the Test Runner lets you go through the first row of test data. The iteration field at the top shows the test row you're currently using. You can navigate to other iterations by using the previous and next buttons. When you file a bug, the parameters for the row you were testing are added to the bug.

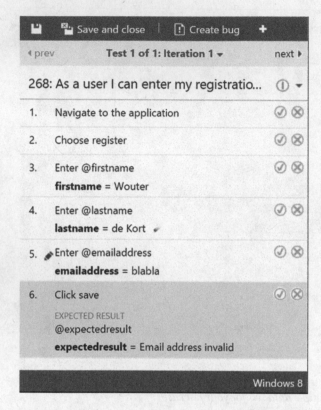

Figure 11-7. *You can run test cases with multiple sets of data*

As you can probably predict, when you have multiple test cases, some steps will be the same for each test case. For example, opening the browser, navigating to your application, and signing in are the required steps that every test case has to take. To help you with this, you can create shared steps. Shared steps are a named group of steps that you can then insert into other test cases. If you then make a change to your Shared step, it changes in all test cases that use the shared step. You can create and insert shared steps by using the toolbar above the steps area in a test case details, as shown in Figure 11-8. In addition to shared steps, you can also create shared parameters (see the bottom part of Figure 11-6). These parameter sets can then be edited through Web Access and shared between different test cases.

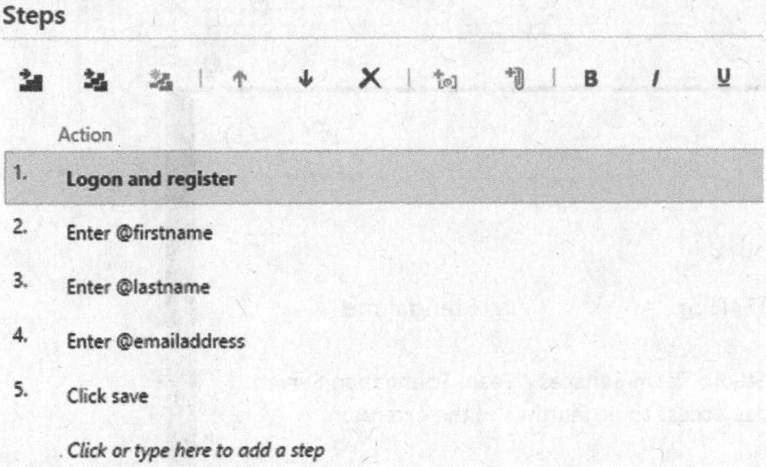

Steps

	Action
1.	**Logon and register**
2.	Enter @firstname
3.	Enter @lastname
4.	Enter @emailaddress
5.	Click save
	Click or type here to add a step

Figure 11-8. *The Steps toolbar allows you to create and insert shared steps*

You now know how to create and run test cases. You can file bugs linked to a test case and structure your cases in suites. If you take a step back, you might wonder if creating a bunch of test cases at the start of each new feature is the way to go. In a DevOps process where things are moving fast, you can't spend much time on creating test cases for every part of your application. Instead, you want to work with the application and pinpoint the areas that need to be covered with manual (or automated) tests. This is where exploratory testing comes in. When you're doing an exploratory testing session, you don't start with predefined test cases. Instead, you just go through the application while keeping track of the steps you've taken. If you find a problem, you can create a new bug and even create a test case so you make sure this defect doesn't return.

Exploratory testing sessions can be started from the Microsoft Test Manager client or from within your browser. For this to work, you install a special extension. The starting point for this is the Exploratory Testing extension in the Visual Studio Marketplace: `https://marketplace.visualstudio.com/items/ms.vss-exploratorytesting-web`. Clicking install takes you to the Chrome Web Store (other browser access is to come). After installing the extension, you can launch it in your browser (see Figure 11-9). You first need to decide if you want to connect to a VS Team Services account (or an on-premises Team Foundation Server) or run in standalone mode. Connected mode allows you to use the full capabilities of this extension.

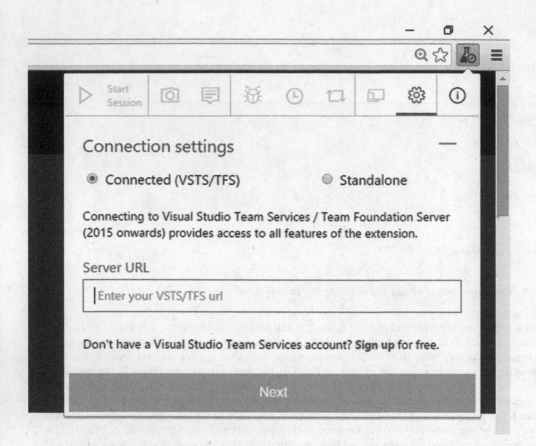

Figure 11-9. *You can do exploratory testing with the extension for Chrome*

Once connected, you start a new session. While the session is running, you add notes and screenshots. The timeline shows the steps you've taken (see Figure 11-10). You can then file a bug (or create a task) and the notes and screenshots are automatically added to the bug together with information on the system you're running, such as your browser, language, dimensions, operating system, and hardware capabilities. You can also select a product backlog item that you want to do some exploratory testing for. If you have a PBI selected, any items you create will be automatically linked to the PBI.

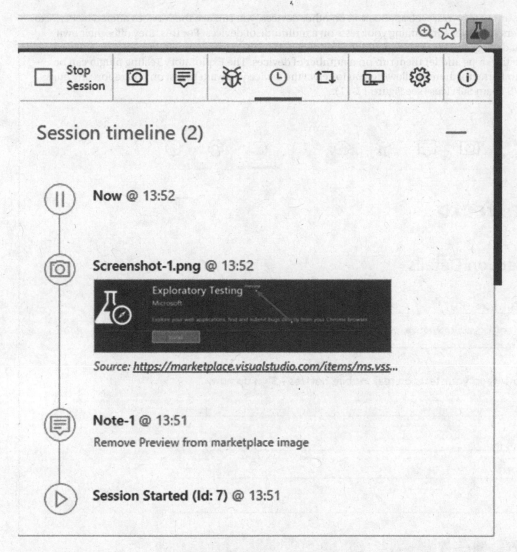

Figure 11-10. The timeline keeps track of the notes and screenshots you make during your session

If you want to test your web application on other devices, you can use the services offered by Perfecto. Perfecto offers solutions for running your tests on a multitude of devices. For this, they offer their own collection of devices but you can also attach your own devices. You can manually run tests on a device or automate the steps and let them run on a number of devices. The Exploratory Testing plugin can be connected to Perfecto, thereby allowing you to select the device you want to test on and report any bugs directly in VS Team Services (see Figure 11-11).

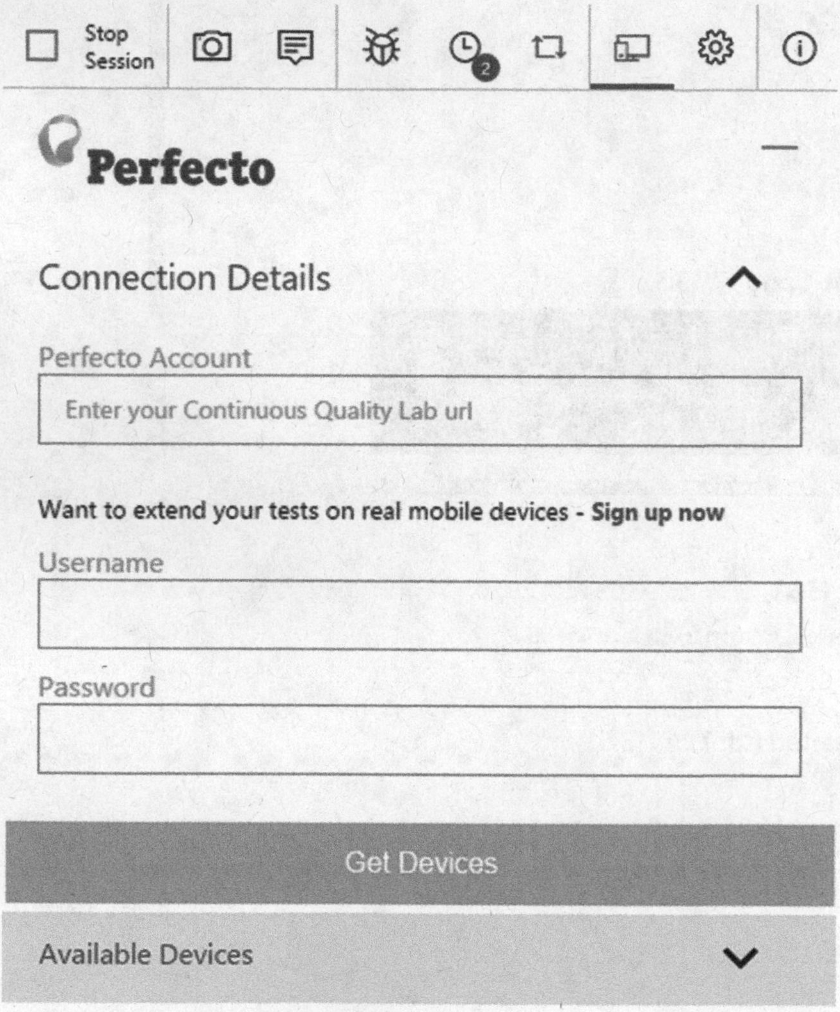

Figure 11-11. *You can connect to Perfecto if you want to test on multiple devices*

While running your tests, you of course want to track the progress of your different test suites and test cases. To help you with this, you can create charts. You can view these charts from the Test hub or you can pin them to your team's dashboard. By default, you get a pie chart that shows the outcome of the different test cases in your plan (see Figure 11-12). You can create charts that show you the status of your test cases (Design, Ready, or Closed), the number of cases assigned to individual testers, the status of tests in each of your suites, and numerous other scenarios (you can find more information on how to create charts in Chapter 6, which covers dashboards and reporting). You can also view a history of your test runs by going to the Runs tab in the Test hub. This allows you to easily see which tests need attention or have completed successfully.

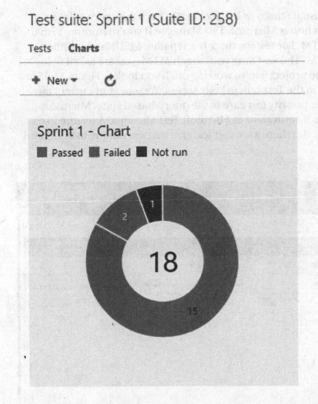

Figure 11-12. *You can create charts to track your test's status*

That concludes the Test hub in Web Access with regard to manual testing. In the part on automation, you'll return to the Web Access but first you're going to learn about Microsoft Test Manager.

■ **Note** The Microsoft ALM Rangers have released great testing guidance that you can find at `https://vsartestreleaseguide.codeplex.com/`. This guidance will help you plan and run your tests.

Microsoft Test Manager

Just as developers use their favorite IDE such as Visual Studio or Eclipse, testers have their own software too. The complement to manual testing in the Test hub is Microsoft Test Manager. If you're running Visual Studio Enterprise, you'll already have access to MTM. For testers, there is a separate MSDN subscription—Test Professional—and it gives them access to MTM. The first time you launch MTM, you are asked to log on to your VS Team Services account and select the project you're working on. If you look at Figure 11-13, a lot of things will look familiar to what you've seen in the Test hub in Web Access. You see your current test plan and the three test suites. You also see the high-priority test case in the query-based suite. Microsoft is working hard on expanding Web Access to make it equivalent to Microsoft Test Manager. A feature like shared parameters is only available in Web Access. But there are other features that are unique to MTM and that's what you're going to explore in this section.

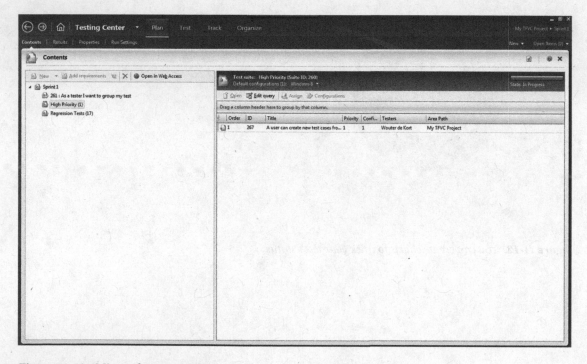

Figure 11-13. *Microsoft Test Manager is the standalone client for testers*

The biggest difference comes from the fact that you are using an actual desktop application that can interact with every program on your computer. This means that when you're running a test case, MTM can track what you're doing and record all your mouse clicks and keyboard keys. When running a test from Web Access, you get a browser popup that doesn't have this intricate relation with your operating system. This is ideal for running cross-platform tests or testing on devices like tablets and phones. When working with Windows, the MTM Test Runner has a lot more capabilities. If you look at Figure 11-14, you see the MTM Test Runner when it's first loaded. The Test Runner docks to the side of your screen and automatically positions other applications next to it. If you click Start Test, you see the test steps from your test case. Just as with the Web Test Runner, you can mark each test as passed (using Win+Ctrl+Q) or failed (using Win+Ctrl+W). You can add screenshots and create bugs just as you've seen with the Web Test Runner.

Figure 11-14. *The Test Runner launched from MTM*

Something that's not (yet) available in the Web Test Runner is the Create Action Recording checkbox shown in Figure 11-14. While you're running a test case, MTM keeps track of your actions. If you launch a program, type some text, or click somewhere with your mouse, this is all recorded. Once the action recording is finished, you can let MTM replay the actions for you. For example, you have a registration form with lots of fields. You have a test case with multiple rows of parameters. Running this test case manually means that you have to enter each parameter in the correct field and then validate the result.

With an action recording, you record the steps to open the registration page and you record one row of data being entered into the correct fields. MTM keeps track of all this and on your next run you can fast-forward steps. This is something you have to see in action to see how great this feature is. I want to encourage you to fire up MTM, create a simple test case that includes steps to navigate to `http://visualstudio.com`, enter a value in the search box, and then close the browser. After recording your actions, you see something like Figure 11-15.

Figure 11-15. *A test case with an action recording can automate manual steps*

You now have a Play button that you can use to automatically replay the recorded actions. On step 3, there is some manual validation required so that step will always pause and ask for your confirmation. This is something I sometimes see go wrong. Testers are often trained to have an expected result for every action they take. If they apply the same process to MTM test cases, you can't fast-forward because MTM will pause on every step to ask if the result is valid. Having expected results only on the steps that offer real value for your test allows you to make better use of action recordings. If steps 1 and 2 are used in multiple test cases, you can create a shared step for them and even a shared action recording. That way, you can always fast-forward the initial steps to get to the situation you actually want to work on. Using action recordings is still far away from actual automated tests, but it can help testers do their work more efficiently.

This recording technique can also be used when you're running exploratory testing sessions from MTM. If you go to the Test menu in MTM, you see the Do Exploratory Testing option. Figure 11-16 shows the repro steps for a bug created in an exploratory session. As you can see, MTM tracks all your steps. Mouse clicks even have a small screenshot attached! This makes it way easier to reproduce bugs. The tester doesn't have to worry about keeping track of how he ended up in a particular state. This is automatically recorded. When your exploratory testing session takes some time, you can edit the steps to make sure that you include only relevant ones by selecting Change Steps at the top of your Repro Steps list.

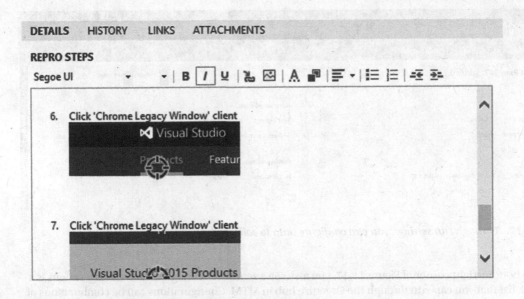

Figure 11-16. *The repro steps recorded for a new bug*

After you've finished configuring your new bug, you can create the bug or you can create a bug and a new test case so you can keep track of this bug and make sure it doesn't return. When you create a test case, you can use the Verify Bugs option in MTM to check if an open bug can be closed.

While running a test, data is collected. You've already seen how actions are recorded and how your system's information is added to a bug. You can record even more information using MTM. If you look at Figure 11-17, you see the Run Settings for your test plan. For manual and automated tests, there is a default plan. This plan captures action recordings and system information. You can also log code coverage, the systems event log, IntelliTrace, screen and voice recordings, test impact, and ASP.NET client proxy data.

Test Impact and IntelliTrace are my personal favorites. Using Test Impact, MTM can help you track what has changed between different versions of your application. MTM also tracks which test cases touch which part of your code base. If some code changes, MTM suggest that you run the test cases that touch that part of the code. This doesn't dismiss you of running a good set of regression tests but it definitely helps you run the highest priority tests first. IntelliTrace is like TiVo for your code. When collecting IntelliTrace data, MTM records exactly what happens in your code—which methods are called, which parameters are used, and what is returned from external calls (SQL queries, for example). You can then use the IntelliTrace log file to debug an issue after the fact. If you're running an application with multiple tiers (such as a client, database, and web server), it makes sense to track event log and IntelliTrace data on these additional machines.

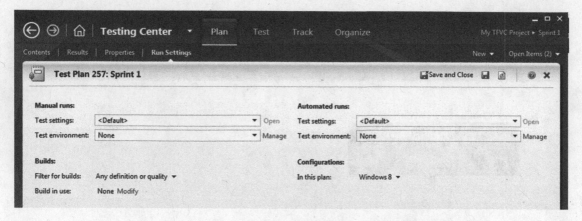

Figure 11-17. *Through run settings, you can configure data to collect while running your test*

In the bottom-right corner of Figure 11-17, you also see a setting for configurations. Configurations is a simple pick list that you can edit through the Organize hub in MTM. Configurations can be combinations of settings like OS and browser version. When you select multiple configurations for your test cases, MTM will automatically let you run the test case for each configuration.

I like Microsoft Test Manager a lot. However, I also know that a lot of organizations aren't aware of the possibilities of MTM. If you're in such an organization, try to experiment with MTM, especially the data recording and action recording features. See if these add value and then be an evangelist in your own organization! In the next part, you will look at different forms of test automation.

Automated Testing

Automated testing is the key to a successful DevOps implementation. Having operations worry about all the changes coming down from developers is natural. Doing something about those feelings is mandatory. And not only operations will be happy, your stakeholders will be too. Automated testing comes in many flavors. In Chapter 8 on managing technical debt, you looked at unit testing and the differences among unit tests, integration tests, and scenario testing. Unit and integration tests are written in code and exercise parts of your application but don't touch the user interface. Scenario tests do touch the user interface and that's what you're going to focus on next.

Visual Studio offers a framework for creating UI tests called *Coded UI*. Coded UI allows you to test client and web applications. You can create a Coded UI test by recording the steps you want to take and then generating code that performs these steps. You can also add assertions that check the UI and validate the result. For example, you can have a simple calculator that adds two numbers. You want to enter the two numbers, click on the Add button, and then verify the result of the addition is correct.

To use Coded UI tests, you need to have Visual Studio Enterprise. You can then create a Coded UI test project and use that to record and modify tests. When creating a new project, you're asked if you want to start by recording a new test or if you want to use an existing action recording (see Figure 11-18). Here you see the link between manual and automated testing. If a tester has a good action recording of a manual test, he can sit down with a developer and then fully automate the test.

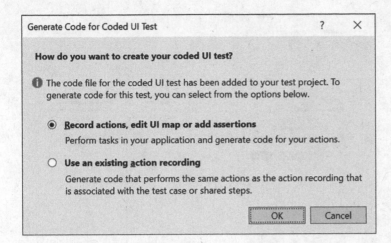

Figure 11-18. *You can create new Coded UI tests by recording your steps or by using an action recording that was made earlier*

If you choose to create a new test from a new recording, the Coded UI Test Builder is loaded (see Figure 11-19). This toolbar allows you to start and pause recording, inspect your steps, and generate code for your test. You can also add a control to the UI map. The UI map is the structure that Coded UI uses to organize the controls you interact with during your test. For example, text fields, buttons, checkboxes, and other controls are added to the UI map. If you want, you can manually add controls to verify values or other settings.

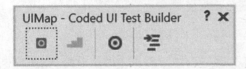

Figure 11-19. *The Coded UI Test Builder helps you record your tests*

Figure 11-20 shows the UI map for a simple Coded UI test recording. The UI map contains steps to open a browser, go to http://visualstudio.com, click on the Marketplace link, and then open the GitHub for Visual Studio Extension. These steps are listed in the left panel.

In the right panel, you see the UI control map. These are the controls that I interacted with while recording this test. The properties of the last control, UIGitHubExtensionforViImage, are shown. Coded UI identifies controls by looking for their IDs and a combination of search properties and window titles. For example, the window title collection contains the Visual Studio Marketplace value since that's the title of the browser when searching for the GitHub logo. Search properties states that Coded UI should look for an image. You can add properties and other search values if those are required to successfully find your control.

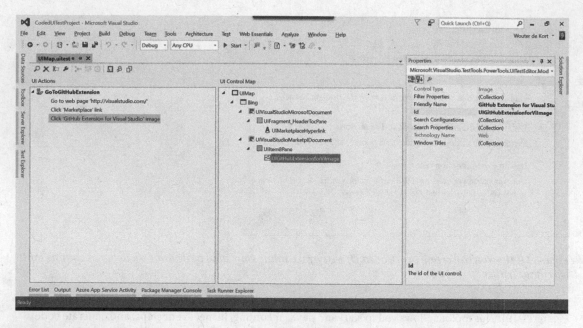

Figure 11-20. *The UI map shows the structure of the controls that are used in your test*

The generated code for this test is located in the code-behind file of your UI map. The code that starts your test is very simple:

```
[TestMethod]
public void CodedUITestMethod1()
{
    this.UIMap.GoToGitHubExtension();
}
```

If you want to modify the GoToGitHubExtension method, you can right-click it in the UI map shown in Figure 11-19 and choose to move the code to a file named UIMap.cs. You can then freely modify the code but you can't update it anymore by using the Coded UI Test Builder. The code that's generated looks like this:

```
public void GoToGitHubExtension()
{
    #region Variable Declarations
    BrowserWindow bing = this.Bing;
    HtmlHyperlink uIMarketplaceHyperlink = this.Bing.UIVisualStudioMicrosofDocument
                                    .UIFragment_HeaderTocPane.UIMarketplaceHyperlink;
    HtmlImage uIGitHubExtensionforViImage = this.Bing.UIVisualStudioMarketplDocument
                                    .UIItem8Pane.UIGitHubExtensionforViImage;
    #endregion

    // Go to web page 'http://visualstudio.com/'
    bing.NavigateToUrl(new System.Uri(this.GoToGitHubExtensionParams.BingUrl));
```

```
// Click 'Marketplace' link
Mouse.Click(uIMarketplaceHyperlink, new Point(65, 32));

// Click 'GitHub Extension for Visual Studio' image
Mouse.Click(uIGitHubExtensionforViImage, new Point(57, 105));
}
```

You can see how in the first region the UI map is used to access the required controls. Then the browser is pointed to the correct URL and mouse clicks are simulated to navigate to the correct locations. Coded UI tests are not meant for use in the parts of your application where the UI is still drastically changing. As you can understand, this code can become quite brittle and hard to maintain. That doesn't mean however, you can't use more maintainable code for your Coded UI tests. If you look at http://visualstudio.com, what do you see? Do you see divs, hyperlinks, paragraphs, and input controls? Or do you see an option to sign in, a menu with navigation choices, and blocks of information with other options? Building your Coded UI test on the level of individual HTML (or WPF) elements is bound to fail. If you have multiple tests that first need to sign in, you can have something like this:

```
browser.NavigateToUrl(new Uri(Params.VisualStudioUrl));
Mouse.Click(signinLink, new Point(65, 32));
// Enter username
// Enter password
// Click on Sign In
```

But what if the Sign In button moves to another location? What if you decide to use two-factor authentication? Do you have these couple of lines spread through all your tests or have you encapsulated them in a simple Signin method? The quality of your test code should be as good as your production code. After recording, refactor your Coded UI tests to a level where you abstract the individual controls and make sure that your tests can be well maintained. A lot of teams fail at test automation because they don't pay enough attention to their test code. When used correctly, automated testing can be very powerful.

■ **Note**   When testing web applications, you can also use Selenium (http://www.seleniumhq.org/) instead of Coded UI. Selenium is a very powerful tool for testing browser applications and something you should look into when you're building complex web applications.

Another important part of automated testing is performance and load testing. Performance testing has to do with how fast your application is. Load testing helps you determine how many users can use your application simultaneously. You can get started very easily by navigating to the root of your VS Team Services project and going to the Load Test hub (Figure 11-21).

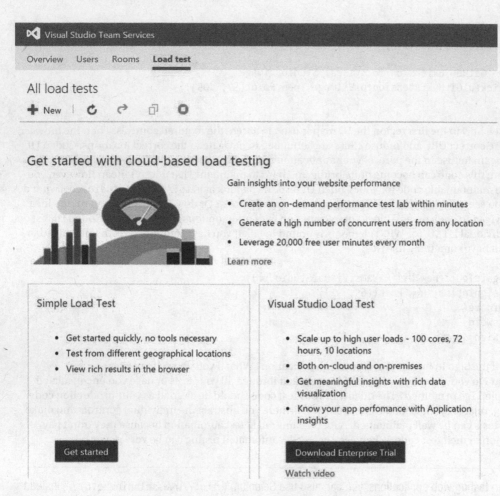

Figure 11-21. *You can run load tests directly from VS Team Services*

A simple load test requires you to configure the options that you see in Figure 11-22. First, you specify the URL of your application being tested. Then you enter a name and select a location. Location is one of the Azure datacenters that is going to be used to simulate the user load on your URL. If you want to make sure that your application is performing well, you probably want to select a datacenter near your users. If you have a worldwide service, you can create multiple load tests and let them run from different datacenters.

In the bottom part of the window, you configure what your load test is going to do. You select the number of users and the time your test should run. These two values form your virtual user minutes and that's what you get charged for when using load testing on VS Team Services. Fortunately, you get 20,000 virtual user minutes for free to get you started. You also configure the think time. When you have 100 users looking at your web application, they won't be constantly active. A user reads something, moves her mouse, and types something while working with your web page. This takes some time and you can configure the delay between certain actions by specifying a think time. You can also choose if your users use Google Chrome or Internet Explorer and the percentages of each by configuring the browser distribution.

Home page (URL)	http://mywebsite.com
	If your app is not publicly available on the Internet, learn more about alternative solutions
Test name	My Load Test
Load location	West Europe (Netherlands) ▾

Test settings

User load	Run duration	Think-time	Browser distribution
Maximum virtual users	The length of time for which the load test runs	Delay between consecutive requests	Percentage of users for different browsers
100 users ▾	5 minutes ▾	5 seconds ▾	IE-60%, Chrome-40% ▾

Run Test →

Figure 11-22. *A simple load test can be created in VS Team Services*

While running your load test, you see a nice graph displaying your results. Figure 11-23 shows an example graph that uses the settings from Figure 11-22. You see that while running for the first 1:45 minutes, no errors were reported. The user load is constant at 100 users and the average request time went to 0 while the requests per second went up to 40. When the test finishes, you see a summary of your average response time, the total requests you made, and the number of errors.

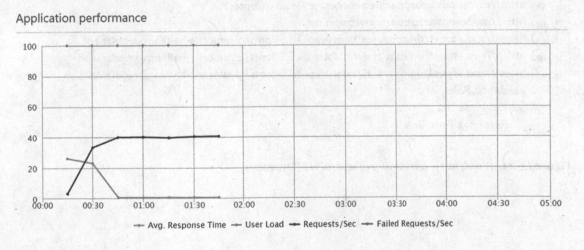

Application performance

— Avg. Response Time — User Load — Requests/Sec — Failed Requests/Sec

Figure 11-23. *While running your load test, you see a real-time graph with the results*

You might wonder how realistic this is. You're now only hitting the root URL of your web application. Things like caching are influencing the results, especially since you are using only one agent and one IP address to run the tests from. A more realistic scenario would hit multiple pages of your web site and simulate a real user. But if you don't have any load testing in place, this is a good place to start. To create more complex load tests, you use Visual Studio Enterprise to create cloud-based load tests. Without using the cloud, this would require you to set up machines that can generate the load with something like Visual Studio Lab Management.

With cloud-based load testing, all this setup is done by VS Team Services. All you have to do is record a web test and send it to the cloud. To get started, you need to create a web performance and load test project. A performance test is different from a Coded UI test. Where a Coded UI test actually opens the browser and interacts with different elements, a load test only captures the web traffic between your client and the web application. This traffic is then scaled to multiple concurrent users and executed against your web application to test its performance.

You start with creating a web performance and load test project. By default, a single empty web test is added. If you look at Figure 11-24 you see a sample web test. The web test lists a series of request to a sample web site that I host on Azure. This is a simple MVC 5 web app without any modifications. The first request is to the homepage. This results in three additional requests that load three fonts. Then a request to the About page and finally to the Contact page. Then I navigated back to the home page, resulting in the last four requests.

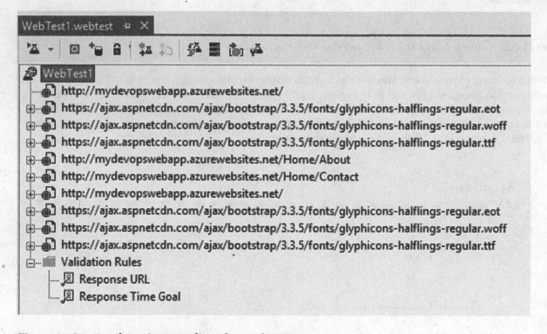

Figure 11-24. *A web test is a recording of several HTTP requests*

It's easiest to create a web test by using the Add Recording button in the toolbar. This launches Internet Explorer with the Microsoft Web Test Recorder Helper plugin. This recorder tracks all the HTTP traffic from your browser. In Figure 11-25, you see the Web Test Recorder active. Navigating to http://visualstudio.com generates the first request. The other requests run when loading the visualstudio.com home page. You can pause the recording if you want to exclude certain steps from your recording. You can also add comments that show up in your recording and of course you can stop the recording. Once it's finished, Visual Studio parses your requests and looks for any dynamic parameters. Dynamic parameters are parameters that are regenerated each time a user runs your application. This can be a session ID, values stored in cookies, hidden fields such as ASP.NET view state for ASP.NET Web Forms applications, and query string or post parameters. All this information is extracted by Visual Studio and added as an extraction rule to your web test. This rule configures how Visual Studio gets the value of the parameter and what you want to do with it. You can also create plugins to interact with your test. You could for example filter out all image requests, modify requests and response data, etc. You can easily run the web test locally and see if it executes the correct requests.

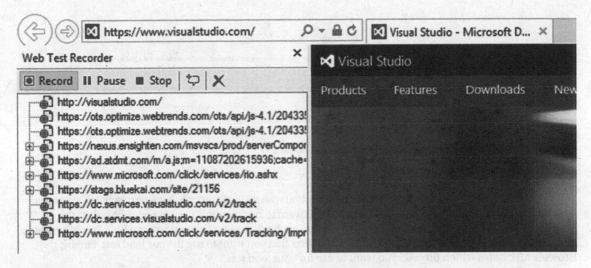

Figure 11-25. *The Web Test Recorder is an Internet Explorer add-on*

Once you have a functioning web test, you can create a load test. A load test takes one or multiple web tests and uses your local PC or VS Team Services to run a load test. Figure 11-26 shows the wizard for creating a new load test. When using VS Team Services, you first need to specify your VS Team Services account. This account is then used for the load test and billed for the virtual user minutes you generate. You then enter the location where you want to run the load test. For example, if I'm testing a Dutch web site for the Netherlands, I would use the West Europe location since that's located in Amsterdam, the Netherlands. Run settings specify how long your test should run and if there should be a warm up period. It could be that the first requests to a web site take longer because the application needs to launch and the cache needs to be built. You can exclude these results from your load test by choosing a warm up period. Scenario specifies what type of test you want to run. Do you want a constant user load (stress testing) or do you want to increase the user count every number of seconds?

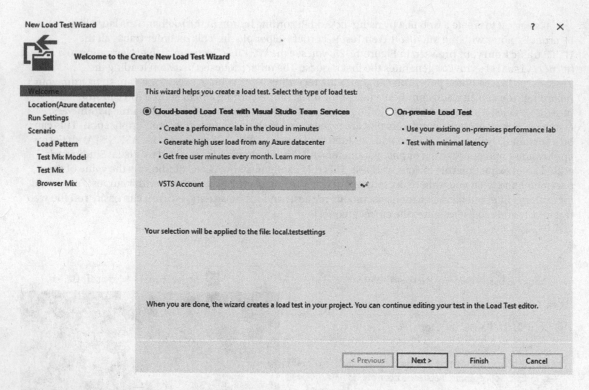

Figure 11-26. *You can create a load test in Visual Studio*

Test Mix is about the distribution of your individual web tests. If you only have one web test, this option isn't very exciting. If you have multiple tests and you want to run tests in a certain order, based on the amount or speed of users or each test proportional to each other, you can specify that with a Test Mix model. Of course you also need to add the individual web tests that you want to use in your load test. Finally, the Browser Mix states which browser you want to use for your load test.

Once finished, you can start your load test. You can use your own PC to generate the load but of course this has its limits. It is however a useful way to validate your load test settings. Once you have a correct load test in place, you can run it with VS Team Services. This gives you a result like the one in Figure 11-27. Here you see a graph of the performance of your application. You can also view detailed data on errors or validation violations that happened during your load test. You can also specify in your load test configuration which properties you want to track—for example, the number of pages/second your application returns or the CPU load that your agents have while generating the load. All this data can be used to create validation rules and monitor the output of your load test.

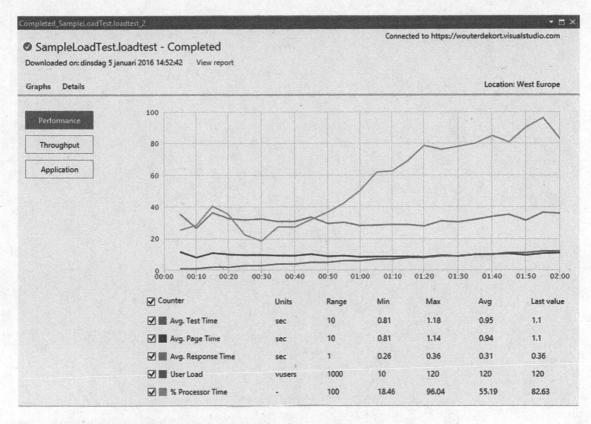

Figure 11-27. *A graph displaying the results of a load test*

Summary

Testing is a huge subject. The goal of this chapter was not to introduce you to every little detail of testing that's possible. Instead, I hope you've seen things you didn't yet know existed and that sparked your interest. You've seen how you can start with manual testing by using VS Team Services Web Access. You can create test plans, suites, and cases. You can insert steps and results and use parameters and shared steps to create a maintainable set of tests. You've seen how exploratory testing can help you when finding weaknesses in an application without much upfront work.

You also explored the possibilities of Microsoft Test Manager: the desktop client for testers. This client lets you collect multiple data sources ranging from audio/video to IntelliTrace data while running your tests. You've also seen how the exploratory testing features of MTM help you track your steps and generate new test cases and bug reports.

Finally, you looked at automated testing. You've seen how Coded UI tests help you create system tests that go through your application's user interface. You've also seen how you can test the performance of web applications by using web and load tests together with VS Team Services.

One thing that this chapter didn't cover is how to run all these tests as an automated step in your release process. The next chapter is all about creating such an automated release pipeline based on VS Release Management. You'll learn how to set up continuous deployment and run the automated tests that you created as a part of your process.

CHAPTER 12

■ ■ ■

Implementing Continuous Delivery with Release Management

Automating deployments is often one of the first steps teams work on when moving to a DevOps process. And that's not without reason. Automating deployments is a huge step. An automated deployment process helps your team reduce errors and lets your team work on important stuff. This chapter shows you how to implement automatic deployments by using Release Management. You'll see what Release Management is and how it works and look at the possibilities for deploying different application types.

Understanding the Deployment Pipeline

I've seen companies deploy in all kinds of ways. Just as there still are companies that don't use version control, there are companies that do their deployments fully manually. The prerequisites for good deployments are version control and a continuous integration build. The build is the start of what's called your delivery pipeline. The *delivery pipeline* is an automated set of steps that takes your code from version control all the way to production. Some of these steps are about the actual deployment but also about running automated tests and making sure that the deployed code is working.

All too often, a developer starts a release by compiling the code locally on her development machine and then copying the output to a server. Your deployment pipeline shouldn't start at the developer's PC. Instead, you want to start at your continuous integration server. That's a location you can control and manage. If you can create a predictable output from your build server, you can then use that output as the start of your deployments. This takes away any uncertainty of a developer following manual steps on her machine to create your deployment package.

After the build server has produced a package, you can take this package through additional steps. This can be deployments to different environments, running automated and manual tests, data migration, and any other step that's required to ensure the quality of your release and for you to be confident to release it to stakeholders.

One of the most important things to understand about a delivery pipeline: built once and only once. The build server outputs the artifacts that you want to deploy. These form the start of your pipeline. Every stage in your pipeline takes these artifacts, configures them, and deploys them to your environment. This guarantees that your artifacts are consistent throughout all stages. This also means that whenever you want to deploy a change, you go through all the stages of your delivery pipeline. You never skip steps; you never deploy directly to production. This means that your deployment is tested several times before it hits production.

W. de Kort, *DevOps on the Microsoft Stack*, DOI 10.1007/978-1-4842-1446-6_12

In addition to the steps in your delivery pipeline, you also want orchestration around your process. You need to establish who's responsible for each stage, which steps are automated, and which require manual approval. You also need configuration management to store the different configuration options for each environment, such as connection strings or other settings, and make sure that the correct settings are applied during each stage.

To build an effective deployment pipeline, you need collaboration between development and operations: DevOps. This is a huge cultural shift. Traditionally, these departments have been silos with very different objectives. Operations is responsible for keeping the applications stable. Each change is a risk. Developers on the other hand are paid to release new features. They are constantly under pressure to keep deadlines. Often operation doesn't trust development because they deliver unstable code that's hard to install and monitor. Developers find that operations is slow and only hinders them in doing all the real work.

Now try getting these two groups to work together. This is a hard problem to solve. Tooling is not the Holy Grail. However, getting both operations and development interested in a single tool is a huge win. DevOps is about breaking down the silos between different departments. Try to get someone from operations interested with keywords like auditability, traceability, and—above all—stability. You need to understand each other's problems and start working as a team.

Having operations fix live production issues in the middle of the night while you tell them "it works on my machine" is not going to make you popular. Work as a team. If you need to get management on board, tell them the advantages of continuous delivery. Customer satisfaction is always a huge argument. Having more frequent, stable, and predictable releases is important. Another important possibility of a good delivery process is hypothesis-driven design. Instead of having a product owner create a backlog based on some customer interviews and intuition, you use your newly found ability to deploy quickly to run small experiments. By measuring how your application is used in production (more on that in Chapter 14), you can quickly deploy small (or larger) changes and measure their effects.

This is what Release Management offers. Cross-platform, web-based orchestration and deployment tooling. Release Management integrates seamlessly with the Visual Studio Team Services build system and offers full traceability from work items, through the code change, build, test, and deploy stages. The following sections go into detail on how to use Release Management in VS Team Services.

Setting Up Automatic Releases with Release Management

Release Management is a very nice, integrated solution in VS Team Services that orchestrates deploying your applications to different environments, be it on (virtual) machines running on-premises or in Azure or to Platform as a Service environments such as Azure apps. Release Management is a cross-platform solution that uses the same agents that the build system uses. Release Management executes a variety of tasks, some out of the box, others created by you, and deploys your application this way. In addition to the task details that do the actual work, Release Management orchestrates the deployment across different environments. It makes sure that the appropriate permissions are followed and that configuration settings are safely stored and applied during deployment.

Just as with Team Build, you get a hosted agent that's completely managed for you by VS Team Services. You can queue a release and it will be picked up by an agent. The hosted pool allows you to connect to Azure. Using the hosted agent to deploy to on-premises environments is typically not possible because of firewall restrictions. In that case, you can deploy an agent on-premises and connect that agent to VS Team Services to run on-premises deployments.

You start your configuration by creating a Release Definition. Within your Release Definition you define the environments you want to deploy to such as integration, testing, staging, and production. This is completely up to you. You can create as many or as few environments as you need. For each environment, you configure the tasks you want to run. In addition to the tasks, you configure variables and permissions. Of course the Release Definition needs to get your application from somewhere. This is where artifacts come in. By linking your Release Definition to a build definition, you can configure artifacts that are taken from your build output. This allows you to create a complete delivery pipeline where version-controlled code is built and released all without manual work. Figure 12-1 shows a very basic Release Definition called Web App Release. There is one environment with only one task: Azure File Copy.

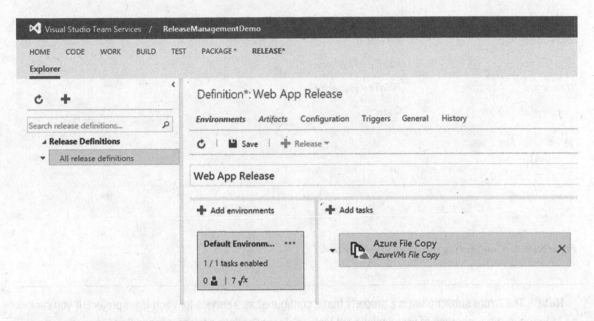

Figure 12-1. *A Release Definition with one environment and one task*

Azure File Copy allows you to copy an artifact to a virtual machine or a storage account in Azure. If you look at Figure 12-2 you see the configuration of the File Copy task. The task is configured to copy a source (more on that in the following paragraph) to an Azure VM. That VM is stored in a storage account with the name `rmtarget5002`. The virtual machine is also part of a Resource Group. Resource Groups can contain multiple items that logically belong together. The VM is selected by name and the login credentials are specified together with a destination folder.

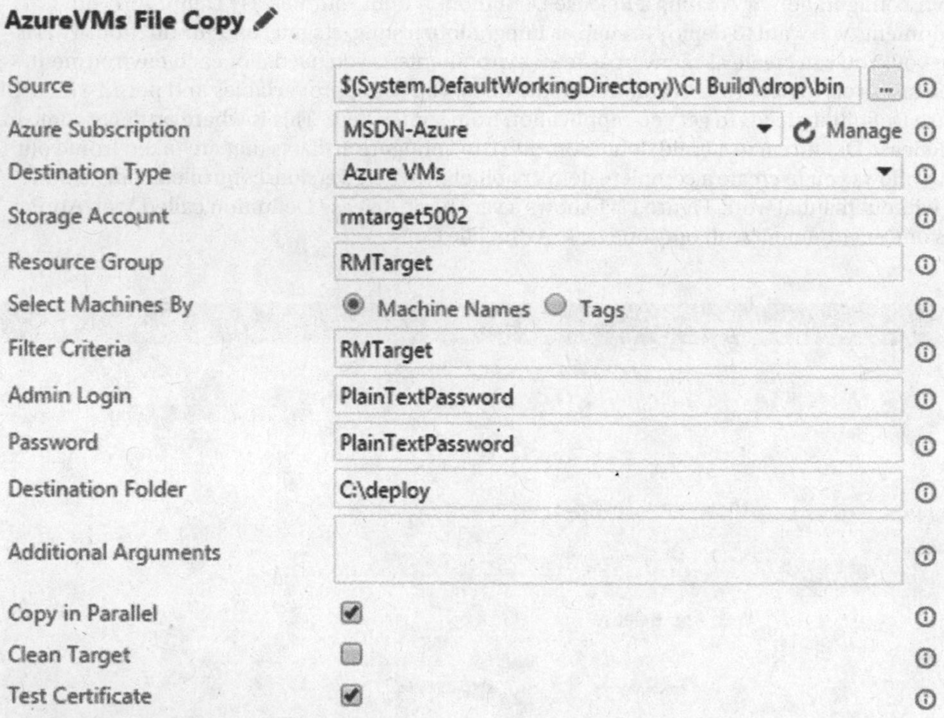

AzureVMs File Copy ✎

Source	$(System.DefaultWorkingDirectory)\CI Build\drop\bin
Azure Subscription	MSDN-Azure
Destination Type	Azure VMs
Storage Account	rmtarget5002
Resource Group	RMTarget
Select Machines By	● Machine Names ○ Tags
Filter Criteria	RMTarget
Admin Login	PlainTextPassword
Password	PlainTextPassword
Destination Folder	C:\deploy
Additional Arguments	
Copy in Parallel	☑
Clean Target	☐
Test Certificate	☑

Figure 12-2. Configuring the Azure File Copy task

■ **Note**   The Azure subscription is a property that's configured as a service for each team project. If you click on Manage in the properties of your deployment task, VS Team Services navigates to the Service section of your project. You can then add Azure subscriptions using a name/password, certificate, or service principal. If you want to deploy to a Resource Group, you need to establish the connection with a service principal. For the classic model, it's best to use a certificate. For a detailed description of the required steps, see `https://msdn.`
`microsoft.com/Library/vs/alm/Release/getting-started/deploy-to-azure#prerequ`.

Having the credentials displayed as plain text is probably not what you want. To help you store and secure variables, Release Management has the ability to store variables accessible to your whole Release Definition and per environment. If you select the ellipses next to your environment name, you see an option to configure variables. This displays the window shown in Figure 12-3. Here I've added one variable named `AdministratorLogin`. You can then enter the value and select the lock icon to securely store the value. This not only hides the value from view but also makes sure that it doesn't end up somewhere in a log file. You can then replace the value for password with `$(AdministratorLogin)`. The `$(...)` syntax can be used for all variables that you define, globally or per environment.

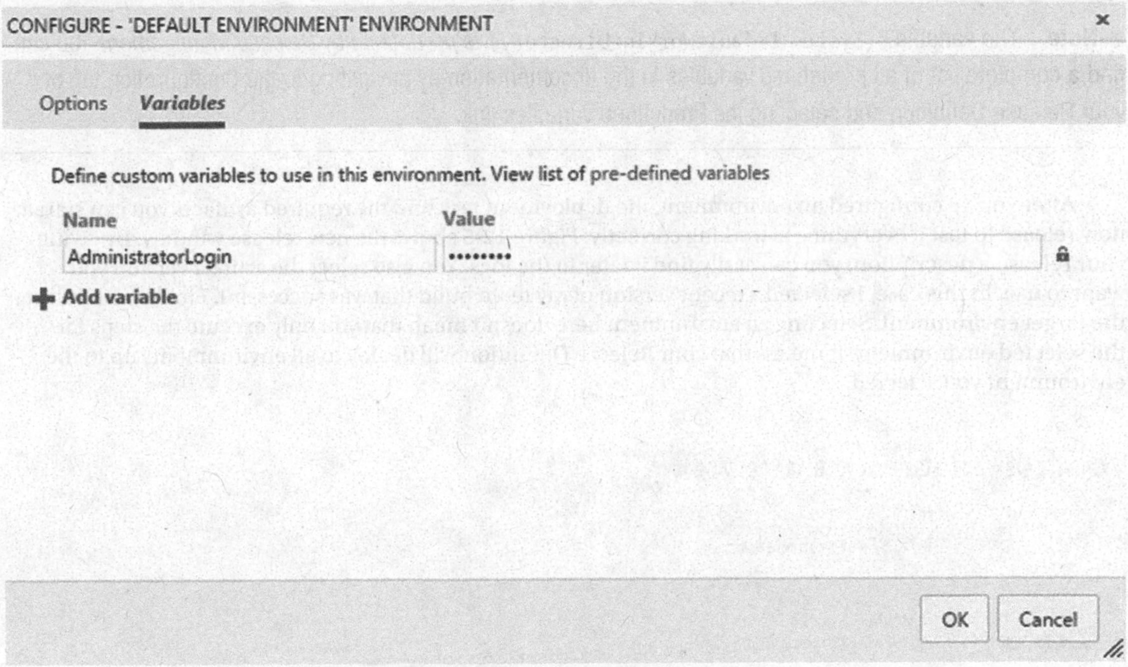

CONFIGURE - 'DEFAULT ENVIRONMENT' ENVIRONMENT   ×

Options   *Variables*

Define custom variables to use in this environment. View list of pre-defined variables

Name	Value	
AdministratorLogin	••••••••	🔒

➕ Add variable

                                                              OK   Cancel

Figure 12-3. Configuring variables used by an environment

The source data from this task starts with $(System.DefaultWorkingDirectory)\CI Build. This data is retrieved from a configured artifact. Artifacts are the data packages that you can use throughout your deployment. Figure 12-4 shows an artifact that gets its data from a VS Team Services Build. Release Management can load artifacts from Team Build and from Jenkins or from an on-premises Team Foundation Server. This allows you to use Release Management in the cloud while the rest of your TFS data is on-premises. At the start of the release to an environment, the agent downloads your artifacts and stores them locally. Other tasks can then access the artifacts and deploy them. The number of supported artifact sources is still growing. If you miss a specific artifact source, you can always skip the linking of artifacts and add tasks that manually download the artifact.

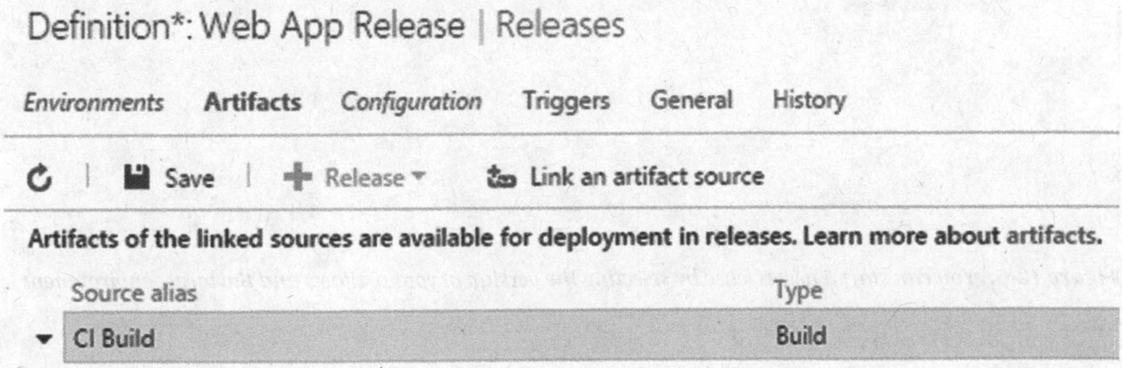

Definition*: Web App Release | Releases

Environments   **Artifacts**   *Configuration*   Triggers   General   History

🔄 | 💾 Save | ➕ Release ▾   🔗 Link an artifact source

Artifacts of the linked sources are available for deployment in releases. Learn more about artifacts.

Source alias	Type
▾ CI Build	Build

Figure 12-4. A VS Team Services Build output can function as an artifact for your release

■ **Note** The variable $(System.DefaultWorkingDirectory) *is predefined by Release Management*. You can find a complete list of all predefined variables in the documentation by navigating to the Configuration tab of your Release Definition and selecting the Predefined Variables link.

After you've configured an environment, the deployment task and the required artifacts you can start a new release to test if everything is working correctly. Figure 12-5 shows the new release window. By giving your release a description, you can easily find it later in the logs. You also select the artifact version you want to use. In this case, I selected a recent version of my team build that was successful. Finally, you select the target environment. Selecting an environment here doesn't mean that you only execute the steps for the selected environment. It means that your Release Definition will deploy to all environments up to the environment you selected.

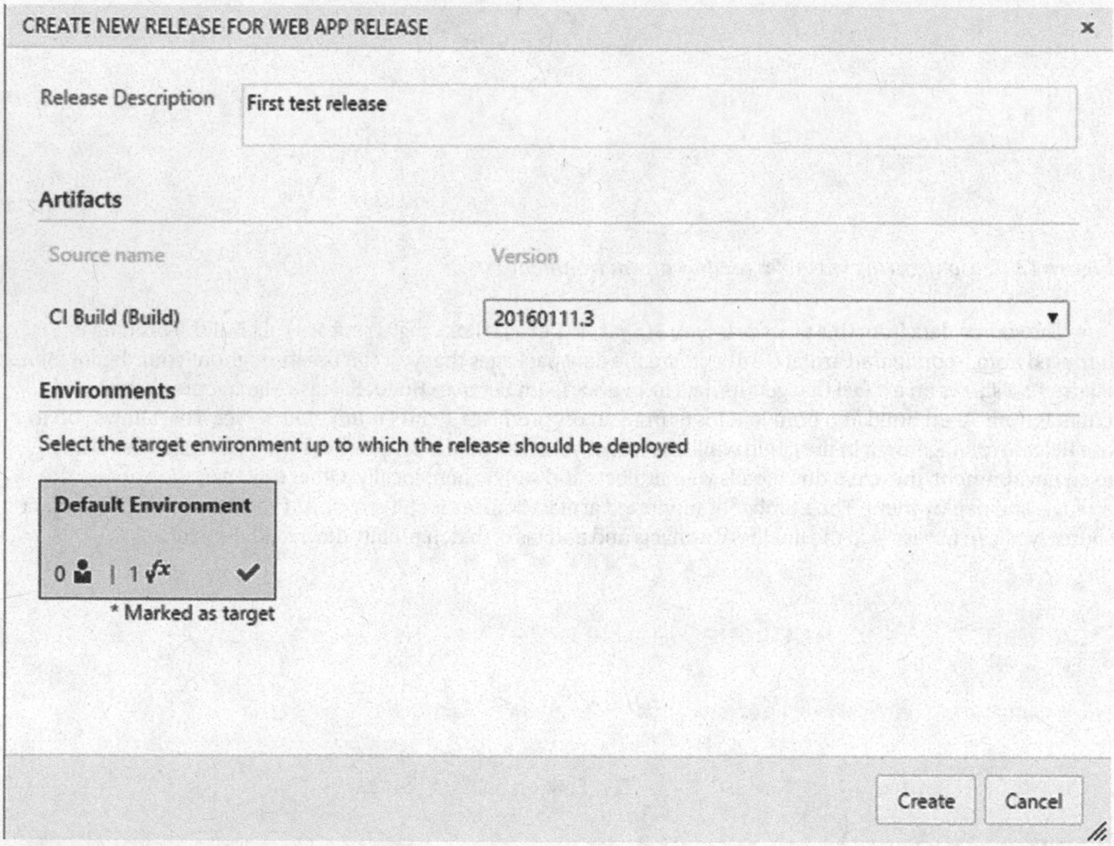

Figure 12-5. You can start a new release by selecting the version of your artifacts and the target environment

While your release is executing, you can see a log similar to the Team Build log. Figure 12-6 shows the log file of an in-progress release. You can see the current environment and the different steps.

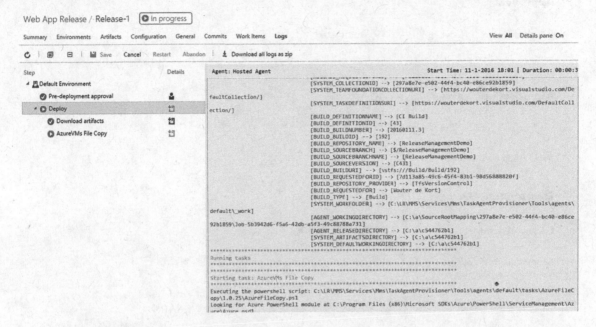

Figure 12-6. *A realtime log file shows the status of your release*

The first step, Pre-Deployment Approval, is part of the orchestration workflow that you can configure. Before and after each environment you have an approval step. You can configure these steps to be automated or have manual approval. If you select the manual option, you also need to select one or more users or groups that are responsible for approving the step. You can also enable to notify these persons by e-mail. They will then receive an e-mail whenever an approval is waiting for them. Figure 12-7 shows the window for assigning approvers.

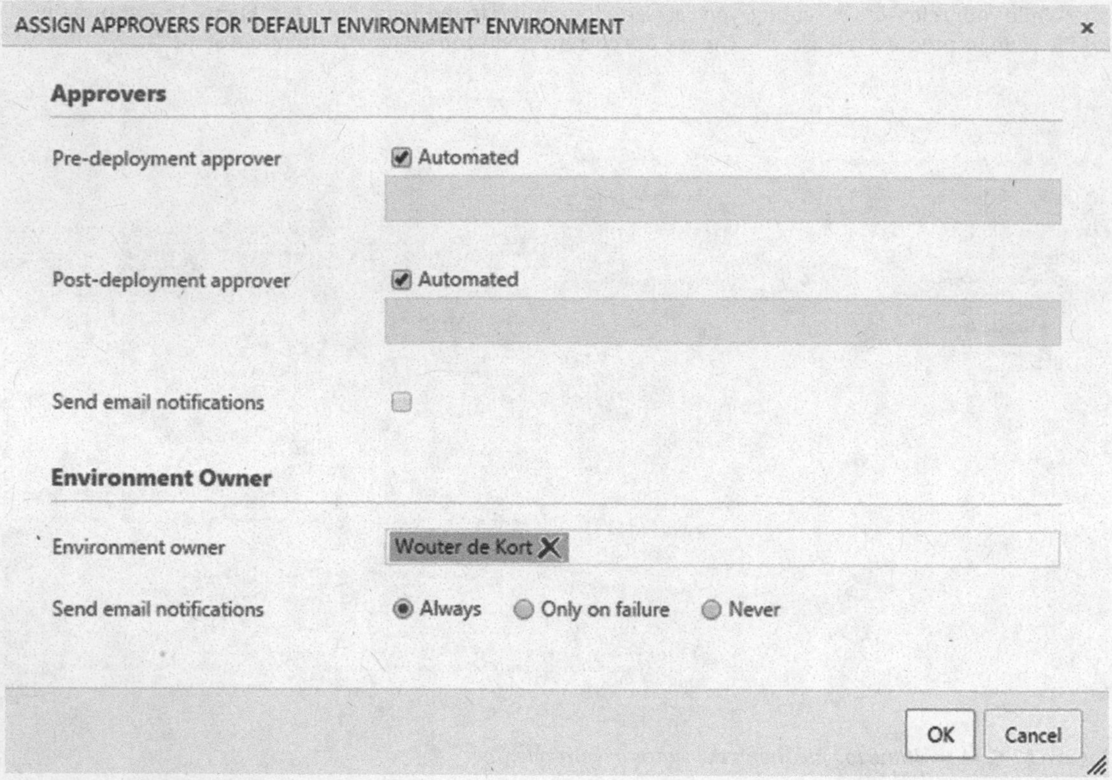

ASSIGN APPROVERS FOR 'DEFAULT ENVIRONMENT' ENVIRONMENT   ✕

Approvers

Pre-deployment approver   ☑ Automated

Post-deployment approver   ☑ Automated

Send email notifications   ☐

Environment Owner

Environment owner   Wouter de Kort ✕

Send email notifications   ◉ Always   ○ Only on failure   ○ Never

OK   Cancel

Figure 12-7. You can assign manual approval or automate the approvals for an environment

The Triggers section allows you to set up continuous deployment. This means that a successful team build triggers a new release. Figure 12-8 shows how to configure this. You can select a build definition from the drop-down. This lists all the build definitions available in your team project. You then select a target environment where you want your release to end. Maybe you want to deploy every check-in to an integration environment and you want to deploy a nightly build all the way to production.

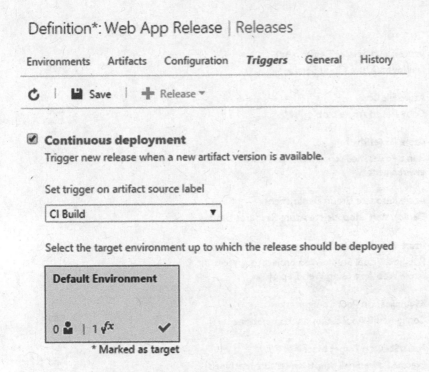

Figure 12-8. *Configuring continuous deployment for your Release Definition*

While creating your Release Definition, you can choose from a number of predefined tasks. You can see the default list of deployment tasks in Figure 12-9. In the same way as you add tasks to team build, you can add release tasks if you miss something (see Chapter 9 for more information). You can also choose to use the PowerShell tasks to run your own scripts.

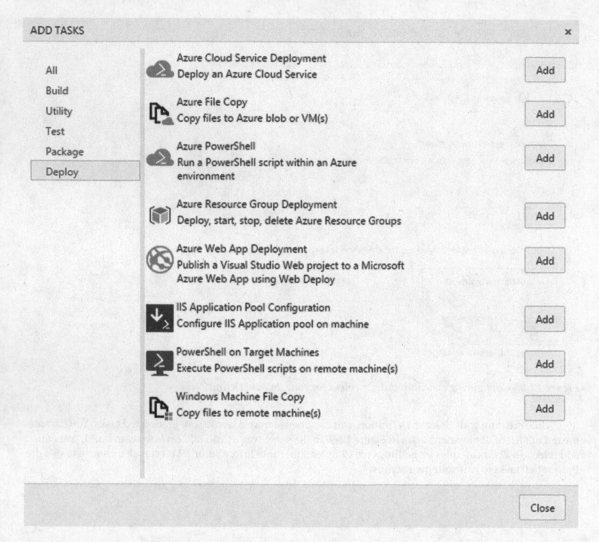

Figure 12-9. *Available deployment tasks*

Release Management also helps you when it comes to traceability. You've already seen the detailed log of a particular release. You can also get a nice overview of your Release Definition, as seen in Figure 12-10. My first release contained only one environment and has succeeded. The second release deploys to three environments. The first one is finished. Currently the second release is running and the third one comes after that. When you assign manual approval steps, you will see an icon of person with a stopwatch. This means that the next stage is waiting for approval. An approver can select this and then enter a comment and reject or accept the approval. If a release fails, you can choose to abandon the release or restart it, as you can see in the toolbar in Figure 12-10.

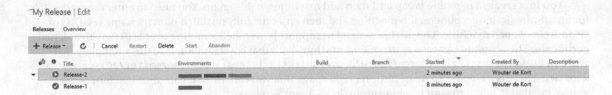

Figure 12-10. *Release Management gives you an overview of your releases*

You've seen what Release Management is capable of. You can create a Release Definition based on environments, tasks, approvers, and variables and then run the release. Another important step in your deployment pipeline is testing. In Chapter 11, you looked at automated testing. The value of your delivery pipeline increases highly when you add automated tests to it.

Imagine that every check-in by a developer is compiled, run, and then automatically deployed on a testing environment, where a set of Coded UI and other automated tests run. A tester can take one of these releases and then approve it be deployed to the manual testing environment. The tester already knows that the basis quality of the release is okay. Additional manual tests are then performed and when stability matures, these tests are also automated.

To run your tests, you will need machines that can perform them. For example, you deploy your web application to Azure Web Apps and want to test it from different client operating systems with different browsers. You need to create these test clients yourself and add them to VS Team Services. This is done in the Test hub under the Machines option, as shown in Figure 12-11.

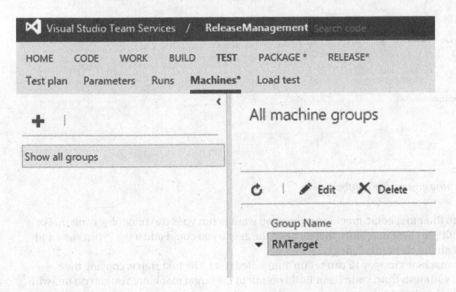

Figure 12-11. *Machine groups can be used to deploy to*

You first create a machine group and then add machines to this group. You need to enter the credentials for an administrator account on this machine and then enter the fully qualified domain name (FQDN) or IP address of each machine. The machines need to support PowerShell remoting over HTTPs with a signed certificate. The absolute easiest way to create a machine with that configuration is to use a template that you can find at `https://github.com/Azure/azure-quickstart-templates/tree/master/201-vm-winrm-windows`. There is a Deploy To Azure button on this page that you can use to create your machine. After you've created it, add it to your machine group in VS Team Services.

Figure 12-12 shows what the machine group looks like after configuring it with a machine that I created based on the previously mentioned template. VS Team Services connects over remote PowerShell with your machine group. Since I'm using a self-signed certificate, I've disabled the CA (Certificate Authority) check. The machine in my group is determined by its FQDN. You can find this name in the Azure portal. I've also tagged the machine. Tags are in the format *key:value*. You can enter any combination you want.

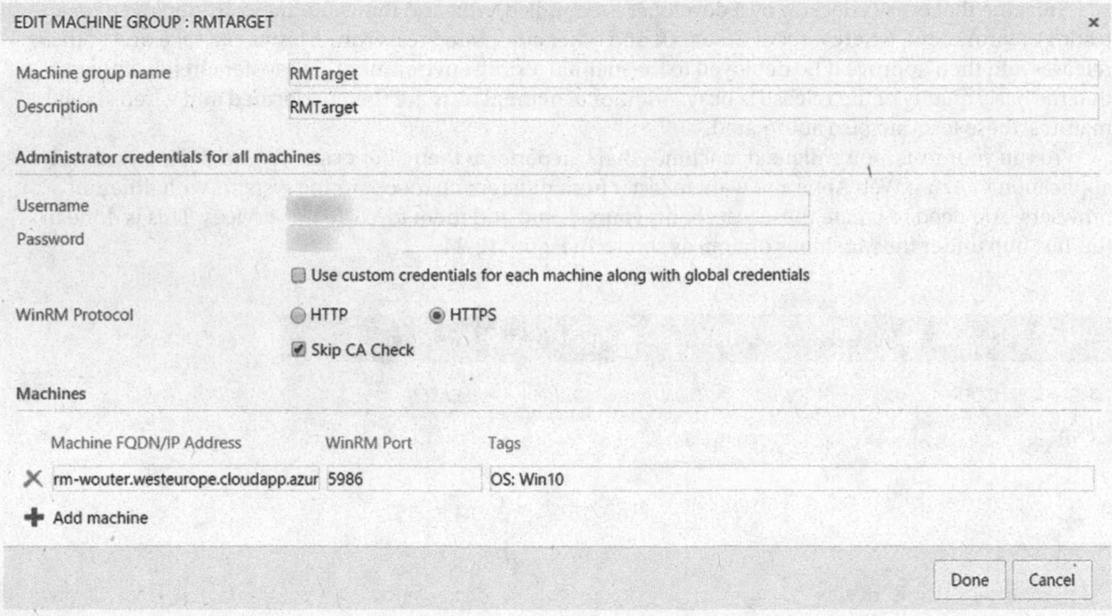

Figure 12-12. *The machine group after configuration*

Later you use this to filter to specific machines when you want to run your test or deploy content. For example, if you have multiple client machines that all need the agent, you could add a tag *Type:Client* and use that as a filter to get all the client machines.

After creating your machine group, you can set up automated tests. The first step is copying the assemblies that contain your tests from your Team Build output to the target machine. You can do this with the Azure File Copy task. You then deploy a test agent to the machine and finally use the Visual Studio Test using the test agent to run your tests. Figure 12-13 shows the tasks you need. The Azure File Copy task is configured with values from the Azure portal such as a resource group and storage account. You also specify the destination folder on the VM where you want to copy your files to. The Test Agent Deployment requires a Machine group and the machines to target. You also specify the credentials that the agent will run with. The final task runs the actual tests. Here you also select a machine group and then specify which tests you want to run. This could be all tests found in assemblies that end with `test.dll`, for example. After this, you can start and run the test.

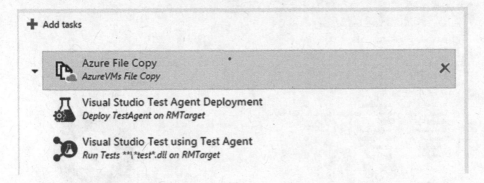

Figure 12-13. Required tasks to run tests using a test agent

Your release will now run tests as a part of it. If you look at Figure 12-14 you see the output of a release that ran some tests. The release failed with the message that some tests didn't pass. If you look at the Test Results section, you see that one of the two tests passed.

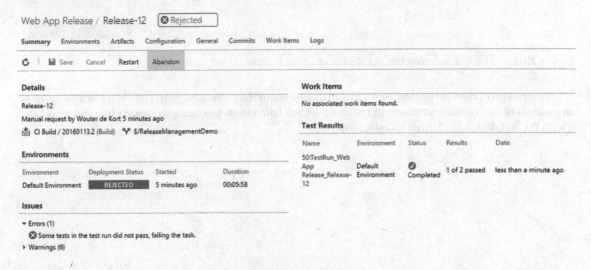

Figure 12-14. Summary of a release that failed because a test failed

By selecting the Test Result name, you're redirected to the Test Hub ➤ Runs page. Here you can see a history of all test runs that you executed. If you look at the current run in Figure 12-15, you see the summary of your test run. On the right side you can find a number of charts that show the outcome of your tests in various formats.

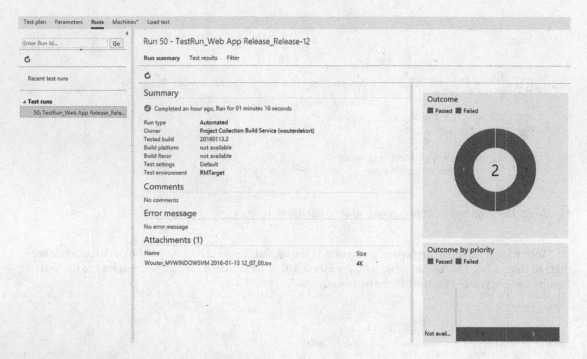

Figure 12-15. *The Test hub contains the details of all the individual test runs*

You can go to the Test Results menu to find details about the individual tests. Here you can also update an analysis of each failure, as shown in Figure 12-16. For failed tests, you can also create a bug and associate it with the test details for further investigation.

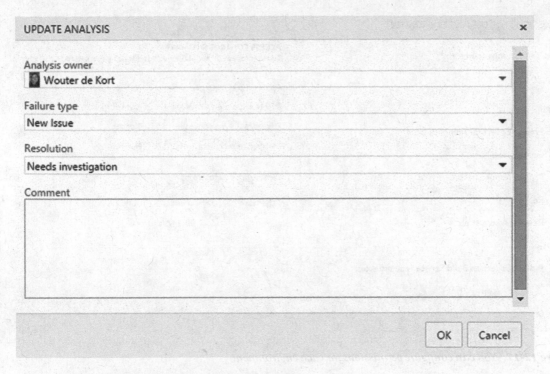

Figure 12-16. *You can update an analysis for a failed test*

Securing your Release Definition is also possible. You can configure who's allowed to make changes to each environment in your Release Definition. The permissions you can set are:

- Administer release permissions

- Delete release environment

- Edit release environment

- Manage release approvers

By default, project collection administrators, project administrators, and release administrators have all these permissions. Contributors can delete, edit, and manage an environment and readers have none of these permissions. If you need more fine-grained permissions, you can edit these from the window shown in Figure 12-17.

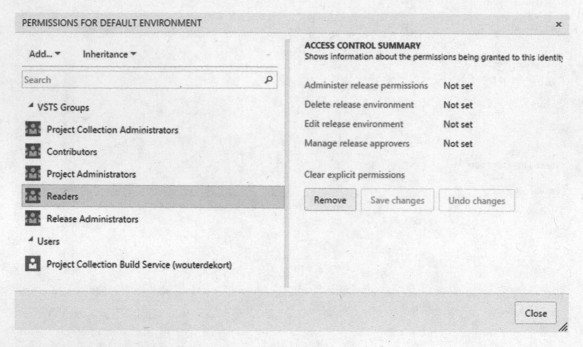

Figure 12-17. *You can configure permissions for each environment*

That concludes the introduction to Release Management. In the next section you'll look at deploying an application consisting of a web application and a database.

Deploying Web Sites

A web application with a backend database is one of the most common types of applications I encounter as a consultant. When you want to deploy a web site, you need to deploy HTML, JavaScript, and CSS files for the frontend. For the backend you deploy a set of assemblies and configuration files. Some of these configuration settings need to be changed depending on the environment. For example, you have a different database connection string for a test environment than for production. The easiest way to deploy web applications is using Web Deploy. Web Deploy is a complete framework for packaging and deploying your application. You install Web Deploy by using the Web Platform Installer (`https://www.microsoft.com/web/downloads/platform.aspx`).

When you have a web application open in Visual Studio, you can select Build ➤ Publish. The Publish Web window opens and you can create a new custom profile by clicking the Custom button and then entering a name for your profile, as shown in Figure 12-18.

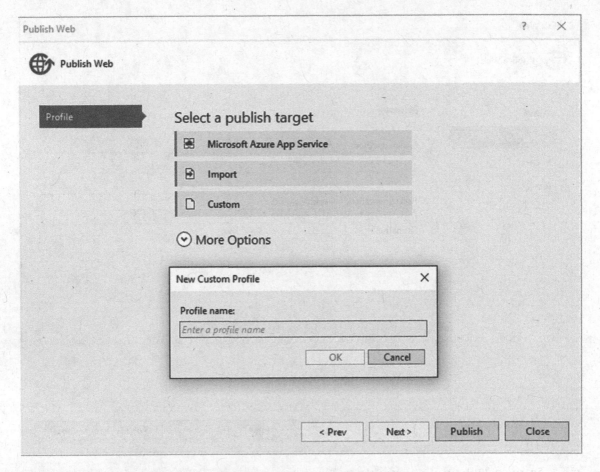

Figure 12-18. *You create a new custom publish profile to use in Web Deploy*

In the Connection step you see a Web Deploy option that allows you specify a server and immediately publish your application from Visual Studio to your server. This is nice for testing your configuration, but it's not a solution that fits nicely in a delivery pipeline. Instead, you can select the Web Deploy package, as shown in Figure 12-19. I've set the package location to a relative path beneath the current project. If you finish the wizard with these settings, you will find a couple of files in the DeployOutput folder beneath your project:

- MyWebApplication.deploy.cmd
- MyWebApplication.deploy-readme.txt
- MyWebApplication.SetParameters.xml
- MyWebApplication.SourceManifest.xml
- MyWebApplication.zip

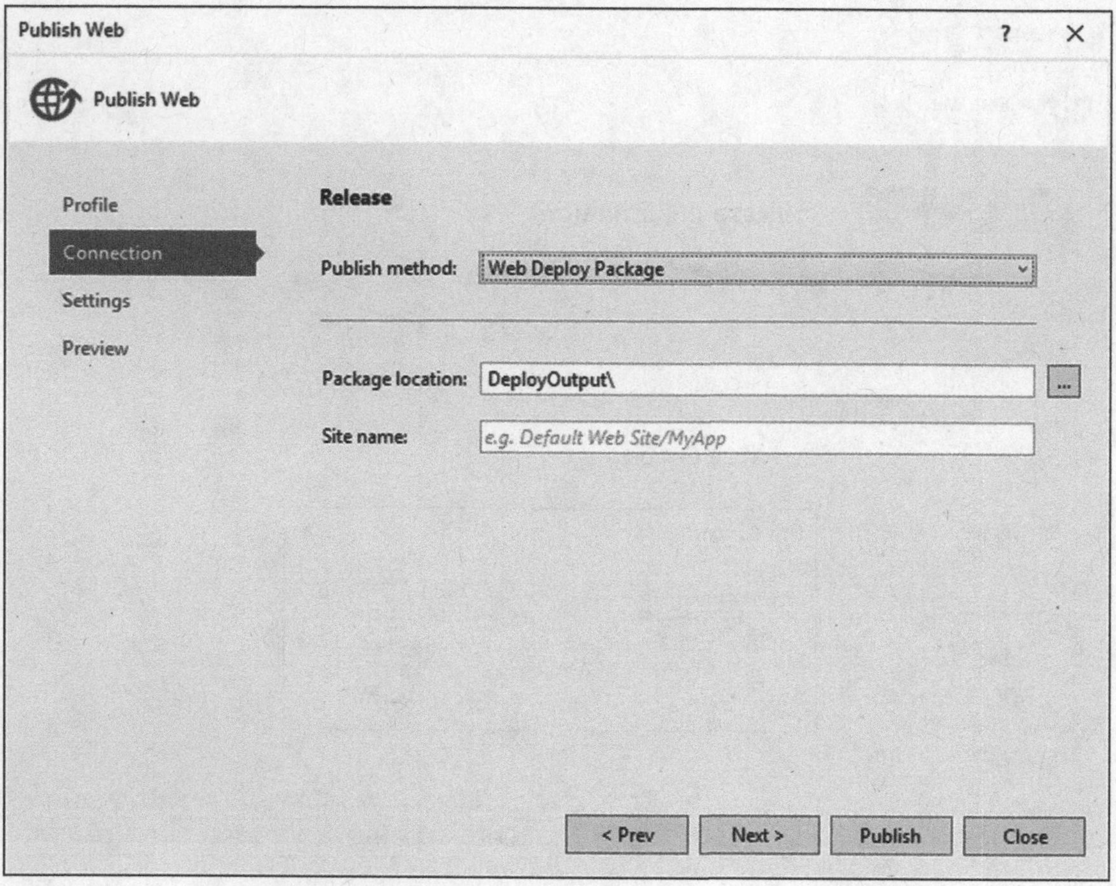

Figure 12-19. *Publish lets you create a Web Deploy package*

The ZIP file is the Web Deploy package. The SetParameters.xml file is used at deployment time to configure your application. The deploy.cmd file contains a batch script that you can run on a IIS web server to deploy the application. To test that this actually works, you can run the batch file locally. Make sure that you've installed IIS and Web Deploy. You can edit the SetParameters file to specify the web application name you want to use in IIS. If you don't want to publish to Azure, you can expand the SetParameters file and add parameters of your own, such as a connection string. In this case, I want to show you how to deploy to an Azure Web App and how you can use the web app to configure settings.

The start of the delivery pipeline is team build. After adding your project to version control, you can set up a new team build that not only compiles the code but also creates the Web Deploy package. To do this, you need to pass two arguments to MSBuild:

```
msbuild /p:DeployOnBuild=true;PublishProfile=<TheNameOfYourProfile>
```

The Publish Profile points to the profile that you created in the wizard shown in Figure 12-19. You can pass these parameters to MSBuild by configuring your Build Definition, as shown in Figure 12-20. This makes sure that your Web Deploy package is created.

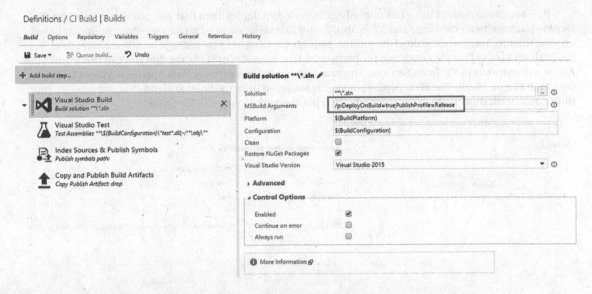

Figure 12-20. Configure MSBuild to create the Web Deploy package

To copy your package to the output of your build, you need to add the DeployOutput folder to the contents property of the Copy and Publish Build Artifacts task. Figure 12-21 shows this. By including DeployOutput like this, it will be a subfolder of your web project. If you want to separate things into different top-level folders, you can add multiple Copy and Publish Build Artifacts tasks. This is the first step of your delivery pipeline. You create an output package and store that in VS Team Services. The next step is to use Release Management to deploy your web application.

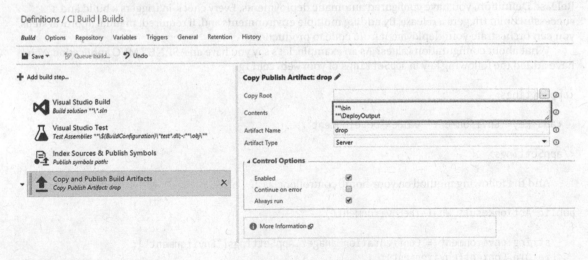

Figure 12-21. You can add the DeployOutput folder to your build artifacts

Release Management has a task named Azure Web App deployment that you can use to publish a Web Deploy package to an existing Azure Web App. To use this task, you need an Azure service endpoint based on a certificate. You can download the publish settings file from `https://manage.windowsazure.com/PublishSettings`. This file contains a property called `ManagementCertificate` that you can use to link your Azure subscription to VS Team Services. You can then configure the Azure Web App deployment task, as shown in Figure 12-22. The Web Deploy package is retrieved from the build artifacts. You need to link your Build Definition that creates the output and then put the path to your ZIP file there.

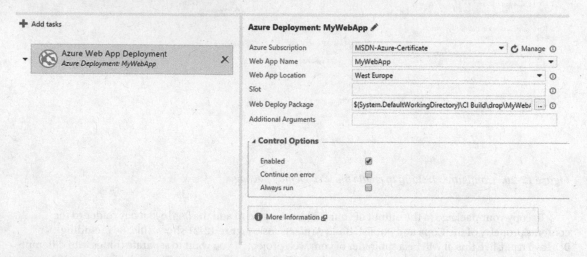

Figure 12-22. *Configure the Azure Web App deployment task to publish your Web Deploy package*

If you now enable continuous integration for your team build and continuous deployment for your Release Definition, you have configured automatic deployments. Every check-in triggers a build and a successful build triggers a release. By adding multiple environments and, if required, manual approval steps, you can orchestrate your deployment from code to production.

What about configuration values? As an example, let's say you have an ASP.NET MVC application. You have added the following key in `appSettings` of your `web.config`:

```
<appSettings>
  ...
  <add key="Environment" value="Development"/>
  ...
</appSettings>
```

And the following method on your home controller class:

```
public ActionResult WhatsTheEnvironment()
{
    string environment = ConfigurationManager.AppSettings["Environment"];
    return Content(environment);
}
```

If you ruin the application on your localhost, you can navigate to `http://localhost:PORT/Home/WhatsTheEnvironment`. This returns the string `Development` from your `web.config` file. When running in production on your Azure Web App, you want the value to be `Production`. To enable this, you can go to the settings blade of your web app and select App Settings, as shown in Figure 12-23. Here I've added an app setting named `Environment` with a value of `Production`. If you navigate to `http://yourwebapp.azurewebsites.net/Home/WhatsTheEnvironment`, you get a value of `Production`. So overriding app settings and connection strings is possible without any code changes. Azure makes sure that if a value is present in the Application settings of your web app, that value is used over anything that's stored in the `web.config` file.

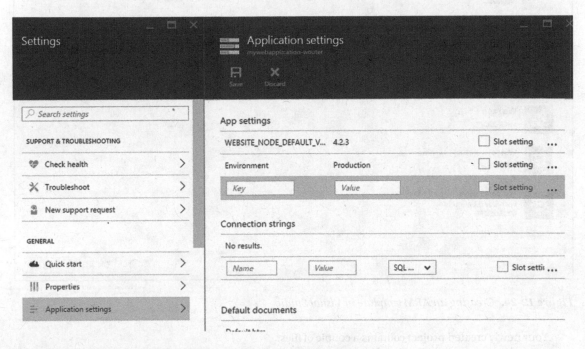

Figure 12-23. *Configuring settings for your Web App in the Azure portal*

> ■ **Note** If you want to store your configuration values in version control and not configure them through the Azure Portal, you can add a script that copies the correct `web.config` to the root of your application or that uses a script to parse the `web.config` and change values based on parameters configured in Release Management. This is a little more work but also works on an on-premises IIS web server. You can find a couple of tasks that help you with this in the Marketplace at `https://marketplace.visualstudio.com/items?itemName=colinsalmcorner.colinsalmcorner-buildtasks` and a good blog article at `http://bit.ly/webrmwebdeploy` that discusses these tasks in detail.

You've now seen how to deploy your project to web app in Azure. You can also use Azure Resource Management templates. If you create an Azure Resource Group project (you can find this template in the Cloud category), you can then select the ARM template you want to start with, as shown in Figure 12-24.

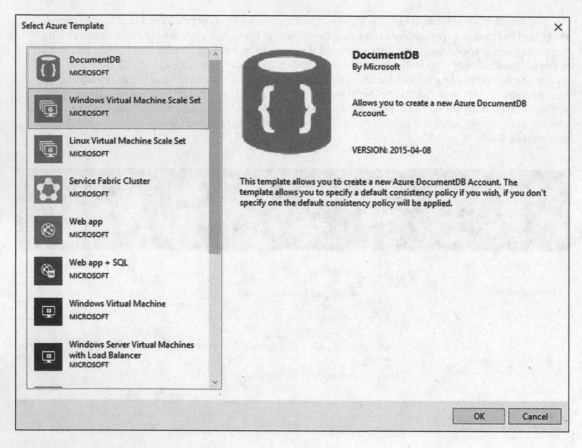

Figure 12-24. *Creating an ARM template in Visual Studio*

Your newly created project contains a couple of files:

- AzCopy.exe: An executable file that's used to copy data to the Azure storage accounts
- Deploy-AzureResourceGroup.ps1: A PowerShell file that starts the deployment of your ARM template
- Website.json: The actual ARM template
- Website.parameters.json: The parameters your ARM template needs for deployment

To start a deployment, you can right-click your Azure Resource Group project and then choose Deploy. Figure 12-25 shows the Deploy to Resource Group window. There you choose the subscription you want to deploy to and then create a resource group or select an existing one. You also need to enter a web app plan (such as free, for example) in the Parameters section. After that you can start your deploy and you'll see how the web app gets created on Azure.

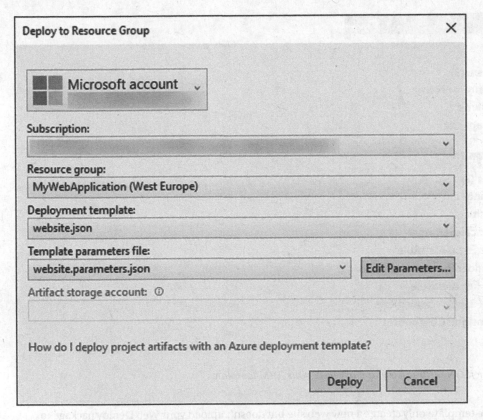

Figure 12-25. *Deploy an ARM template from Visual Studio to a resource group*

■ **Note** If you get an error during deployment, make sure you have installed the latest PowerShell tools. You can find instructions and downloads at `https://azure.microsoft.com/nl-nl/documentation/articles/ powershell-install-configure/`. Also don't forget to reboot after installing.

To extend the ARM template, you need to open the WebSite.json file. You can then open the JSON outline (View ➤ Other Windows ➤ JSON Outline) to inspect the template. Figure 12-26 shows the outline. The parameters are values that your ARM template needs to be deployed. Both skuName and skuCapacity have a default value so you're not required to enter those. The hostingPlanName value is required and you can enter a value like Free.

The Variables section defines calculated values in your ARM template that you can later reuse. For example, webSiteName:

```
"webSiteName": "[concat('webSite', uniqueString(resourceGroup().id))]"
```

The final section, Resources, contains the actual resources you're creating with this ARM template. As you can see in Figure 12-26, it's more than a simple web app. You also configure your hosting plan, auto-scale settings, and use Application Insights (see Chapter 13 for more information on Application Insights).

Figure 12-26. *The JSON outline lets you work with your ARM template*

Currently, the template only creates a new web site but doesn't upload your Web Deploy package to it. You can extend your ARM template by clicking on the cube with a green + in the top left, as shown in Figure 12-26. In Figure 12-27 you see how to add the Web Deploy for Web Apps part to your ARM template. This adds `MSDeploy` as a child node of the web site. One property that's important to note is `PackageUri`:

```
"packageUri": "[concat(parameters('_artifactsLocation'), '/',
parameters('WebDeployPackageFolder'), '/',
parameters('WebDeployPackageFileName'),
parameters('_artifactsLocationSasToken'))]"
```

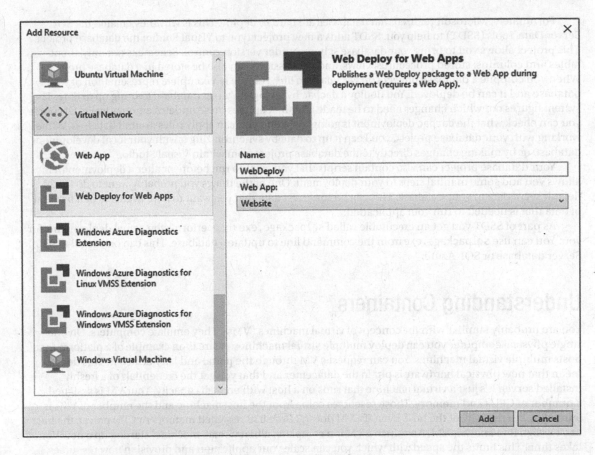

Figure 12-27. *Add Web Deploy for Web Apps to your ARM template*

This property contains the location of your artifact and an access token. You can't store the Web Deploy package on your local machine and then reference it from an ARM template running in Azure. Instead, the PowerShell template takes care of uploading your Web Deploy package to Azure storage and then passes the correct URL and token to the ARM template. To deploy the package, you can copy it to the folder of your Resource Group project and then include it as a project file in Visual Studio. This makes sure that the file gets uploaded to storage.

You can then enter the relative path and name of the ZIP file in the parameters section of your deployment. If you want to verify that your content is uploaded to Azure storage, you can open the Cloud Explorer (View ➤ Cloud Explorer) in Visual Studio and navigate to Storage Accounts ➤ Blobs. Look there for your content uploads. To use ARM templates in Release Managements, you can use a PowerShell task to execute a deployment script or use the Azure Resource Group deployment task. You can use the Azure File Copy task to move your Web Deploy package to Azure storage and then run the ARM template.

Almost all web applications that I see at customers use databases, yet almost all teams are having problems with automatically deploying databases. Renaming columns, changing stored procedures, and having a basic set of test data are only some of the problems teams face when it comes to automatic database deployments. Unfortunately, there is almost no project that doesn't use a database. Bear in mind that I'm talking about relational databases like SQL Server. NoSQL databases like document databases have other challenges and advantages that are outside the scope of this book.

Fortunately, Microsoft realized that databases are hard to deploy. This is why they created the SQL Server Data Tools (SSDT) to help you. SSDT adds a new project type to Visual Studio: the database project. This project allows you to bring your database schema under version control. Schema is not only about tables and columns; stored procedures, views, and permissions can also be stored in a database project. When you compile a database project you get a `dacpac` file. This file is a complete representation of your database and it can be deployed. You deploy a `dacpac` by giving it a target database to bring up to date. The system figures out which changes need to be made and then applies these updates automatically. Of course you can check what the `dacpac` deployment is going to do and you can apply rules around data loss. While working with your database project, you keep it up to date by synchronizing it with your local development database or by making changes directly to the database project from within Visual Studio.

Your database project can also contain scripts that you want to run before or after a deployment. This allows you add some manual steps to your deployment. One of the things you probably want to do is add a default set of data to your database. This can be some test data that you want to have available or a base set of data that is needed to run your application.

As part of SSDT you get an executable called `sqlpackage.exe` that performs the actual deployments for you. You can use `sqlpackage.exe` from the command line to update a database. This can be a regular SQL Server database or SQL Azure.

Understanding Containers

You are probably familiar with the concept of virtual machines (VMs). They emulate computers. On one single physical computer you can deploy multiple virtual machines. Azure is an example of a platform that hosts multiple virtual machines. You can request a VM through the portal and later access it. This doesn't mean that new physical hardware is put in the datacenter and that you get the credentials of a freshly installed server. It's just a virtual machine that runs on a host with enough capacity. Your VM is assigned a number of CPUs and memory. Those resources come from the host machine and the number of VMs is limited by the capacity of the host. Even if a VM doesn't use all its assigned memory or CPU power, the host can't assign it to another VM. And since a VM is a complete, albeit virtual, machine, starting up a new VM takes time. This limits the speed with which you can scale your application and provision new resources.

A concept that's gaining a lot of popularity are containers. A container looks a lot like a VM but is much lighter. Instead of having dedicated CPU and memory, a container uses these resources dynamically. If a container needs 2GB of RAM, it will use 2GB of RAM. If it needs less, it uses only what it needs. Containers boot very quickly. You still get an isolated environment with an external IP address, but you don't have the disadvantages of VMs.

A very popular container platform is Docker. *Docker* containers run on Linux. Since Microsoft understands the importance of containers, Windows Server 2016 will also be able to host containers. A container is built out of images. These images are layered on top of each other to form an application. Images are also shared between different containers on the same host. This saves memory and disk space. Sharing these resources doesn't mean that there are security risks for your application since the container host makes sure that each container runs in its own process. A container has a configuration file that specifies which layers you want to put on top of each other. A layer can be a web server or an ASP.NET stack. Layers have a version number and are immutable once created. These images are stored in a central registry. There is a public version of a Docker registry that you can find at `https://hub.docker.com/`. If you do a search for ASP.NET, you can find a Microsoft ASP.NET image at `https://hub.docker.com/r/microsoft/aspnet/`. This is the cross-platform version of ASP.NET that lets you run your web applications written in .NET on Linux.

Since containers are a stack of components in the form of images, you can easily move containers around. This allows you to redefine the idea of a delivery pipeline where an application goes through multiple environments. The environment for a Docker container doesn't change. You just push the complete environment to another location with another set of configuration parameters.

As an example of how you can to deploy to Docker, you can create a new ASP.NET 6 application. If you create a standard application from the installed templates and then open the Publish Web wizard, you see the options in Figure 12-28.

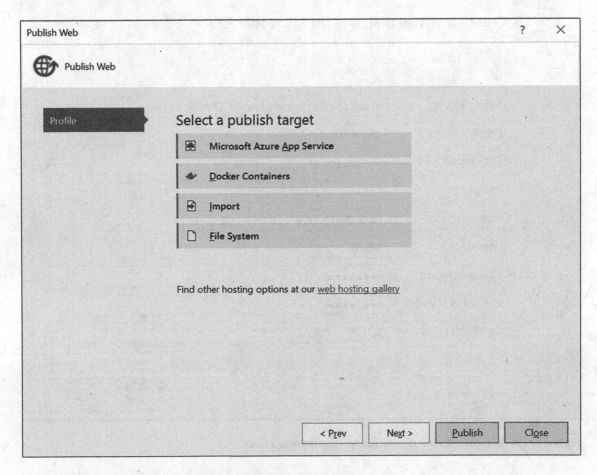

Figure 12-28. ASP.NET 6 applications can be deployed to Docker

After selecting the Docker option, you're asked to select a host machine or create a new one. Figure 12-29 shows the settings for a new Linux host. This creates a new ARM file that's stored in your project. Visual Studio then deploys this ARM file to Azure to create your host. After the host is created, you can deploy your application to it. This is nothing more than selecting your created Docker host as the target. Visual Studio makes sure that the correct ASP.NET image is loaded and then puts your application in an image on top of it.

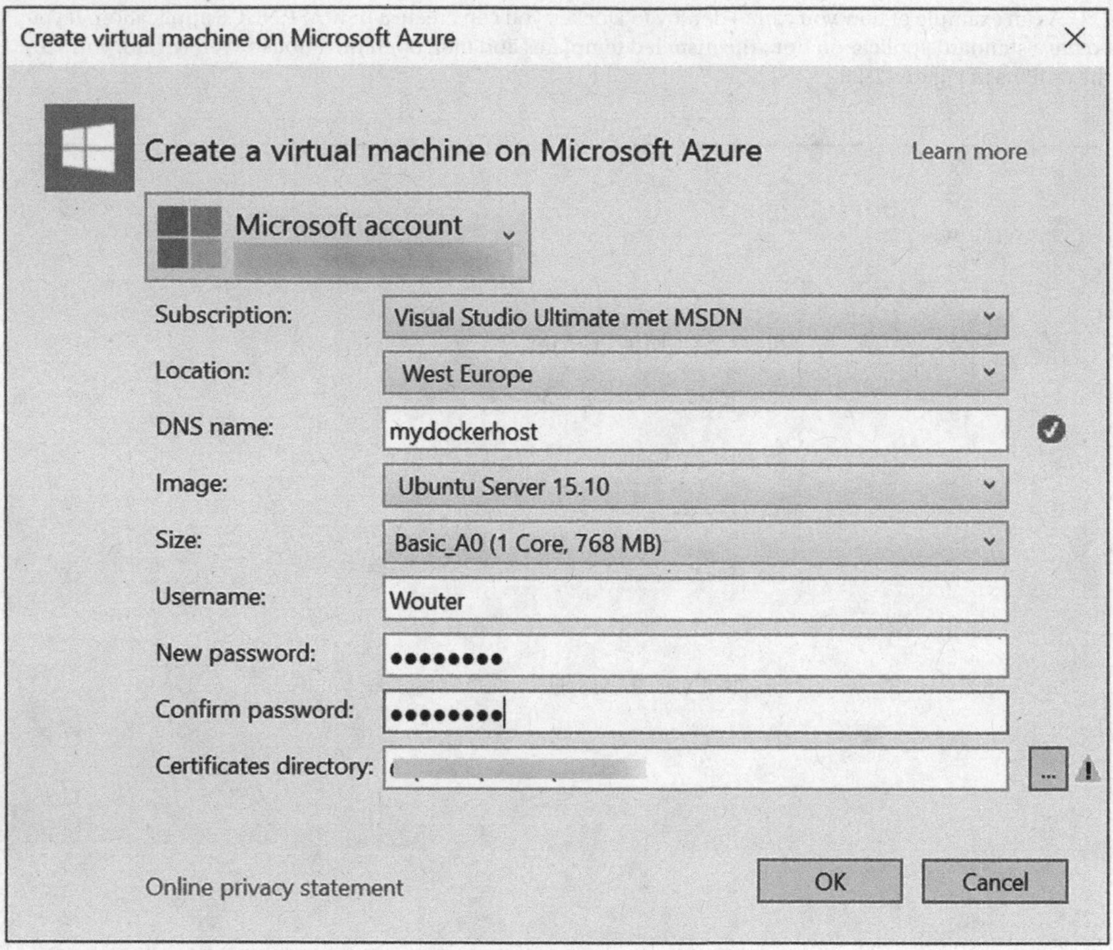

Figure 12-29. You can create a new container host running Linux

---

■ **Note**   This is only a short introduction to the concept of containers and they are becoming more and more important. For a deep dive into containers, I recommend *Docker: Up & Running,* by Karl Matthias and Sean P. Kane.

Summary

This chapter introduced you to the concept of a delivery pipeline, which is a series of steps that takes your application from code to deployment. You've seen how you can use Release Management for the orchestration of your deployments. You can create a Release Definition with multiple environments and tasks that perform the actual steps required for your deployment. You've also seen how you can integrate automated tests into your deployment pipeline.

Then you looked at the different options for deploying a web application. You've seen how you can create a Web Deploy package and how you can deploy the package to an Azure Web App. You also saw how you can leverage Azure Resource Manager templates to automate the creation and configuration of resources. Finally, you looked at an introduction of containers and learned why they are so popular.

In the next chapter, you learn about Application Insights. You'll see how AI lets you monitor your applications to understand what your users are doing and how your application is working.

CHAPTER 13

■ ■ ■

Using Application Insights

A key idea of DevOps is the build-measure-learn cycle that you go through. Throughout this book you've seen how the planning, build, test, and release management tools that Visual Studio Team Services offers help you with building and releasing your app. This sets you up for the DevOps cycle that you can now run in an automated, efficient way. This chapter introduces you to the measure step and how you can use that to learn things about your application and your users. You will learn what Application Insights is and how you can you use it to monitor your applications.

What Is Application Insights?

Application Insights is a service offered by Microsoft as a part of Microsoft Azure. Microsoft develops and runs the service for you and you can use it to monitor web, client, and mobile applications. Monitoring compasses different areas such as:

- Availability: Is our web application running and accessible to our users?

- Performance: Can we handle the load on our application?

- Usage: What are users doing with our application? Which features are popular and which aren't?

- Failures: Do users run into errors or is there something else wrong with our application?

- Dependencies: What's the performance and availability of applications we depend upon?

Application Insights tracks all those metrics and you can expand it with your own metrics. For example, by adding a couple of lines of code, you can start following the path that users take through application. You can see where they run into errors or where they leave your application. This can help you to prioritize new work and see where investments should be made. Figure 13-1 shows an example of the Application Insights dashboard that monitors my public blog (http://wouterdekort.com). You see things like server response time, server request count, and page view duration metrics. At the bottom you see some tiles which we'll look into later in this chapter.

© Wouter de Kort 2016

W. de Kort, *DevOps on the Microsoft Stack*, DOI 10.1007/978-1-4842-1446-6_13

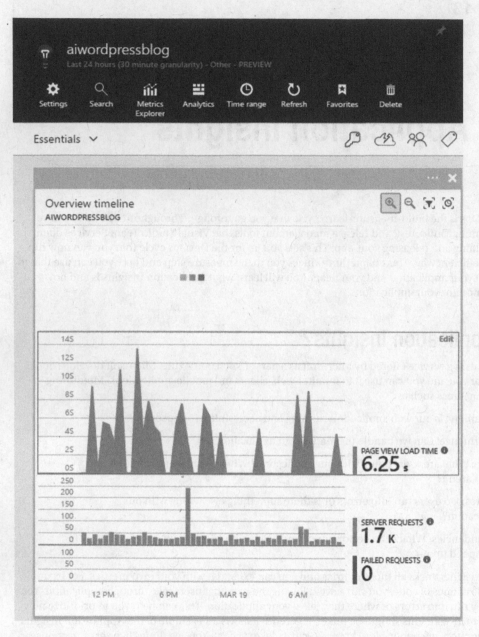

Figure 13-1. *Application Insights helps you with understanding the usage and performance of your application*

You can add your own charts and pin these to your dashboard or mark them as favorite for you and your team. This allows you to easily set up a dashboard that you can display in your team room or at other places where people want a quick overview of how your application is doing. The dashboard also allows you to zoom in for further detail. You can go down to the level of individual requests to inspect them for further details. Since Application Insights is offered as a service, the payment is based on data volume. Fortunately, there is a free plan that you can use to monitor small- to medium-sized applications. When you reach your quota, you can choose to start paying for additional monitoring or do nothing and only monitor session data. At the start of each month, your quota is reset.

Another important aspect of using Application Insights is privacy and data retention. In most countries you will get into trouble if you start collecting private user data. It's good to know which data Application Insights collects and how it's stored. At the time of writing, all data is stored in servers in the United States. The data is encrypted when in transit but not when residing in the servers. Recall that Chapter 2 covered how Azure protects your data and how only a select group of people can access data with your explicit permission. The same is true for Application Insights. The Application Insights Software Development Kit (SDK) collects out-of-the-box data from your application. This doesn't contain sensitive data but instead data for load, performance, usage, and diagnostic metrics. You can also add your own data collection and since you control what's monitored, you could send sensitive data to Application Insights. When adding custom monitoring, make sure that you understand which data is considered sensitive and make sure that your code reviews check for these types of issues.

Configuring Monitoring for Your Application

Getting started with Application Insights is made very easy by the integration between Application Insights and Visual Studio. If you create a new web application, you get the option to configure Application Insights, as shown in Figure 13-2. (If you've already created your application, you can add Application Insights by opening the context menu of your solution and choosing Add Application Insights.) Your project now contains an extra ApplicationInsights.config file. This file specifies which metrics you want to monitor. A references to the Application Insights SDK is also added. None of your code is modified; having the configuration file and a reference to the SDK is enough.

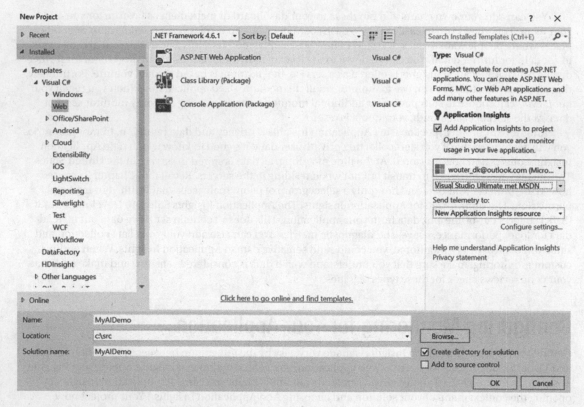

Figure 13-2. *Add Application Insights while creating a project*

If you now run your application locally in Debug mode, you will send your first Application Insights telemetry data to Azure. In the taskbar, you can find a new button named Application Insights (see Figure 13-3). Between the brackets you can see how many events have been sent to Application Insights. When you open a couple of pages in the web application running on your local host, you will see the number of events increasing.

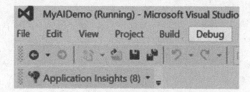

Figure 13-3. *While running your application, Visual Studio tracks the events sent to Application Insights*

After sending a couple of events, you can navigate to the Azure portal to see the collected metrics on the dashboard. Figure 13-4 shows the dashboard blade. The metrics show server response time, page view duration, server requests, and failed requests. The first peak was while I was navigating the web site. The flat line after that was while the application wasn't running.

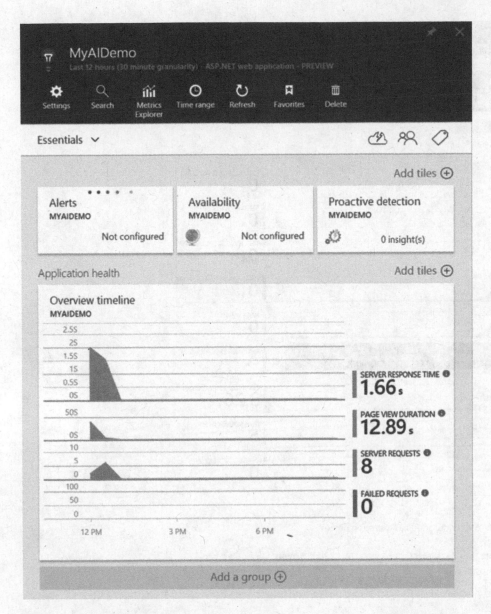

Figure 13-4. Application Insights shows the events that you send from your local development machine

If you select one of these charts, a second blade opens showing the details for that particular metric. For example, if you select Page View Duration, you see the details, as shown in Figure 13-5. Here you see the details as viewed from the user's browser. You can see how long it took to render a page, how long it took to request individual pages, and even dependencies like AJAX calls are tracked. It's worth it to explore the blades. While doing this, look at the time range and filters options. Time range is the last 24 hours by default but you can change this to any period you are interested in. Filters allows you to choose from a wide range of properties such as country, IP address, or even device type and filter your data down to that. For example, in Figure 13-5 you see that a filter for browser is applied.

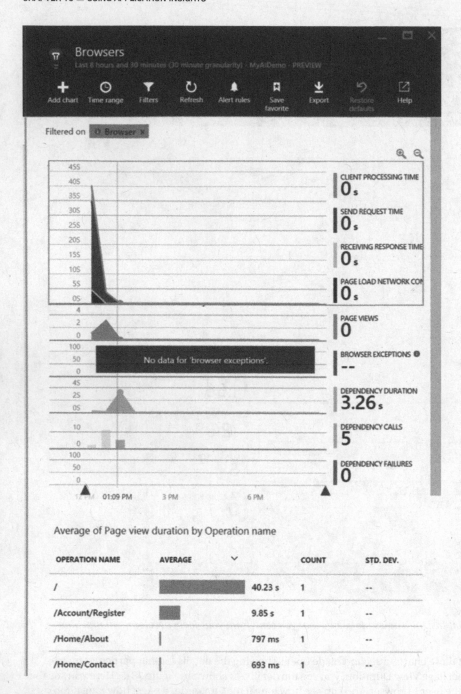

Figure 13-5. Application Insight automatically tracks page view details

You can also set alerts for all the available metrics. Figure 13-6 shows how to configure a new alert. An alert becomes true whenever a certain condition for a selected metric becomes true over the period of time that you select. So a single peak value won't trigger an alert but peaking over a period of five minutes, for example, will trigger the alert. Having alerts for things like CPU usage, memory usage, or request count can help you track the health of an application.

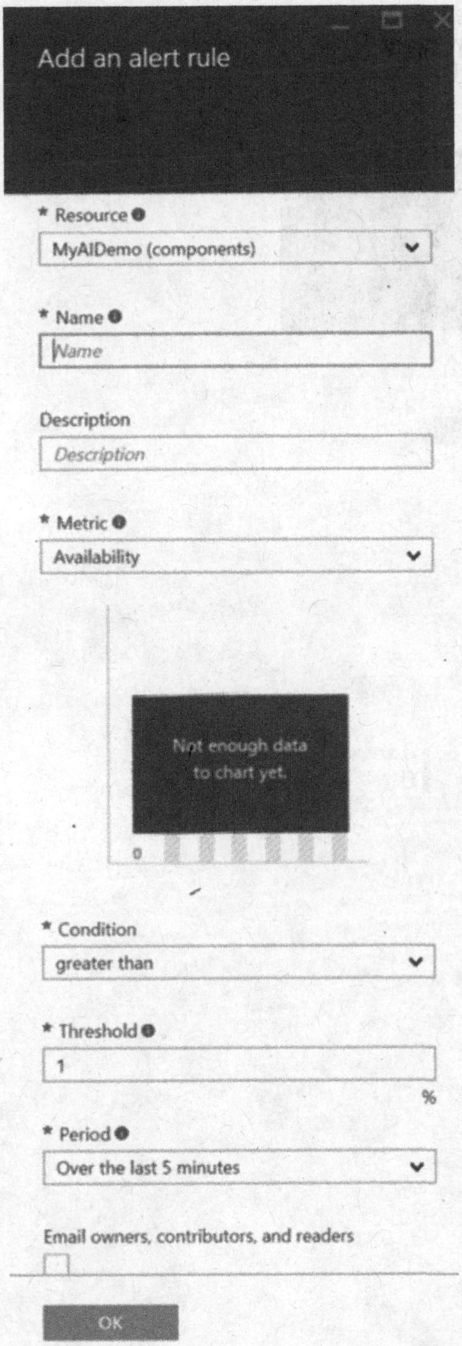

Figure 13-6. *You can configure alerts for the different metrics in Application Insights*

Another useful way to inspect the telemetry data, is by using the search blade. This blade shows you a list of all the different events that Application Insights tracks for your application. For example, the search blade shows you individual AJAX requests and server responses but also things like exceptions and other diagnostic data. Figure 13-7 shows the search blade.

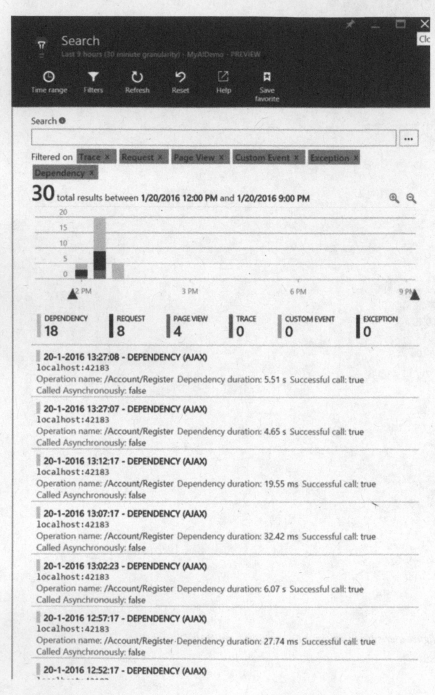

Figure 13-7. *The search blade allows you to inspect individual events*

Now that you've seen how you can set up Application Insights and some of the charts and dashboards it gives you, it's time to further inspect the different Application Insight features that you can use.

Availability Monitoring

Making sure that your web application or web service is available and responsive is an important part of delivering a great user experience. If users can't reach your application or the application is slow, you will start getting complaints and maybe even start losing users. This is where Application Insights availability monitoring can help you. You can set up a web test that will check the availability of your web site on regular intervals from multiple locations around the world. Figure 13-8 shows the configuration for a new web test.

Figure 13-8. *You can configure a URL ping test for availability monitoring of your application*

You can configure a URL ping test or a multi-step test. A URL ping test checks the URL that you enter and confirms that it's available by checking the resulting HTTP status code. You can also check for certain content being available, like a sentence or other phrase that lets you know the web site loaded correctly. By default, parse dependent requests is checked. This means that Application Insights parses the response it gets from your URL and then also tries to load any links or images that you have in your HTML. This makes sure that your page not only loads but also that the dependencies of your page are available. By default, a failure is recorded when a retry fails three times. This makes sure that you don't get too many false positives. You also configure how often and from which locations the test should run.

Location corresponds with Azure data centers all around the world. This allows you to check if your application loads for users in different countries and also avoids failing the test if there is a network issue in one of the locations. By default, when three of the five configured locations fail, the test fails.

Figure 13-9 shows the results from the URL ping test that I have running for my blog. The data shows the availability in different time ranges. In this case, there are no failed request and the availability is 100 percent. If there were failures, you would see red dots in the chart for the tests that failed. You can inspect individual failures and drill down into the response to diagnose the issue.

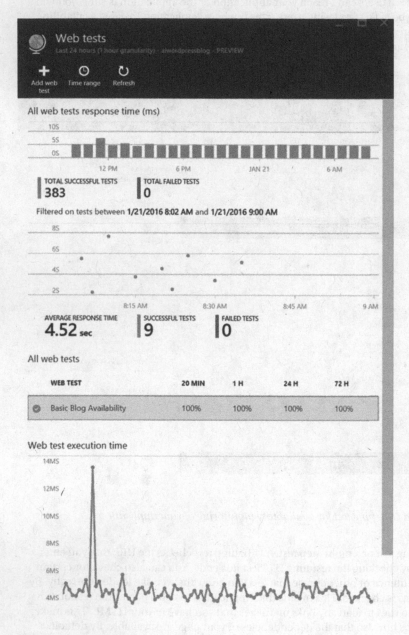

Figure 13-9. *The results of a URL ping test*

When it comes to responsiveness, it's important to know what the performance of your application is. In Chapter 12 you saw how you can use VS Team Services to set up load and performance testing. Application Insights automatically records performance data for your application. Figure 13-10 shows the performance blade for my blog. What immediately stands out is the top request, which is on average quite a lot slower than other requests. By selecting this specific URL, you can then drill down into individual requests and responses and see why this particular page is slow. In this case, there were some uncompressed images that made the page load slower. It's also important to check if there is a relationship between server requests and server response time. If the number of requests goes up (meaning your web site is more popular) and the server response time also goes up, this could mean that you have too few resources allocated for your web application.

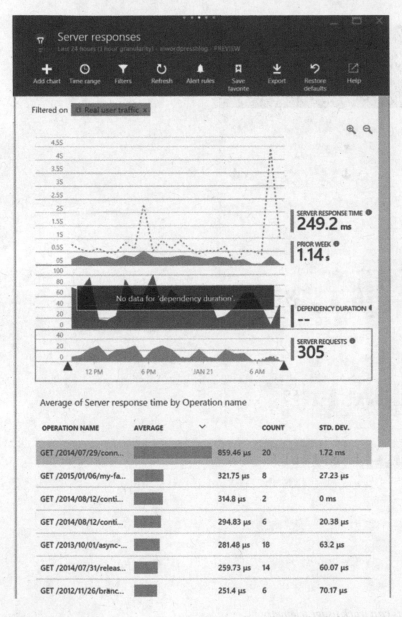

Figure 13-10. *The performance blade of Application Insights helps you monitor the responsiveness of your application*

Usage Monitoring

Measuring how your users use your application and learning from it is a critical part of DevOps. Out of the box, Application Insights already tracks usage statistics for you. Figure 13-11 shows the usage blade of Application Insights. You see the number of users, sessions, and page views. There is a filter that excludes synthetic traffic. This means that the web tests you set up or traffic you get from search engine bots is not added to these metrics. You can further drill down into these statistics and find information as how long your users stay with your application, which pages they visit, and how long they look at them. You can also find from which country your users visit and what types of devices they are using.

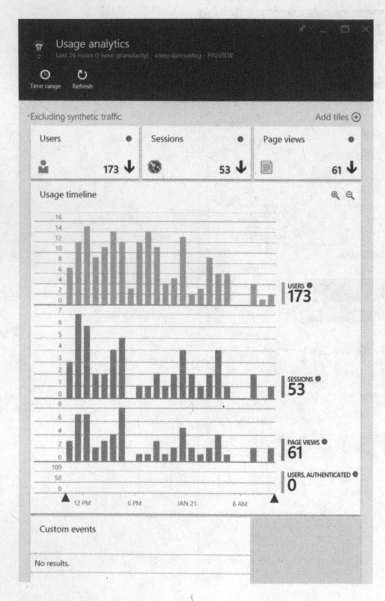

Figure 13-11. *Application Insights can track usage telemetry*

Some of these metrics are tracked server side, but you can also add some JavaScript to your HTML pages to track metrics from the browser. This allows you to see how long a user visits a page, which dependencies load successfully, and what the responsiveness from the client side is. If you've created your web application with Application Insights enabled, the JavaScript code is automatically added. You can also get the JavaScript you need from the Application Insights portal. Figure 13-12 shows what this looks like. The client-side telemetry pane contains the JavaScript code that you need to insert into your pages. The instrumentation key is unique for your Application Insight instance on Azure. By specifying this in the client, your application can send data to your Application Insights instance.

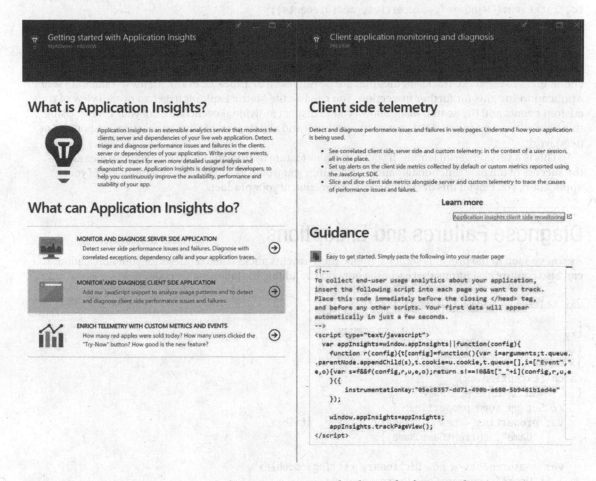

Figure 13-12. *By inserting some JavaScript, you can monitor the client side of your application*

In Figure 13-12, the bottom option shows that you can also enrich your telemetry with custom metrics and events. This is a very cool option since it allows you to monitor how users are using your application. Adding custom events does require changes to your code. The following C# code snippet shows how to add custom telemetry:

```
var tc = new TelemetryClient();
// Set up some properties:
var properties = new Dictionary<string, string>{{"Game","GameName" }, { "Difficulty", "Hard"}};
var measurements = new Dictionary<string, double>{{"GameScore", 20 }, { "Opponents", 1}};
tc.TrackEvent("WinGame", properties, measurements);
tc.TrackMetric("GameScore", 20, properties);
```

TrackEvent is used to monitor specific events in your application. This can be anything that makes sense for your application: starting a new game, adding a product to a shopping card, creating a new client, etc. TrackMetric tracks metrics that are not attached to a specific event. All these values are sent to Application Insights for further inspection. You can use the Metric Explorer to get an overall view of your custom events and the search blade allows you to inspect individual occurrences of your events. Using this data allows you to see what your users are doing and which parts of your application are popular or need work.

This is a very powerful feature. If you start a new feature by thinking about how you can measure the success of the new functionality and which things you would like to know about the usage of your application, you can let this data influence the direction of your product.

Diagnose Failures and Exceptions

As you've seen in the previous sections, Application Insights tracks failed requests for your application. You can also capture exceptions that occur in your code by adding the following C# code:

```
var telemetry = new TelemetryClient();
...
try
{ ...
}
catch (Exception ex)
{
    // Set up some properties:
    var properties = new Dictionary <string, string>
      {{"Game", currentGame.Name}};

    var measurements = new Dictionary <string, double>
      {{"Users", currentGame.Users.Count}};

    // Send the exception telemetry:
    telemetry.TrackException(ex, properties, measurements);
}
```

The TrackException method sends the exception data combined with the properties and measurements you specify to Application Insights. You can then inspect this data and combine it with the other events you track to diagnose and fix problems in your application even before a customer reports them.

Another important metric to track is when you deploy a new version of your application. If exception counts start rising after an update, you can immediately correlate this with the code changes you made. To allow Application Insights to show when a new deployment happens, you need to install an extension into your VS Team Services account. You can find the extension at `https://marketplace.visualstudio.com/items/ms-appinsights.appinsightsreleaseannotations`. After installing the extension, you have a new task for Release Management. Figure 13-13 shows this task and its configuration.

Figure 13-13. *You can add the Release Annotation task to your release definition*

You need the ID of your Application Insights resource and an API key. You can create the API key through the API blade in the Azure portal. After configuring this, a deployment annotation is automatically added to all your charts in Application Insights.

Summary

Application Insights is a powerful tool that you can use to monitor your application. It helps you track the availability and responsiveness of your application. You can also monitor the usage of your application and even extend it with custom events that give you insight into how your application is being used. You can also track exceptions and view these in Application Insights to quickly discover the cause of errors. By adding release annotations, you know when an error was introduced and determine the root cause of the problem.

The next chapter is the final chapter of this book. You will look back at everything you've learned and come up with a plan to introduce all these possibilities into your organization.

CHAPTER 14

■ ■ ■

The Path Forward

This is the final chapter of DevOps on the Microsoft stack. In this chapter you'll look back at what you've learned. The chapter also covers the order in which I normally try to introduce all the different components of DevOps to a company. This chapter will help you come up with a plan that fits your situation.

The Basics

Introducing change to an organization is difficult. If you are in the situation where you've read this book and want to start implementing some of the steps, you will face challenges when working in a team. I think the best way to introduce Agile, DevOps, and Application Lifecycle Management to an organization is by example. You can show what can be achieved and then deliver a proof of concept that shows that the principles can be applied to the types of projects your organization works on. If there is a Greenfield project coming up, that's often a good fit for introducing DevOps. But Greenfield projects don't happen that often. If you're on a Brownfield project, the challenges are harder but not insurmountable. You need to find the biggest painpoints that you and your colleagues have to deal with every day.

Some of the issues you can look at are:

- Are there many recurring bugs?

- Are the specifications clear and does everyone know what to build?

- Are deployments done manually? Does this often lead to frustration and errors?

- What is the quality of your codebase? Do you have a lot of technical debt?

- Can developers work together on an application? Are there sometimes problems to find the right version of the code when a bug is filed? Is time lost due to merging being difficult?

- Do you share code? Is there a lot of duplication between projects? How is code shared?

- When do your testers start working on a project—once the first version is released or before that? Do they have their own professional tools or are they mostly using things like Excel and manual testing?

- Do you know when your production environment is having problems? Can you easily diagnose and triage failures?

You know your situation best and you can probably come up with more questions and problems that are specific to your situation. I've noticed that using these types of questions often brings the problem areas to the surface.

As a general approach, I try to implement the following components first:

- Version control

- Technical debt management

- Continuous integration

Why these three? Because as developers, we can implement these features without needing the help of other teams in the project. This is all technical and deals with code. Version control is an absolute must. If you're still using shared folders and copy/paste merges, start with version control. If it's hard to convince your fellow developers of the benefits of version control, start with using it yourself (or look for another job). Git's distributed architecture makes it very easy to install it locally on your machine and use it only as a local repository. This allows you to have a history of your own changes and easily rollback to a previous version or create a feature branch to do some experimentation without having to deal with copying folders and restoring backups.

The key to getting others enthusiastic about your ideas is to show them that they work. Lead with your example and not with your words. Ending up in a discussion about whether certain features are good for the team is often a discussion you're going to lose as long as your colleagues haven't seen the benefits in action. Try to make them enthusiastic by showing what's possible. A local Git repository is a good way to get started.

The same is true for technical debt management. Running the analysis tools that are a part of Visual Studio just to inspect the overall quality of your code is something you can easily do. Maybe you don't have the time to start fixing some of this code. If this is true, at least run the analysis for the new code you are working on and make sure that you don't introduce any new technical debt. You can even install a local version of SonarQube on your development machine and run the analysis on your project.

The best way to get others enthusiastic is to open the dashboard on your PC at the moment a visually oriented colleague or even a manager drops by. Show them what's possible and how easy it is to implement. Adding unit tests for the new code you're writing is also a good step. You can even use IntelliTest to create a test harness that allows you to safely refactor code without worrying about breaking anything.

Continuous integration is a little more difficult because you need to have version control in place and have access to a build server. If you can motivate your team to move to Visual Studio Team Services, you have all the required resources in place. If going to the cloud is (not yet) an option, you can also install Team Foundation Server on-premises. Your MSDN subscription already gives you access to the required licenses, making the whole process a lot cheaper. Continuous integration is the start of your delivery pipeline. If setting up a complete Team Foundation Server environment is too hard, you can install the agent on your local machine. Of course this isn't the best solution when it comes to performance and scalability, but it at least will get you started.

The moment you have a version control system and a continuous integration platform, you can start improving the life of your fellow developers. Set up SonarQube to have a nice visual display so that others can see what your team is doing. If you can find a spare monitor, attach a simple device such as a Raspberry Pi to it and display it somewhere in your team area.

These are often the first steps I try to take with a team. Most teams already have version control. Sometimes they are on older platforms like Visual SourceSafe, which means you need to help them migrate to Git or TFVC. Continuous integration is something that a lot of teams still don't have. If you have continuous integration in place, you can centralize your technical debt management and show others which improvements you're making. This also requires a change in behavior. Checking in broken code and failing the CI build is not an option anymore (technically, it's still an option but a bad one). Making the current build status visible to the team is a good way to improve culture. Table 14-1 shows a checklist that you can use when starting with the basics.

Table 14-1. *Checklist for DevOps Basics*

Area	Feature	Description
Overall	Tooling	Decide on using Visual Studio, VS Team Services, or Team Foundation Server and Microsoft Azure. Enable access for all team members.
Version Control	Type	You need to choose between Git and TFVC for your project. You can find some great information to help you decide at https://msdn.microsoft.com/en-us/Library/vs/alm/code/overview.
	Branching	You need to decide on a branching scheme. This depends on the type of version control you choose. For TFVC, the simplest branching structure is the best. For Git, you will create more branches but still need naming conventions and retention policies.
	Policies	Decide on check-in policies such as requiring comments, requiring a linked work item, building and testing locally, etc.
	Code Reviews	Decide if and how you are going to do code reviews. TFVC has support for code reviews in Visual Studio. Git has pull requests that function as a review mechanism.
	Feature Toggles	Decide if you are going to use feature toggles. Choose a framework and create policies around the retention of toggles.
Technical Debt Management	Unit Tests	Unit tests are a must for DevOps projects. Decide on a unit test framework and other helper libraries at the start of your project. Set a goal for code coverage.
	Code Metrics	Set thresholds for the different code metrics and validate these during the project.
	Duplication	Set a threshold for the amount of duplicated code that's allowed. Fix all the strong and medium duplicate findings.
	Architecture Validation	Decide if architecture validation is beneficial for your project. Implement the architecture in a modeling project.
	Custom Code Analyzers	Decide on the usage of custom Roslyn-based code analyzers. Build and distribute your analyzers in the team.
Continuous Integration	Build Definition	Define one or more build definitions at the start of your project. Configure the triggers for continuous integration and scheduled builds. Make agreements with your team as to the penalty for failing a build.
	Agents and Pools	Decide if you can use the hosted agents or that you need to add your own build agents.
	Custom Build Tasks	Decide if you need custom build tasks to simplify your build definitions.
	SonarQube	Install and configure SonarQube to continuously measure your technical debt.
	Visibility	Make sure that all the stats on your project are visible on a monitor or TV in the team room. Enable all stakeholders to monitor the project's statistics.

Stepping It Up

After having the basics of version control, technical debt management, and continuous integration in place, I start looking at continuous delivery. Speeding up the release process, even if it's only to a test environment, allows you to increase the feedback cycle. You can deploy agents to your on-premises infrastructure or use Azure and spin up virtual environments or Platform as a Service (PaaS) resources to deploy your application to. If some of your configuration settings are hard to manage automatically or if the setup of an environment isn't automated, that's not a reason to wait to build a delivery pipeline. If some of the steps aren't optimal, that's not a problem. As soon as the feedback cycle starts rolling, you can start improving on the steps and immediately see the benefits of your actions.

In the meantime, teams can start looking at what they build. Introducing the Agile Project Management tool is something that will take time. The same principle applies: lead by example. Why not have your own small Kanban board on a piece of paper with some post-its? You can then start monitoring your own flow of work. Are you finishing items before picking up new work? Do you have enough information to process a new work item from start to finish? Showing the Kanban board to colleagues makes the idea visible. Introducing concepts from Scrum such as the daily standup and the continuous improvements is important.

If your team or management isn't open to these ideas, you could distribute a few copies of books like *The Phoenix Project* (`http://www.amazon.com/Phoenix-Project-DevOps-Helping-Business/dp/0988262509/`) or *Software in 30 days* (`http://www.amazon.com/Software-30-Days-Customers-Competitors/dp/1118206665/`). Invest in this area if it's a painpoint for your team. If you're not clear on certain functionality, why not use PowerPoint storyboarding to sketch an idea and discuss it with others? Why not send a feedback request to someone to validate that you've build the right thing?

Test management is another area where you can probably make some improvements. In my experience, a demo showing the data collection options of Microsoft Test Manager is enough to get testers enthusiastic. Combine this with action recordings and exploratory testing and testers are often ready to get started with MTM. When you have automated releases in place, testers can push a new version to their test environment whenever they're ready and without having to ask a developer for a new deployment. If you use the Agile Project Management tool, you can also start filing bugs from within MTM and add these to the team's backlog.

If you have version control, technical debt management, continuous integration, continuous deployment, Agile planning, and test management in place, you are a professional team that can make huge improvements. Table 14-2 shows an overview of the different steps.

Table 14-2. *Checklist for DevOps Next Steps*

Area	Feature	Description
Continuous Delivery	Configuration Management	Bring all your artifacts under version control. This applies to source code, the database schema, configuration settings, and all the other data that's needed for a deployment.
	Environments	Decide if your dev/test environments are running on-premises or in Azure.
	Release Management	Configure Release Management for automatic deployment. Configure the stages, approvers, and configuration variables.
	Feedback Cycle	Don't wait with CD until everything is perfect. That will never happen. Start the feedback cycle and improve on it to grow your team and its processes.

(*continued*)

Table 14-2. (*continued*)

Area	Feature	Description
Agile Project Management	Agile	Make sure that your team is well educated in the aspects of the Scrum process. Choose a Scrum Master and make sure that you have a product owner. Start working with a backlog and follow the Scrum meetings.
	Kanban	Map your process to a Kanban board. Define work in progress limits. Create the required swimlanes. Start looking for bottlenecks and keep optimizing your flow of value.
	Portfolio Management	If you have multiple teams that use VS Team Services, map these teams to teams in VS Team Services. Use epics and features to schedule work and divide it across the different teams.
	Dashboards	Set up dashboards with the information that your team needs to focus and improve.
	Storyboarding	Use Microsoft PowerPoint (or another storyboarding tool) to create storyboards for your product backlog items. Attach the storyboards to the PBIs to create traceability.
	Feedback Management	Involve stakeholders by asking them for feedback.
Testing	Manual Testing	Involve testers by helping them to use VS Team Services. Give Microsoft Test Manager to your testers and help them set up test suites, plans, and cases.
	Exploratory Testing	Start using exploratory testing to help speed up the testing process.

Finishing Touches

For the finishing touches, there are just a couple of areas left:

- Automated testing
- Monitor and learn
- Performance and load testing

Automated testing saves the testers a lot of time and gives you the ability to speed up your deployments because you have a safety net in place that runs on every new deployment. Asking the testers which tests they have to run over and over to make sure that an application is ready for production will show which tests are prime candidates for automation. If it's hard to write unit tests for your application because of the architecture, you can start with creating Coded UI tests that run your application through the UI. This gives you the ability to refactor pieces of your code while still being sure that the application isn't broken to introduce a better testable design.

Another area that's easy to automate is performance and load testing. You can set up a simple load test through VS Team Services in a couple of minutes. Expanding it to have real web tests that affect multiple parts of your application is the next step. Combine this with Application Insights and you can start to monitor the availability and performance of your application in production. This allows you to be proactive when problems occur and fix them, hopefully before the first customer reports the problem. Application Insights can also be used to monitor the usage of your application. Which features are popular? How are users using your product? These questions can then help you define the direction of your investments.

All these features are a lot to implement. I've seen that showing what's possible and making people enthusiastic is often the best way to go. Of course the road doesn't end here. The tools that Microsoft offers through VS Team Services are evolving rapidly. Staying up to date and learning how new tools can help your organization is important and will only become more important when more organizations, including your competitors, apply DevOps principles.

You can find a features timeline at `https://www.visualstudio.com/en-us/news/release-archive-vso`. Microsoft uses this page to lay out their roadmap for VS Team Services. You can see which features are being worked on and often there are links to blog posts discussing these new features. Most of these blogs can be found at `http://blogs.msdn.com/b/visualstudioalm/`. Adding these blogs to your favorite RSS reader will help you stay up to date.

There are also some great conferences organized by Microsoft where new features are released and discussed. The yearly Build conference, Ignite, and Visual Studio Connect all contain sessions that will help you. Fortunately, you can find most of these sessions online at `https://channel9.msdn.com/`. Table 14-3 summarizes these last points.

Table 14-3. *Checklist for the Finishing Touches*

Area	Feature	Description
Testing	Automated UI tests	Start speeding up your testing work by automating stable regression tests.
	Performance and load testing	Set up performance and load tests. A `ping` test can be set up in a couple of minutes. Web tests require more attention and can be added during the project.
Monitoring	Application Insights	Configure Application Insights for your application and start monitoring the key metrics.
	Add events	Add custom events to Application Insights from your code to start learning what your users do with your application and how you can improve it.
Staying up to date	Features Timeline	Regularly look at the Features Timeline on `visualstudio.com` to make sure you don't miss any new features and you know what's coming.
	Blogs	Start following popular blogs to stay up to date with all the new features coming out.
	Conferences	Visit conferences or use Channel9 to inform you of all the new possibilities and how to apply them to your team's projects.

Summary

DevOps is a huge subject. Hopefully this chapter gave you an idea of the features you can introduce to your team and organization. Start with version control, continuous integration, and technical debt management. Then move on to continuous delivery, Agile Project Management, and test management. Finally, you can apply the finishing touches with test automation, performance and load testing, and monitoring.

I hope your DevOps journey is a success!

—Wouter de Kort

Index

A

Agile Manifesto
  methodologies, 6
  phrases, 5
  Scrum, 4
  software development, 4
  Sprints, 4
  testers and developers, 4
Agile project management. *See also* Kanban and
      Lean techniques
  basics checklist, 281
  coding, 20
  developers
    overview dashboard, 40
    team explorer (Visual Studio), 39
    work panel, 41
  feedback loop, 20
  functional design, 19
  methodologies, 20
  scrum, 20
  ScrumBut, 21
  team rooms
    automated message, 38
    communication, 36
    configuration events, 37–38
    VS Team Services, 37
    widget dashboard, 37
  tooling
    bugs, 30–32
    capacity, 32–36
    impediments, 28–29
    product backlog items, 24–27
    Scrum template, 22
    sprints, 22–24
    tasks, 27–28
    team web access, 22
  waterfall project, 19
Alerts and notifications
  configuration, 94
  features, 93
  mention, 96
  mentions, 95
  SOAP, 95
  web access, 93
Application Insights
  configuration file
    creation, 263
    events, increase in, 264
    local development machine, 265
    metrics, 267
    search blade, 268
    page view details tracking, 266
  diagnose failures and exceptions
    C# code, 274
    release annotation task, 275
    TrackException method, 274
  differences, 261
  monitoring application
    performance blade, 271
    results of, 270
    URL ping test, 269
  privacy and data retention, 263
  usage and performance, 261–262
  usage of monitoring
    C# code, 274
    JavaScript inserted, 273
    TrackEvent, 274
    track usage telemetry, 272
Automated testing, 281
  checklist, 282
  Coded UI, 220
  features, 282
  graph displays, 228–229
  HTML elements, 223
  HTTP requests, 226
  load test, 228
  load test hub, 223–224
  performance, 281
  recording UI test, 221
  source code, 222
  structure, 222

Automated testing (*cont.*)
  time graph, 225
  VS team services, 224–225
  web test recorder, 227
Azure, 9
  IaaS, PaaS, and SaaS, 10
  MSDN subscription, 11
  portal, 12
  security, 11
  shut down, 14
  virtual machine, 12–13

B

Backlog, 7
Baseless merges, 121
Branching strategies, 134
  feature toggle, 135
  scenarios, 134

C

Centralized version control systems, 99, 102
Code search
  ASP.NET MVC code, 89
  code elements, 91
  feature, 89
  filters, 90–91
  keyword search, 90
  repositories/projects, 89
Coding, 20
Communication, 19, 43
Containers
  ASP.NET 6 applications, 257
  concept of, 256
  docker, 256
  Linux, 258
  VMs, 256
Continuous integration, 161, 279
  build agents configuration
    control panel, 173
    installation, 174
    pools, 173
    queue and agent, 173
  build definition, 162
  configuration options, 165–166, 172
  custom tasks creation
    command creation, 179
    JSON file, 177
    personal access token, 179–180
    PowerShell task, 175
    task directories, 180
    task.json file, 175–176
    task upload, 180–181
    tfx-cli installation, 178
    tfx command, 178–179

  default build template, 163
  general tab, 169
  hosted build agent, 162
  infrastructure, 163
  queue, 171
  repository configuration, 167
  retention tab, 170
  SonarQube
    begin and end steps, 186
    dashboard, 181–182
    demo environment, 182–183
    generic service, 186
    issues page, 185
    parameters, 185
    Roslyn project, 184
  templates, 164–165
  timeline, 172
  triggers tab, 168
  variables configuration, 167
  Web Access portal, 164

D

Dashboards
  default overview, 92
  widgets configuration, 92–93
Definition of Done (DoD), 64
Dependency Inversion Principle, 142
Deployment pipeline
  delivery pipeline, 231–232
  development and operations, 232
  operations fix, 232
DevOps
  Agile Manifesto, 4
  backlog, 7
  capabilities, 6–8
  definition, 5
  developers and operations, 5
  key phrase, 5
  need for training, 16
  phases, 4
  practices, 6–7
  process, 5–6
  Scrum, 4
  self-assessment, 8
  sprints, 4
  waterfall project, 3
Distributed version control
        systems, 100–103
  Git (*see* Git version control system)
Docker, 256

E

E-mail requesting feedback, 50
Enterprise Agreement (EA), 12

■ F

Feedback management
  communication, 43
  configuration, 49
  e-mail requesting feedback, 50
  overview page (other links), 48
  queries, 53
  request work, 47
  response tool, 50–52
  screenshots, 51
  Storyboards, 44–46
Functional design, 19

■ G, H

Git version control system
  branches
    creation, 129
    merges, 129–130
    structure, 128–129
  clone, 124–125
  commit and push
    commit changes, 125–126
    remote server, 127
  distributed control system, 124
  fetch and pull, 127
  key points, 124
  pull request
    branches panel, 130–131
    code hub, 131
    comments, 133
    creation, 131–132
    web access, 133
GoToGitHubExtension method, 222

■ I, J

Infrastructure as a Service (IaaS), 10
Interface Segregation Principle, 142

■ K

Kanban and Lean techniques
  different phases, 55
  Kanban board, 57
    analysis column, 64
    backend tag, 63
    backlog items, 60
    column configuration, 63–64
    Definition of Done (DoD), 64
    Doing and Done state, 58
    extra swimlanes, 65–66
    fields adding, 61
    navigation, 60
    reordering cards configuration, 66–67

ScrumBut, 59
style rule, 61–62
tag colors configuration, 62–63
task directories creation, 60–61
team's process, 57
work in progress limit (WIP limit), 58
pipeline speed, 56
principles, 56
process, 55
Scrum, 55
steps of, 57

■ L

Linux, 258
Liskov Substitution Principle, 142
Load testing, 281

■ M, N

Manual testing
  charts, 215
  exploratory testing sessions, 211–212
  insert shared steps and creation, 211
  notes and screenshots, 212–213
  parameters-multiple data sets, 209
  Perfecto, 214
  program running, 210
  query-based suite, 206
  runner window, 208
  test hub, 205
  test suite and cases, 205, 207
  toolbar, 207
  Web Access, 205
Microsoft Azure. See Azure
Microsoft Test Manager (MTM)
  automation of manual steps, 218
  repro steps, 219
  standalone client, 216
  Test Impact and IntelliTrace, 219
  Web Test Runner, 217

■ O

Open/Closed Principle (OCP), 142

■ P

Package management, 189
  App.config file, 191
  ASP.NET MVC application, 193–194
  configSection, 191
  copyleft license, 193
  EntityFramework package, 191–192
  jQuery web site, 189
  npm, 193

Package management (*cont.*)
  NuGet package manager, 190
  NuGet packages, 193
  Package Source, 192
  uncompressed version, 190
  VS team services
    AllowedExternalPackages feed, 196–197
    configure package sources, 198
    extension, 195
    feeds, 195
    nuget.config file, 199
    nuget.exe file, 196
    NuGet.org, 196
    NuGet Packager and NuGet
      Publisher, 200
    PowerShell session, 198
Path forward
  basics
    approach, 278
    checklist, 278–279
    continuous integration platform, 278
    issues, 277
    technical debt management, 278
    version control, 278
Platform as a Service (PaaS), 10, 280
Portfolio management
  areas, 68
  backlog items, 74
  backlog navigation levels, 68–70
  capabilities, 67
  details view, 72–73
  epic and features, 72
  features, 67
  hierarchical area configuration, 71
  mapping panel, 73
  mobile strategies, 67
  overview page, 70
  processes, 67
  product backlog item, 74
  SAFe, 72
  sub-areas, 71
  team project, 68
  visible iterations, 71–72
PowerPoint
  animations, 45
  links, 45
  Lorem(), 45
  product backlog items, 45
  Storyboarding plugin, 44
  VS Team Services project, 46
Product backlog items (PBIs)
  business value, 26
  criteria, 26
  details, 25

  effort field, 26
  overview, 24–25
  tags, 27

■ Q

Queries
  bugs, 77
  charts
    area chart, 84
    column chart, 86
    dashboard, 85
    horizontal bars, 86
    line chart, 89
    pie chart, 83
    pivot table displays, 87
    snapshot, 84
    stacked area chart, 88
    stacked bar graph, 87
  search box
    backlog items, 77
    detail page, 78
    filters, 79
    keyword search, 79
    product/product backlog item, 79
    search filters, 78
    states drop-down, 79
  work item query
    clauses, 80
    definition, 79
    direct links, 81
    explorer, 82
    filter options, 81
    operator, 80
    results, 80
    tab creation, 80
    tasks/bugs, 82

■ R

Release management, 232
  automated tests, 242
  Azure File Copy task, 234
  configuration, 242
  configure permissions, 246
  definition, 233
  deployment tasks, 240
  key points, 245
  machines option, 241
  manual/automated approvals, 238
  overview, 241
  realtime log file, 237
  summary, 243
  target environment, 236

test agent, 243
test hub details, 244
triggers section, 238
update, 245
variable configuration, 235
VS Team Services Build output, 235
Roslyn
  code fix project creation, 157
  CodeFixProvider, 158
  DiagnosticAnalyzer, 158
  execution, 159
  namespace, 159
  source code, 156
  uppercase class names, 158

■ S

Scaled Agile Framework (SAFe), 72
Scrum, 4
  Kanban and Lean techniques, 55
ScrumBut, 21
Scrum templates
  bugs, 30
    detail view, 31
    links, 32
    unique fields, 31
  capacity
    assign hours, 36
    forecasting sprints, 32–33
    members management, 34–35
    overview, 33–34
    sample capacity plan, 35
  impediments
    creation, 29–30
    definition, 28
    details, 28–29
  items, 22
  PBIs (see Product backlog items (PBIs))
  sprints
    Configure Schedules and Iterations
      link, 22–23
    iterations, 23
    schedule, 23–24
  tasks
    default fields, 28
    sprint backlog, 27–28
  team web access, 22
Single Responsibility Pattern (SRP), 142
Software as a Service (SaaS), 10
SonarQube
  dashboard, 181–182
  demo environment, 182–183
  generic service, 186
  issues page, 185

parameters, 185
Roslyn project, 184
SQL Server Data Tools (SSDT), 256
Storyboards. See PowerPoint

■ T

Team Foundation Server (TFS), 9
Team Foundation Version Control (TFVC)
  annotate option, 112–113
  branches
    baseless merges, 121–122
    creation, 121
    merging submenu, 119–120
  changeset, 106
    check-in pending
      changes, 108–109
    code hub, 109
    source control, 107–108
    team explorer, 107
  check-in-policies
    policy warning, 123
    team project, 122–123
  CodeLens, 112, 114
  comparation, 113
  Get Latest command, 110
  history, 112
  key concepts, 104
  merge conflict, 111
  shelvesets, 114
    code review request, 117–118
    pending changes windows, 115
    response request, 118–119
    suspend and resume work, 117
  workspace, 104
    check-out, 105
    cloak folders, 105–106
    configuration options, 104–105
    mapping configuration, 106
    Visual Studio widget, 105
Technical debt, 149
  architecture validation
    context menu, 151
    errors, 151
    layer diagram, 149–150
    modeling project, 149
    properties, 152
  basics checklist, 279
  code analysis
    built-in dictionary, 140
    code, 138
    configuration, 139
    errors, 140
    file properties, 140

Technical debt (*cont.*)
    SuppressMessage attribute, 140
    warnings, 138
  code metrics
    calculation, 146–147
    concepts, 141
    coupling, 144
    cyclomatic complexity, 144
    depth of inheritance, 146
    lines of code, 142–143
  custom code analyzers (*see* Roslyn)
  duplications cause
    code clone analysis results window,
      147–148
    comparison, 148
    groups, 147
  overview, 137
  SonarQube, 137
  unittesting (*see* Unit testing)
Testing process, 281

U

Unit testing
  continuous delivery model, 152
  coupling, 153
  creation, 155
  integration tests, 153
  IntelliTest, 154
  overflow exception, 156
  testing pyramid, 152–153

V

Version control systems. *See also* Git version
    control system
  basics checklist, 279
  centralized server, 99–100

distributed server
    branching, 101
    design, 100–101
  feature toggling, 102
  Git and TFVC, 103
  PaaS, 280
  steps, 99
  strategies, 101–102
Virtual machines (VMs), 256
VS Team Services, 9
  advantage, 15
  security options, 15
  timeline, 14–15
  Twitter account, 15
  web site, 15–16

W, X, Y, Z

Waterfall project, 3
  disadvantage, 20
  stages, 19
Web deploy package
  application, 246
  ARM template creation, 252
  Azure Web App deployment task, 250
  configuration, 251
  creation, 248
  custom publish profile, 247
  DeployOutput folder, 247, 249
  home controller class, 250
  JSON outline, 254
  MSBuild, 249
  project files, 252
  resource group, 253
  SSDT tool, 256
  Web Apps, 255
  web.config file, 250
  ZIP file, 248

Get the eBook for only $5!

Why limit yourself?

Now you can take the weightless companion with you wherever you go and access your content on your PC, phone, tablet, or reader.

Since you've purchased this print book, we're happy to offer you the eBook in all 3 formats for just $5.

Convenient and fully searchable, the PDF version enables you to easily find and copy code—or perform examples by quickly toggling between instructions and applications. The MOBI format is ideal for your Kindle, while the ePUB can be utilized on a variety of mobile devices.

To learn more, go to www.apress.com/companion or contact support@apress.com.